William Sokolin

The Complete Wine Investor

COLLECTING WINES FOR PLEASURE AND PROFIT

PRIMA PUBLISHING

DISCLAIMER
Investment decisions have certain inherent risks. Prima therefore disclaims any warranties or representations, whether express or implied, concerning the accuracy or completeness of the information or advice contained in this book. Any investment a reader may make based on such information is at the reader's sole risk. You should carefully research or consult a qualified financial adviser before making any particular investment.

Interior Design by Trina Stahl
Illustrations by Lisa Cooper
Graphic images by Image Quest
Interior photos by Mick Rock/Cephas, Ted Stefanski/Cephas, and Bruce Flemming/Cephas

Library of Congress Cataloging-in-Publication Data

Sokolin, William.
The complete wine investor : collecting wines for pleasure and profit / William Sokolin.
p. cm.
ISBN 0-7615-1676-X
1. Wine as an investment. 2. Wine industry.
HD9370.5.S648 1998
332.63—dc21 98-35912
CIP

98 99 00 01 02 HH 10 9 8 7 6 5 4 3 2 1
Printed in the United States of America

How to Order
Single copies may be ordered from Prima Publishing, P.O. Box 1260BK, Rocklin, CA 95677; telephone (916) 632-4400. Quantity discounts are also available. On your letterhead, include information concerning the intended use of the books and the number of books you wish to purchase.

Visit us online at www.primalife.com

To Gloria, David, Deanne, and Glenn
with all my love.

To Joe Dimaggio, Ted Williams,
Jackie Robinson, and Roy Campanella
who started me on my way to an early dream—
the Brooklyn Dodgers—
and on my way to the greatest game on earth—Wine.

Contents

Introduction

THOMAS JEFFERSON HAS always been an inspiration to me. He was an astonishingly accomplished person. During the 84 fruitful years Jefferson lived he was the author of the Declaration of Independence, the third president of the United States, and ambassador to France, among other things. President Kennedy once aptly described Jefferson's soaring intellect to a group of 12 Nobel Prize winners who had gathered at the White House for dinner:

"This is the greatest assemblage of intellects ever gathered in the White House—except when Thomas Jefferson dined alone."

For all his intellectual, human, and professional achievements, Thomas Jefferson counted one achievement above all others: the lowering of America's wine tariffs, which allowed more wine into the country. At the time, alcoholism was rampant in the Colonies, the favored drink being rum. Casks of it were used as ballast on ships—and then consumed by a populace with a bottomless thirst.

Jefferson saw wine as a low-alcohol alternative. Said he: "No nation is drunken where wine is cheap; and none sober, where the dearness of wine substitutes ardent spirits as the common beverage. It is, in truth, the only antidote to the bane of whiskey."

Jefferson put his wine where his mouth was, and was America's first serious wine collector. He surveyed the vineyards of Bordeaux, Burgundy, the Loire Valley, and elsewhere; engaged in a variety of tasting; kept meticulous notes; talked to vintners; and shipped—literally, in those days—thousands of bottles of wine to his home in Monticello. He was the driving force behind many people starting to drink wine in America.

But while Jefferson has always been an inspiration, it was a less well-known man who made all the difference, wine-wise, in my life. I'm sure that if Jefferson himself had heard the story of how this occurred he would have liked it.

My father passed away in 1958, and I inherited the liquor store he had founded in 1934 and operated on 34th Street and Madison Avenue in New York City. I was never enamored of the liquor-store business, and at first I considered selling it to pursue something else. Then a glass of wine, and the man—Ray Milland—intersected with my plans, altering my life forever. I went to see a motion picture that he starred in. He was handsome, debonair, and sophisticated—one of the leading men of the time.

One scene mesmerized me: He poured himself a glass of wine—Mateus—and drank it with fitting stylishness. It struck me as the quintessence of sophistication and just blew me away. Never mind that the Mateus was a quite ordinary rosé that I later learned was favored by hippies on drugs; I perceived it my way, and I decided to try to convert the store into a place where the Ray Millands of the world could purchase their wine.

When I made my intentions known to my wife, Gloria, and the rest of the family, they responded logically: "Why don't you consider checking into a mental hospital?" After all, wine was not popular in the United States at that time; most people perceived it as a mysterious, high-society, snobbish beverage drunk only by the rich because it was very expensive. And, in fact, for years that was mostly the case.

However, I would not be dissuaded, and in a short time, I gradually transformed the store. We culled the liquor, offering less and less of it, and more and more stocked our shelves with wine.

I also educated myself about wine, and over the next few years it came to dominate the offerings in the store. I bought fine wine, storing some of it in a cool, dark basement that I converted into a very good wine cellar.

The store started to enjoy some success, and the reason was simple: dumb luck. A variety of forces were at work in America, particularly the more general availability of excellent California wines. That meant that Americans were starting to drink more wine.

No one knew at the time—or if they did they didn't advertise it—that wine would grow more valuable. But I sensed that it would, and as I had followed my nose (a vital organ in wine appreciation) in developing a wine shop, I started to buy wine that I felt might increase in value as the years went by.

At the time, this meant one thing: the wines of Bordeaux, that storied region of France that had been making wine for hundreds, perhaps thousands, of years and which has long been considered the first and last word on fine wine. More specifically, it meant buying more red wine than white because, of the two general wines the region produces, red lasts longer than white, though there are some whites that can last for decades. And to have it appreciate significantly in value, I knew I would have to hold onto it for a long time.

In 1982, my daughter was set to go to Tufts, the same Boston-area college that I had attended. All she needed was tuition. As it happened I had hundreds of bottles of vintage Taylor Port in my shop. I had paid only $2,000 for it but was able to sell it for $90,000—enough to pay for my daughter's entire four years at Tufts.

The '60s and '70s saw wine sales grow, then explode in the '80s (see Chapter 1, "The Year That Shook the Wine World"). It became evident to me that wine was here to stay—it was a collectible—and could be a spectacular investment product. While an investment in stocks might yield 20 percent a year, wine could break the bank: People holding wine saw its value soar hundreds of percent.

In the mid-'80s—after 25 years of selling, buying, investing in, and drinking fine wine—I felt qualified and compelled to tell people how to buy not only for profit, but for pleasure and fun. That's the way I've always done it, making money but also buying a little extra wine with my profits for drinking. As I am fond of saying, if a wine investment doesn't work out perfectly, you can always liquidate—pleasurably.

Back in 1986, I bottled my know-how in the book *Liquid Assets: How to Develop an Enjoyable and Profitable Wine Portfolio*, in which I furnished specific predictions on which wines to invest in. Happily, many people profited—some greatly—and were able to enjoy a delicious drink at the same time.

Indeed, the ideal reader for this book is someone who sees wine as an investment and as something to enjoy—the type of person who would buy a collectible like a painting with the intention of someday selling it for a profit. In the meantime, however, this investor could enjoy standing in front of the painting to contemplate its beauty.

The same goes for the wine investor/lover I envision: someone who can enjoy wine as much as he or she enjoys making money.

Now it is time for a fresh look at wine investment, to supply a new vintage of information. (Clearly, I am wine-obsessed!) Much wine has gone under the bridge, and while many of the principles I detailed in *Liquid Assets* still apply, there's quite a bit of new information that one must know to do well—to liquidate pleasurably in more ways than one.

I have lost one thing since I wrote my first book, however: snobbishness about wine. In truth, when I first started out and gradually increased my know-how, I developed a slight patina of arrogance. Happily, a comment from my daughter brought me crashing back to earth:

"You know, Daddy," she said, "I don't know why you're getting all crazy about it. Wine is just fermented grape juice."

I was remiss before in not thanking one person who made my career in wine possible, and I want to do that now:

To Ray Milland, wherever you are, I lift a glass of magisterial Bordeaux Claret to you, and I hope to see you one day (but not too soon). It's been a hell of a ride!

William Sokolin

CHAPTER ONE

The Year That Shook the Wine World

THE 1960S AND 1970s—particularly the '70s—were a time when America started to notice wine—and drink it. I like to think I did my share. Over the years, I had educated myself on the subject during visits to important winemaking regions of France—particularly Bordeaux. I passed on what I learned to others—people who came into my busy wine shop, those who attended weekly wine tastings at my apartment on 35th Street in Manhattan, and just about anyone else who would listen to me hold forth on the subject.

I was not only enthusiastic, but devious in spreading the word. In the '60s the *National Review* had its offices on the floor above where I lived. Whenever I printed a new wine catalogue I would wait until everyone at the magazine went home and then slip it under the door. I was also a member of the New York Athletic Club, and more than once, members would open their lockers to find that the latest Sokolin wine catalogue had mysteriously appeared.

First Glimmerings

In the '70s I had started to see that some wines had investment potential. No great mental legerdemain was required on my part. Some wines were increasing in price. It was elementary. If you could hold them long enough, prices would rise significantly. Eventually you could sell and reap a profit. Or if you were a wine lover and investor such as myself, you could use part of your investment earnings to finance buying more wines to drink. So I started to tell people about wine's investment potential, and I suddenly found myself in demand to speak on a variety of radio shows on the topic.

My message spread. American investment bankers and others started to invest in wines, and the so-called "great growths"—coming out of the Médoc region of Bordeaux, which then indisputably produced the finest wines in the world and, crucially, ones that had in-the-bottle staying power. In fact, because of their chemical makeup, many of these wines were not really drinkable until at least a decade after they were in the bottle. (For more on Bordeaux wines, see Chapter 7.)

The '70s were not all nirvana for investors. While wine prices surged upward in the first two years of the decade, 1973 saw them flatten and fall—typical of any market that cannot sustain endless growth. The downturn lasted about five years, and then in 1978 prices started to inch up again.

1982: A Pivotal Year

To be sure, the '70s were an exciting period for wine drinkers and investors—and those, like me, who did both. But as scintillating as it was, the decade gave no hint of the huge upturn in wine prices that the '80s would bring. A variety of factors contributed to the fact that certain wines ballooned in value. Expected, but pedestrian, reasons included an increase in wine manufacturing costs—prices for glass, cork, and other materials went up—and as wine became more popular, dealers charged more. But the single most important reason, in my view, can be traced back to the fateful confluence of one year, one place, and one person.

The year was 1982, the place was Bordeaux, and the person was Robert M. Parker, Jr.

Great for Wine Growing

Looking back on it one can only say that 1982 was an extraordinary year for wine growing. The creation of fine wine depends chiefly on the skill of the winemaker, but no winemaker—from Helen Turley in California to the great André Tchelistcheff—can work miracles. Nature must cooperate first.

Nature was not only cooperative in 1982: She beamed ear to ear. The winter and spring that preceded what is known as the "flowering" of the vines had been mild. April was also mild, and very dry: There were only 6 millimeters of rain recorded. There was no frost, which could do damage, and it was quite sunny.

The result was that the vines remained very healthy and were able to produce a prolific number of buds.

The good weather continued, and then in June there was a "mini heat wave," according to wine critic Clive Coates in his book *Grands Vins.* This resulted in the vines flowering one week earlier than normal, but it was "uniform and the fruit setting was accomplished very quickly, thus gaining a further week on the norm and ensuring that all the berries would arrive at fruition at the same time."

July was hot, but a much-needed rain started to fall at the end of the month and returned intermittently through an otherwise uneventful August. The main idea with grapes is that they get some moisture, but not too much.

By August 20, the grapes, started to mature—again, earlier than usual. And then the rain went away and Bordeaux enjoyed three weeks of heat which, Coates said, also had a positive effect: "In the great heat the grapes galloped not only towards maturity, but towards concentration."

The harvest began on September 14, one of the earliest on record. Winemakers kept a wary eye on the sky for signs of rain. At that point too much rain would have been bad because it could swell the grapes and dilute their flavor.

But there was no rain, and the winemakers completed the harvest quickly and efficiently. They carefully handled what seemed to be an extraordinarily large harvest, virtually completing it by early October.

The winemakers were acutely aware that they had some special raw material on their hands. They carefully monitored and nurtured the grapes through the winemaking process (see Appendix A, "How Wine Is Made").

Even in the cask the wine gave an indication of its greatness. Young Bordeaux red wines typically have a deep purple color, but the 1982 harvest (vintage) went beyond that to a purple that was almost black. Coates says that one day after 50 tastings his tongue had turned black!

Also, there was a surprising amount of concentrated fruit. The grapes contained the largest amount of natural sugar since the 1947 harvest and had what Coates said was almost the richness of port wine.

Word spread. Growers and merchants, naturally exuberant about wine, waxed rhapsodic about it. Ironically, it was wine that the merchants could not possibly have tasted yet. Firms started running ads in magazines and other spots. Word spread like a brushfire.

Enter Robert M. Parker, Jr.

FIFTEEN YEARS EARLIER, in 1967, 29-year-old Maryland native Robert M. Parker, Jr., went to France to visit his fiancée, Patricia, who was in her junior year at college. At the time, his experience with wine was virtually nonexistent. One day he ordered some high-quality French wine simply because it was cheaper than Coca-Cola. He got a pleasant shock. "I was fascinated," he told *Money* magazine in 1990, "to find this beverage that enhanced food, prolonged a meal, offered such variety, and made me mellow but not blurry or bloated like liquor and beer."

Upon his return to the States, he drank up wine books by such savants as Frank Schoonmaker, Alexis Lichine, André Simon, Hugh Johnson, and others. Gradually, he became obsessed with the beverage, and after he and Patricia got married, they visited the great vineyards of Europe and formed wine-tasting groups in Baltimore.

Parker noticed something: Just because a supposedly knowledgeable critic said a wine was good didn't mean it was so. "We'd buy expensive labels that the critics raved about and find them disappointing. Gradually I realized that many of the critics were swayed by free samples and expense-paid tasting trips."

The Ralph Nader of Wines

Out of that experience Parker had an epiphany. "There was no Ralph Nader in the field. It dawned on me that I could become that objective voice for consumers."

And that's what he strove to become. In his Baltimore tasting group, friends and others came to value his opinions on wine quality. He started to publish those opinions in a publication he founded by borrowing $2,000 from his mother and sending it out free to some 7,000 people. He called it the *Wine Advocate.*

He expected an avalanche of paid subscriptions. That didn't materialize, but he got enough—at $10 a subscription—to put together another issue, and he was off and running. He was still a practicing lawyer, and with wine tasting and writing he was working 90 hours a week. But it wasn't long before his income from the *Wine Advocate* enabled him to devote all his time to critiquing wine.

As time went by his voice became more and more heard—and respected. For one thing, he did his homework—or mouthwork. Parker tasted—smelled and savored but spit out—over 100 wines a day, according to Tony Hendra in a *Forbes* magazine article. By contrast, the well-respected printed oracle of the wine business, the *Wine Spectator,* has a panel of a half a dozen or so wine tasters; in 1997, they collectively tasted just over 10,000 wines (approximately 4–5 wines per person, per day).

Also working in Parker's favor was his sense of taste. He could detect subtle differences in wine that others missed (someone once commented that his mouth was more like a holding tank than a mouth). He devised a point system that was easy for consumers to understand.

The wine-rating system in use when Parker came onto the scene was based on 20 points, as follows:

19.0–20.0	Excellent.
16.5–18.5	Very fine.
15.0–16.0	Good to very good.
13.5–14.5	Quite good.
12.0–13.0	Average.
10.0–11.5	Disappointing, perhaps poor.
Less than 10	Disagreeable.

Parker based his system on higher numbers—like grades in school—and consumers found it more readily understandable. To wit:

90–100	Outstanding to excellent.
80–89	Like getting a "B" in school—but, Parker said, wines in the 85 to 89 range were very good.
70–79	"Represents a 'C,'" Parker said in the 1995 edition of *Parker's Wine Buyer's Guide,* "but obviously 79 is a much more desirable score than 70."
Below 70	"A 'D' or 'F,' depending on where you went to school; for a wine, too, it is a sign of an imbalance, flawed, or terribly dull or diluted wine that will be of little interest to the well-informed wine consumer."

Parker was not afraid to accompany the points awarded to—or withheld from—a wine with acid commentary, some of it blunt to the point of insult. He described some wines as having "foul barnyard odors" or, as he was quoted in *Money* magazine, "smelling like cat urine."

Since the great wines were being produced in the Bordeaux region, Parker and his wife started making three trips a year there, tasting the new wines and predicting what kind of vintages the various châteaux were producing from barrel tastings.

The "Wrath of Grapes"

By 1982 Parker was well respected—and feared—variously known as the "Wrath of Grapes," "Carnac of the Cask," and the "Mouth That Roars." Wine-literate consumers knew who he was, and retailers and others had started putting his ratings on ads for wines they sold. Parker's rating made a difference in sales. Today it is acknowledged that if Parker gives a wine a score above 90 it can boost its price 25 percent; if it scores between 96 and 100, the price can jump an additional 33 percent!

Everyone found out just how influential Parker was when he started publishing reports characterizing the 1982 vintage as the "wine of the century." He gave a bunch of wines from the noted vintage scores in the 90s; he gave six Bordeaux blended wines—Cheval Blanc, Latour, Léoville-Las-Cases, St. Julien Grand Vin, Mouton-Rothschild, and Le Pin—a score of 100!

Although there was a lot of hype, Robert M. Parker, Jr., could be believed. Prices of wines from the 1982 vintage went though the roof. He put wine and its worth on the map as never before.

Overall, the so-called "first growths" of Bordeaux went up in price some 1,500 percent between 1970 and 1984—an average increase of 100 percent a year, with most of the growth after 1982. The value of wine has continued to escalate, and cold hard numbers are bracing. For example, here are the prices of some wines in 1965 compared to prices in 1998:

Wine	1965 Price per Case	1998 Price per Case
1959 Lafite	$162	$12,000
1961 Mouton-Rothschild	188	14,000
1962 Pétrus	120	12,000
1964 Lafite	66	6,000
1953 Margaux	195	9,000
1955 Montrose	59	4,000
1959 La Mission Haut Brion	78	10,000
1961 Palmer	140	9,000
1961 Romanee Conti	200	43,000
1964 Lafite	56	4,500
1966 Latour	90	4,000
1966 Pétrus	110	12,000
1967 Lafite	78	5,000
1970 Pichon-Lalande	70	4,500

Some Say It Can't Be Done

Robert M. Parker, Jr., is not perceived as the "god of wine" by all. He has his critics. Some claim, for one thing, that he is not the guru he purports to be because it is physically impossible for him to taste 100 wines a day and still retain an objective taste sensation. After a while, they argue, one's taste buds become numb.

There is some scientific evidence to support this. Tony Hendra wrote critically of Parker in the Sept. 22, 1997, issue of *Forbes*. In Hendra's article, Dr. Ann Noble, a researcher in the Department of Viticulture and Enology at UC Davis, says that when "tasting (young) wine . . . astringency—caused by acidity and tannins—induces 'fatigue,'" meaning your ability to make tasting judgments is impaired. If you're tasting very astringent wines—for example, young Bordeaux barrel samples—the messages coming from your mouth and your nose get confused so that you "become less sensitive to aromas." She notes that the ethanol inhaled during a large tasting might also adversely affect judgment. When she asks her own subjects to rate aromas in wine, she tends not to set out more than four reds—which are more astringent than whites—or six whites. Her bottom-line judgment on what she sardonically refers to as "tasting wine for quality" is not that accurate. "Obfuscation has reached a fine art here," Noble concludes.

> To be sure, the '70s were an exciting period for wine drinkers and investors—and those, like me, who did both.

So Parker may not be tasting 100 wines a day. In fact, in the 1995 edition of *Parker's Wine Buyer's Guide*, he says that he deplores it when people do marathon tastings. Unfortunately, Hendra did not cite a source for the 100-wines-a-day figure in his *Forbes* article.

There is also ample evidence that some wines Parker rated highly were not worthy of such scores. Some of those wines became essentially undrinkable as they matured, even some of the vaunted '82s. On the other hand, who's right all the time?

No matter what one thinks of Parker, a central fact remains, and it is critical to remember when collecting wine with an eye on investment: A great mass of wine consumers perceives Robert M. Parker, Jr., as a savvy, honest wine critic. He is the clock by which the wine world runs, though—as you will see later in this book—there are other critics whose opinions also carry great weight. But to go against Parker's scores when investing is to run the risk of failure, because you can have difficulty selling the wine unless he has rated it well. This may sound a bit unbelievable and outlandish. It is. But it is also true.

The Lucky Profited Too

IT WASN'T ONLY a few astute investors who made money during the '80s wine boom, but also many people who were just plain lucky. They happened to be holding wines that skyrocketed in value. My friend Bill Buckley, Jr.'s father, Bill Sr., had bought approximately 20,000 bottles of fine wines for $1 a bottle in the 1930s and was holding them when the wine boom started. Had he ever sold any, he would have made a huge profit! Buckley and his horde are people after my own heart. They drink a lot of the wine, but still have plenty in store.

The most surprising price rise I've seen has been for a 1945 bottle of Mouton-Rothschild. *Wine Spectator* magazine—which also rates wine using the 100-point system—gave it a perfect score of 100 points. In 1945, my father was selling it for $11.50 a case—less than a dollar a bottle (a standard case holds 12). By 1970 the price was $400 a case, and the price continued to rise. By 1982 it was about $15,000 per case, and by 1994 it was close to $20,000. A few people bought it—and profited greatly. By 1996 the price had ascended to a nutty $126,000. Sanity returned, to a degree, in 1997 when the price plummeted to a mere $60,000 a case.

More than a few grapes have been changed into wine since I first wrote *Liquid Assets*, but the essential fact remains: One can still make a lot of money investing in wine—as many people have already—and at the same time let some of those profits pay for the fine wine they drink. The chapters that follow will detail some different approaches.

Important Points

- In 1982, wine value exploded. One big reason was the praise heaped on the vintage by Robert M. Parker, Jr., the most influential wine critic in the world.
- The older method of rating wine is based on a 20-point system; the newer one, established by Parker and used by *Wine Spectator* magazine, is based on 100 points.
- The number of points a wine has received by Parker or *Wine Spectator*—particularly Parker—must be respectable before a wine can be considered investment grade wine, or IGW (see Chapter 2, "What Are Investment Grade Wines?").

Chapter Two

What Are Investment Grade Wines?

IN THE MOVIE *The Jerk*, actor Steve Martin portrays a new millionaire who is not very bright. The film contains a classic scene that had wine aficionados worldwide howling with glee. Martin's character is sitting at a table in a posh restaurant and a haughty waiter comes to the table.

"Monsieur," the waiter says, "do you want another bottle of Château Latour 1966 wine?"

"Yes, but no more 1966. No more 1966! Let's splurge! Fresh wine. The freshest you've got! This year. No more of that old stuff!"

The Importance of Longevity

IN THAT SCENE, Martin articulates one of a number of characteristics that are commonly associated with wines that increase in value, or as I call them, investment grade wines—IGW for short. That characteristic is longevity. Wines that can last a long time—20 to 30 years or more—and taste delicious when you finally drink them have the most investment potential. Such wines yield what wine lovers call "complexity" in taste: not just one taste sensation but a variety of flavors that explode on one's palate and add up to extreme pleasure.

> This ability to get better with age is the single most important characteristic that distinguishes fine wine from other beverages, as well as other lesser wines. I owned a bottle of 1870 Lafite that was sensational when I opened it in 1981.

This ability to improve with age is the single most important characteristic that distinguishes fine wine from other beverages, as well as other lesser wines. I owned a bottle of 1870 Lafite that was sensational when I opened it in 1981. Several months after this historic opening, I had lunch with the Baron Elie de Rothschild, the owner of Château Lafite, and I mentioned the ancient bottle. He gave me a cool look and replied, "My dear man, you drank it too young."

People have been aware of some wines' aging potential for a long time. The Bible seems to suggest that St. Luke understood the influence of age on a wine's flavor, and there is some evidence of wine being allowed to age in ancient Greece. But, it's the ancient Romans who are credited with being the first to truly allow wine to age. Wines that had a high sugar content were aged in an amphora (a two-handled, narrow-necked, big-bellied vessel), and certain wines could be kept for 15 to 20 years, or even decades.

Artificial Aging

Interestingly, the Romans were also involved in artificially aging wines with smoke and heat. (Today, if wine is stored in an area where the temperature is too high, it will age prematurely). The famed Roman physician, Galen, noted that while wines could be artificially aged, they did not taste as good as naturally aged ones. But, for a time, wines that had been aged by smoking came into vogue.

When the Roman Empire fell, so did the love of aged wines. For 1,000 years, cheap, diluted, low-alcohol wines reigned supreme. Such wines lasted only a few months, then turned to vinegar and were sold off very cheaply. There were only a few better wines available during this period, and they were higher in alcohol and sweeter, such as Sack.

Until the 17th century, there was no such thing as bottled wine. The English invented bottles and corks, and wine took a giant step forward out of the cask, where it had been routinely stored, and into the bottle. Specifically, port and fine red wine, or claret as the English call it, were bottled. Gradually, storage of the wine to allow it to age became common, and during the 18th century the enjoyment of aged wine once more came into vogue—just as it had during Roman times—this time to stay.

Only a Few Wines Age Well

Again, the essence of IGW is longevity. Relatively few wines are suitable for aging: I figure 0.1 percent of all the wines produced yearly, which amounts to perhaps 50 wines worldwide. Most wines, whatever the type, are meant for drinking when they are "young"—within one to two years of bottling. With fine wine, age is not only a virtue, but a necessity.

In general, you can tell if a wine is meant for early or later drinking by the way it's packaged. Wines that come in boxes or jugs are synonymous in this country with cheap, lower-class wine. Also designed to be run quickly are branded wines; most fighting varietals (low-cost wines labelled with the predominant grape used to produce the wine), perhaps excluding those made from Cabernet Sauvignon grapes; almost all pink-colored wine; the great majority of German QbA wines and almost all French Vins de Pays; all wines released for sale within six months after the vintage is declared, such as those marked "nouveau" as well as dry sherries, fino and manzanilla; and most wines named Asti Spumanti and Moscato.

Many Factors Affect the Aging Process

A variety of factors go into how long wine takes to mature, including how it is made (what winemakers call "vinification"), and the types of grapes used. In general, red wine is capable of aging much longer than white.

When additional liquor is added to wine, the liquor acts as a preservative, and the wine is said to be "fortified." This is done with wines such as sherry and port in order to make them last longer. Vintage port is made so that it ages extremely well—sometimes more than 100 years.

Vineyards normally release sparkling wines for sale quickly, and in many cases before they are fully mature. They have high acidity (tartness), so if they were allowed to mature in the bottle another year this would be helpful. But commerce often wins out.

Champagne is another wine that does well when aged. Some champagne has been in the bottle for decades and has improved greatly. For example, perhaps the hottest investment grade champagne now (for reasons to be explained later) is Dom Perignon 1990, which won't be ready for drinking until sometime in the 21st century.

> With fine wine age is not only a virtue, but a necessity.

Aging is also affected by other factors. One is the size of the bottle. The larger the bottle the more slowly the wine matures. So, for example, wine in standard-size bottles will mature more quickly than wine that is in magnums (which hold two times the standard bottle). The reason is said to be the greater amount of oxygen, proportionately speaking, that is found in smaller bottles. The more oxygen, the quicker the maturation process.

Temperature is also a factor: The cooler it is, the slower the maturation process—just like the cold slows down body functions.

Aging can also be affected by filtration or fining, two separate winemaking processes both of which are used to remove sediment and strip the wine of solids that, if left in the wine, will accelerate aging.

As wine matures, it becomes more valuable without the expense of any additional processing other than storage. Obviously, the longer a wine lasts the more valuable it becomes. This is due in part to the fact that as it ages it gets scarcer. Like any collectible—which is what wine essentially is—the less of it that is available, the more valuable it becomes in the eyes of collectors.

A Dispute About Aging

SOMETIMES PEOPLE DOUBT wine's capacity to age. I remember one wealthy client in his early 20s who knew a great deal about fine wine. He once disputed my claim that a few bottles of 1870 Lafite I was selling would still taste delicious. He was convinced I was selling high-priced bottles of French vinegar. He used to needle me whenever we met: "Sold any of that vinegar lately?" To settle the argument once and for all I invited him for lunch at my apartment, where we would open one of the bottles—on one condition. If he liked the wine he had to purchase my remaining stock (four bottles).

Even though the bottle had been recorked (a process by which wine that has evaporated is replaced with wine of the same vintage and a new cork inserted), at the château (the estate vineyard in Bordeaux, France, where the wine was produced), I was still nervous as I inserted the corkscrew and eased out the long cork. My client smiled at me. I gently tilted the bottle and poured each of us a glass. The wine had a deep brick-amber color and I remember a heartbreaking scent of faded violets, like the contours of youthful beauty in the face of an elegant older woman.

He tasted it. His eyes nearly popped out of his head as he exclaimed, "My God, Bill, we're drinking history!"

And so we were—tasting our way back into the previous century. By way of apology he purchased my remaining four bottles. I was a little sad to see them go.

THE OLDEST WINE I EVER DRANK

How old can wine be and still be drinkable? Old.

The oldest wine I ever drank started with a terrible disaster. It was a $220,000 1787 bottle of Château Margaux that

Thomas Jefferson himself had shipped over from France during the time he had served as ambassador. I was bringing the bottle, which I owned, to display (or should I say promenade) at a wine dinner at the Four Seasons Restaurant in Manhattan. This event also proved that my cardiovascular system was in good shape when I didn't have a heart attack upon discovering (at the restaurant) that I had somehow damaged the bottle at the top, to the point that the wine had leaked. Despite being in a state of near collapse, I was able to get the bottle to my apartment, drain off what was left of the wine, and refrigerate it.

I was amazed a few days later when I drank this 200-year-old wine. It wasn't bad at all. And I can tell you that drinking the same wine that Jefferson liked was a mystical experience. (The bottle was insured, and the publicity generated by its breaking ultimately drove up its worth. Today, its value is more than $990,000. A man once offered me a house as an even trade for it!)

A Wine Must Be Easily Recognizable

PUBLIC RECOGNITION IS a factor that can help a wine become an IGW. It's part of a slightly vague but crucial concept called mystique. If the public recognizes a wine as being valuable, it is regarded as a Cadillac, or Mercedes, or Jaguar, rather than a Ford or Chevy. It occupies a high-quality niche in the public's mind. Historically famous vineyards steam along year after year with a momentum so well established that nothing short of natural disaster could unseat them from their positions in the vinous heavens. Bordeaux châteaux in France are one example. Châteaux such as Lafite, Latour, and Mouton-Rothschild—the legendary names—evoke hours of anecdotes about ancient wines drunk on important occasions, fabulously expensive bottles, and celebrity patrons quaffing entire cases of the stuff at parties.

Take Part In a Legend

Part of the pleasure—as the customer who doubted the quality of the 1870 Lafite discovered—in drinking these wines is the sensation of participating in a legend. Winston Churchill liked port, champagne, and Bordeaux reds. (Between his daily box of cigars and the gargantuan quantity of alcohol he was consuming, it's a wonder he managed to squeeze in any time for the war.) Benjamin Disraeli liked Château Latour. Napoleon liked a different wine. History provides many more examples of historical personages drinking fine wine. When we drink them, we somehow become part of that history.

There are also modern legends, which you can be sure contemporary wine lovers are aware of. In addition to a host of Hollywood people like Danny DeVito, Francis Ford Coppola, Mel Brooks, and many more, Ed Bradley of *60 Minutes* is known for his love of fine wine, which he developed while stationed in Paris in the 1960s.

President Richard Nixon was another celebrity who loved wine. He was quite knowledgeable about it, and he certainly understood the importance of mystique. He said: "What makes a memorable wine? Far more important than the type of wine, the reputation of the winemaker, or the vintage, is the ritual of serving it and the conversation about it. Don't get me wrong. While the ritual is 90 percent nonsense, it is 100 percent fun."

Nixon certainly had a cache of wine stories. One he told frequently. During a luncheon at "Chequers, the British Prime

Minister's country residence, where I was seated next to the Queen. There were no printed menus, but I knew enough to recognize that the red wine which was served was outstanding. I discovered a year later that it was a 1947 Château Margaux, a great year, and a British favorite because they used to own the winery. For this occasion they served, as I recall, just eight bottles to 25 luncheon guests; the Chequers wine steward had rejected six bottles as not being up to par. My guess is that those rejected bottles ended up in the drainpipes of the waiters rather than the drains of the sink."

Mystique Sells Wine

Mystique, producers have learned, sells wine—and it can be a function of more than just famous people drinking it. Not for nothing have winemakers developed reputations as the greatest hosts in the world. I remember tasting the 1982 Mondavi Cabernet in circumstances that were less than ideal for rational assessment; everything was tipped in the wine's favor. Wine great Robert Mondavi had invited a group of us for an evening's entertainment at the vineyard. We sat at picnic tables arranged among the rows of vines, sipping vintage (here meaning *superior*) Cabernet while Bobby Short sang from a temporary stage erected on the lawn. A dreamy California night, supper music from a premier entertainer, a bowl of stars overhead—even if a cold-blooded tasting the next day had revealed the wine to be less than appealing (it wasn't), how would I ever forget my first experience of that wine?

In addition to his contribution to innovative wine production methods, Mondavi is a marketing and public relations genius. I'm sure many other wine drinkers have been introduced to Mondavi wines under similar circumstances. And you can be damn sure that every time they introduce a friend to one of his wines, the story of their night at the vineyard gets trotted out.

Normally, I'd warn you against buying wines for investment simply because you fell in love with the vineyard, but sometimes, as in the case with Mondavi, a visit will show you if a proprietor is prepared to go the promotional distance necessary to bring his wines before the public. In the case of a fine, but not necessarily famous wine, its investment value can depend on whether the owner is willing to cultivate publicity and distribution.

> Châteaux such as Lafite, Latour, and Mouton-Rothschild—the legendary names—evoke hours of anecdotes about ancient wines drunk on important occasions, fabulously expensive bottles, and celebrity patrons quaffing entire cases of the stuff at parties.

Probably the most important way that the public gets to know a wine is via print publicity. Among members of the wine trade, the spring tasting tour of Bordeaux châteaux is known as the "gout route"—an occupational hazard for traveling wine writers and critics.

Writers often provide the first wave of enthusiasm or disenchantment regarding a vintage's prospects. As you saw in Chapter 1, Robert M. Parker, Jr., mounted such a persuasive campaign in favor of the 1982 Bordeaux vintage in his publication, the *Wine Advocate*, that members of the trade and the public were raving about the "vintage of the century" before the wine was old enough to provide even a remote confirmation of his opinion. For speculators, the actual worth of the wine was almost of no consequence next to the public perception of its value—not that a gulf between the reputation of the 1982s and their actual worth in terms of longevity would last for long. If the 1982s didn't prove as long-lived as some writers believed, then the market would have ultimately corrected the wines' prices. What's important to note is the power of a collective belief in the value of a wine.

Price Considerations

ANOTHER CHARACTERISTIC OF IGW is significant price escalation over time. A wine's price must have risen, or have the potential to rise. It's really simple: If a wine doesn't appreciate, then it's not IGW. A bottle of wine that retails for $50 in 1990 and is resold for $500 in 1999 is investment grade. A delicious wine that costs $50 in 1990 and $60 in 1999 is not IGW. The very mention of its name may reduce a wine lover to a salivating imitation of one of Pavlov's dogs, but that's irrelevant to the cool-headed investor.

So in order to detect IGW we have to look at its price history. IGW shows a dramatic increase in price—usually over a relatively lengthy period of time. An average increase is at least 15 to 20 percent a year consistently. Before you invest in a wine, you should get answers to the following questions. The information is easily obtainable and it will enable you to get a better sense of whether you're dealing with IGW or not.

- What price does the wine generally command at auction?
- Does the wine usually make its first retail appearance at a low initial price, then increase in value over time?
- How many years has the vineyard or estate produced IGW?
- How many times has the vineyard or estate produced wine that annually increased in value by 50 or 100 percent over 10 years?

- How does the vineyard or estate's output compare to other vineyards or estates in the same geographical area and climate?

High Price May Mean Nothing

A breathtakingly high price does not necessarily denote a good investment. There are times, for example, when I have not recommended that clients buy a variety of world renowned wines, such as Lafite, Mouton, Pétrus, Latour, Cheval Blanc, and Haut-Brion because of their astronomical prices. The high degree of excellence of these wines remained unchanged, but that wasn't the point. If a wine's purchase price is so high that it cannot reasonably increase over the coming years, it's not IGW.

The Point System

THE BIG CHANGE in characterizing wine as investment grade since the mid-'80s is the point system born in that decade.

Before you invest in any wine, check out its point score, both that given by Parker and its score in the *Wine Spectator*. To ignore a wine's score is foolhardy.

While the *Wine Spectator* and Parker have been known to disagree, many times they agree on the overall quality of a particular wine.

Clive Coates is one other critic I like, and many people who buy only very high-end wine seem to favor him too. Coates uses the older 20-point system in rating wines. (For details about both scoring systems, see Chapter 1.)

Purple Prose

WINE CRITICS COMMONLY attempt to describe how wine tastes. Their verbiage is, in many cases, as noninstructive as it is colorful—the same color as many grapes, purple. For example, in *The Wine Spectator's Ultimate Guide to Buying Wine*, a critic describes a wine from a Graves Château in Bordeaux as "giving a dazzling combination of ripeness and maturity in flavor. It has concentration, depth and a mouth filling but lively texture. The flavors are exotic without becoming extreme, evoking chocolate, pepper, ripe fruit and tobacco."

In striving for precise description, critics sometimes go too far. Robert M. Parker, Jr., for example, once compared the smell of a particular wine he liked to "road tar." Not exactly an image to start one salivating with anticipation.

All this notwithstanding, you should understand what the critics mean when they describe wine in certain ways. A number of these commonly used terms are contained in Appendix B, "A Glossary of Wine Terms."

The Wine's Birthplace

ANOTHER CHARACTERISTIC OF IGW is the sound reputation of the area that the wine comes from. Certain areas are known by buyers to generally produce high-grade wines, just as Idaho has a reputation for producing good potatoes, the state of Washington delicious apples, and Maine succulent lobsters.

When it comes to wine, there is a variety of contenders for the crown, but many critics would likely still consider Bordeaux, France, as the world's top wine-producing region. From its storied châteaux have come most of the greatest wines ever made, and the winemakers there have a reputation for excellence (see Chapter 7).

The Bordeaux area is classically known for red wines—75 percent of its production is red—but it also produces some delicious whites, which amount to the remaining 25 percent of its annual production.

Its geographical sidekick, Burgundy, also has an excellent reputation for producing fine wine, but it has not quite achieved Bordeaux's stature.

Challengers: California and Beyond

While Bordeaux may still be number one, a number of regions are starting to gain a reputation equal to that of Bordeaux in winemaking. This is partly because these regions have adopted some of the methods used in Bordeaux for growing the great grapes that lead to great wines. Innovative winemakers like California's Helen Turley, for example, have planted vineyards on the sides of gravelly hills in the same kind of seemingly inhospitable soil found in Bordeaux. Turley has also replanted cuttings from Bordeaux.

And she's had great results: Some of her wines now sell for $1,000 per bottle.

The thing that really put California wines on the map can be traced back to a place far from California—Paris, one crisp morning in May of 1976 at the Academie du Vin. What happened there was equivalent to an atomic blast—wine-wise—heard 'round the world.

Gathered there, as Robert Finigan writes in his book *Essentials of Wine*, was an "assemblage of learned palates" that even impressed Steven Spurrier, co-founder of the Academie and the person who dreamed up the event. Also there were

Pierre Brejoux, inspector general of the Institut National des Appellations d'Origine; Micael Dova of the Institut Oenologique de France; Aubert de Villaine, co-director of the Domaine de la Romanee Conti; and Christine Vanneque, wine steward of the Tour d'Argent.

> It's really simple: If a wine doesn't appreciate, then it's not IGW.

This prestigious group had come together to do a blind tasting (in which wines are unlabeled) to compare California Chardonnays (white wines) with the finest white Burgundies and some of the greatest red wines of Bordeaux with California Cabernet Sauvignons.

The experts rated the wines using the 20-point scoring system. When Spurrier read the scores, his announcement was greeted with shock. First place for Chardonnays went to a 1973 Chardonnay from Château Montelena in the Napa Valley. Among the red wines, Stag's Leap Wine Cellars nosed out the 1970 Château Mouton-Rothschild!

Warren Winiarski of Stag's Leap told *Essentials of Wine* author Finigan, "The phone began to ring before I'd even heard the results myself, and it didn't stop for weeks."

California wines were suddenly on the world's wine map.

Other Up-and-Coming Areas

In the last few years, other parts of the United States as well as Australia, South America, New Zealand, Lebanon, Italy, and South Africa have garnered a reputation for fine wines, in part because today's winemakers travel and bring their considerable skills with them. For example, the winemaker at Château Margaux in Bordeaux, Paul Pontellier, traveled to South Africa. No small wonder that the wines coming out of there are Bordeaux-like in taste and quality.

Another up-and-coming area is the North Fork of Long Island, which has a Bordeaux-like climate—even though you can get snow there in December, it can be warm enough to grow flowers too. As of this writing, four Bordeaux winemakers have settled there.

Though they're not there yet, certain South American countries are also coming on strong. Chile is one example. At this writing, two different Chilean vintners are just introducing two high-quality red wines (each priced at $50 or more per bottle). One of the partners in the Chilean vineyard is Tim Mondavi, son of the famed Robert, which is further indication that today's winemakers travel worldwide.

Availability

No matter how great the wine, it doesn't do you much good if it can't be bought. Later chapters provide more details, but the main source for IGW is auctions (see Chapter 4). Auction catalogs are also an excellent place to get information on wines. Chapter 4 lists relevant information on a variety of auction houses that regularly conduct wine auctions.

At auctions—or anywhere else for that matter—the overwhelming majority of wines sold are red. Again, most white wines simply do not age as well. By far the largest entries are for prestigious red Bordeaux wines, followed by true vintage port, that is port from years when the wine was especially good. In the United States, you will also note the abundance of California wines offered at auction. In England, it is old vintage champagnes. On both sides of the Atlantic you will see a smattering of activity in a small group of Burgundies, both red and white, one or two offerings from the Rhine, some German dessert wines (all of which are white), and a handful of Italian reds like Brunello di Montalcino. Traditionally, the investment market has focused on two types of wine: estate-bottled Bordeaux and true vintage port. Their longevity, their history of appreciation, and the public confidence in their consistency have set them apart. Most of the Bordeaux first-growths will survive at least 40 years in the better vintages.

Investment Strategies

SOME WINE LOVERS follow a conservative investment strategy, restricting their purchases to the great French châteaux, relying exclusively on the dozen or so blue-chip wines that fall into the category described previously. But if that were the only investment avenue, or even the most practical one, you wouldn't need this book. You could choose your wines by watching reruns of "Lifestyles of the Rich and Famous."

Unfortunately, there aren't enough of these great wines to go around, at least not at prices that most of us find practical. The late President Nixon related a stunning example of this scarcity. It occurred when he had lunch with the Baron Guy Rothschild—a wine legend—at Nixon's Saddle River, New Jersey, home. Nixon served Rothschild a Lafite Rothschild 1961, rated by some people as the greatest Bordeaux of the century, three cases of which Nixon had received from a friend after winning the presidential election in 1960. "When the Baron tasted it," Nixon said, "he immediately recognized it and told the assembled guests how lucky they were to have it served to them. He said that it was so rare that he did not have any of it left in his own private cellar."

Speculators sometimes cause a scarcity of blue-chip wines. They buy in large quantities, which drives the prices of many of these wines sky-high. In 1984, a Wall Street brokerage firm purchased almost 1,000 cases of the 1982 Bordeaux vintage. The firm netted a 65 percent profit (after taxes) one year later. This made wine the number one item in the firm's collectible portfolio that year. It also fueled a frenzy in an already tight market for the top wines.

Most Fertile Opportunities

The most fertile opportunities for someone new to the investment side of wine is in the produce of less-well-known estates. The competition to obtain these wines is not as keen, they're more affordable, and there's greater room for price movement. You also stand the chance to make a coup. And who wouldn't wish to have been one of those fortunate few who recognized the potential of Pétrus before it became the wine world's equivalent of platinum? In 1964, a client of mine purchased several cases of 1961 Château Pétrus. The price was $120 per case; in December 1985 he let one case go—for $10,000. Today it's worth $30,000 to $40,000 a case.

Later chapters discuss a host of these potentially valuable wines.

Important Points

- IGW stands for investment grade wine.
- IGW is wine that is a collectible. It has a number of characteristics:

  Longevity—the ability to last years and still taste good—is the essence of IGW.

  It comes from a respected vineyard with a history of producing fine wines.

It tastes better at maturity than when young.

It is relatively scarce (and gets scarcer as the years go by and it is consumed).

Prices rise significantly and consistently over time.

Like any other fine wine, IGW has a "complicated" or multi-flavored taste.

- Taste in wine is essentially decided by the winemaker.
- In general, red wine ages better than white, hence red wines are more frequently IGW than white.
- Vintage port is an excellent IGW because it can last so long (more than 100 years).

> The most fertile opportunities for someone new to the investment side of wine is in the produce of less-well-known estates.

- Bordeaux is the main producer of IGW; 75 percent of its wines are red, 25 percent white.
- Mystique helps sell wine.
- California exploded on the world wine scene after some of its wines beat Bordeaux wines in a tasting in Paris in 1976.
- While Bordeaux is still the main producer of IGW, other areas such as California, South Africa, New Zealand, Australia, Lebanon, Italy, South America, and the North Fork of Long Island are starting to, or have also been, producing IGW.
- Wine auctions are the most popular places to find IGW.

Chapter Three

Rules for Collecting Investment Grade Wine

One night, a few months before I started this book, I sat down to a steak dinner my wife had prepared, complete with baked potatoes, vegetables, salad—the succulent works. Our choice of beverage was, of course, wine, in this case a red, bottled and bought locally at Lenz Wineries on the North Fork, one of the wineries in that area that I feel is up and coming.

Not to belabor the point, the meal was delicious and the bottle of wine, which had cost only $12, was excellent and a perfect complement to the meal. I thought to myself, "This would be an excellent IGW." But then I added a fateful word: "someday." As good as it was, it was not yet IGW—it was missing many of the characteristics or aspects of IGW, except taste.

But this was not enough. If I had stored it away as an IGW, I would have been violating one of the rules I am about to lay down for buying IGW wine: *Don't buy based on taste alone.*

An educated palate is an asset, as long as it is kept in its place. Wine writers often confuse taste with value. Taste is not the only measure of a good value and, from the standpoint of investment, it's almost secondary. Many excellent investment grade wines, as suggested in Chapter 2, taste pitiful during their first years of existence because aging is what improves taste and increases value. For example, I have tasted some wines in the cask that were so astringent they left my mouth feeling as if I had been sucking on a sour pickle. Particularly powerful vintages can take a decade to mellow, which allows the more appealing features of their flavor to assert themselves.

However, some exceptional vintages, or specific wines within a vintage, do manage to combine immediate drinkability with an ability to age. Wine critics who favored the Bordeaux 1982s singled them out for that specific reason. By comparison to the pleasurable 1982s, wines from the vintage of the following year, the 1983s, taste like tough customers indeed. Here's an example of two superior vintages appearing back-to-back, each highly unlike the other. Wine writers have dubbed the 1982s "precocious," meaning they're pleasant to drink years ahead of the time one would expect; the 1983s, on the other hand, are "classically structured," an allusion to the sort of wine that everyone thinks Bordeaux used to make in the good old days before nouveau vinification.

Predictions Are Tricky

As mentioned earlier in the book, predicting how young wine will taste at maturity is a notoriously tricky business, the confidence of some wine writers notwithstanding. The great wines of 1961, another "classically structured" vintage, were followed by the easy-drinking 1962s, wines whose early palatability caused many writers to predict they wouldn't last. Nevertheless, I sometimes find myself tasting a 1962 that's still wonderful, still capable of proving the critics wrong.

Buying Rule: Buy Good Wine Only in Good Vintage Years

WINERIES AND CHÂTEAUX have good years and not-so-wonderful ones, but one should only buy wine from the good years (or good *vintages*). The wisdom of this would seem obvious, but speculative frenzy and the fear of being shut out of a boom market tempts many novice wine buyers to consider buying wines even from off vintages (assuming the year hasn't been a total disaster). Technology has so weighted the odds in the winemakers' favor that only bizarrely bad weather can ensure a truly catastrophic vintage. Taking this as their cue, buyers mistakenly continue to pay the high prices demanded by vineyards for inferior vintages, hoping that high opening prices guarantee that the wine will appreciate in value, just as its more highly regarded predecessors have.

Exceptional wines may be found in almost any vintage; these are wines whose taste runs completely counter to the trend that year. Don't mistake them for IGW, however.

It's been my experience that it takes a while for most people to get into the habit of distinguishing between IGW and wines purely for drinking. For my purposes, anything that is not IGW is a drinking wine. The previous discussions emphasized formal distinctions between wines that taste good and wines that make money. Learn to think of IGW as a collectible that you can make money on but that can also taste good itself.

Ironically, the very qualities that have contributed to some Bordeaux wines' success as investment vehicles—their mystique and their popular reputations for occult complexity—inhibit many wine lovers from thinking of them as investments. Instead, they continue to regard them as drinking wines, albeit drinking wines for those with deeper pockets and more sophisticated palates than themselves.

> An educated palate is an asset, as long as it is kept in its place. Wine writers often confuse taste with value. Taste is not the only measure of a good value, and from the standpoint of investment it's almost secondary.

Not so. Wine knowledge certainly has its specialized aspects, but you needn't master those aspects to become a successful investor. Nor should the exalted positions of certain châteaux in the world of wine inhibit you from buying their products as investments. If it helps, think of IGW as financial building blocks in the elevation of your own cellar.

The biggest mistake of wine lovers new to investing is their insistence on purchasing wines that will not appreciate. The criteria for IGW are simple and straightforward: The wine must be long-lived, it must be of high quality, and it must have a prestigious reputation and be known as a tradable collectible. If you compromise these standards, then you compromise your investment.

Every wine lover has his or her treasured favorites, the obscure *cru bourgeois*, the *petite château* from Bourg or Blaye, the Zinfandel discovered while driving through the Carneros district. Years ago, I discovered that former President Reagan's favorite wine was a Parducci Cabernet–Merlot (I know because he called me personally to complain that I hadn't delivered it). He told me that he and Mrs. Reagan had liked the wine ever since they'd spent an afternoon touring the winery when he was still governor of California. Another client, a physician who vacations in Europe with his wife, purchased Schloss Vollrads from me. On one trip they stayed in Wiesbaden. On their first day they spent the morning soaking in the spa's mineral baths, then made the short drive to Winkel and toured the vineyard at Schloss Vollrads, returning to Wiesbaden that evening for dinner and a night at the casino.

> The criteria for IGW are simple and straightforward: The wine must be long-lived, it must be of high quality, and it must have a prestigious reputation and be known as a tradable collectible. If you compromise these standards, then you compromise your investment.

Any wines first encountered under such circumstances have an enduring charm and appeal. Quite naturally, we'd like to nudge these favorites onto the list of IGW to see them elevated in the eyes of the world to their rightful stature (and see our own pioneering cleverness validated in the investment arena). But this sort of logic confuses apples and oranges. If a wine doesn't meet the criteria spelled out in Chapter 2 (or isn't likely to in the near future), then it isn't IGW. Likewise, some wine lovers delight in seeking out small wineries and, finding one whose taste seems out of proportion to its price, they think they've discovered a future IGW. Perhaps they have, but much more information should be considered before making a decision. Are other people talking about the wine? Does it have a production large enough to establish a market? Is the proprietor, winemaker, or manager of the winery a significant figure willing to publicize and push the wine until it impresses itself onto the public palate? Is there anything about the specific vineyard to lead you to believe its wines will soon develop into collector's items, giving rise to a history of being traded? For the selections of the wine drinker fresh to investment the answer is almost always no.

Nor should you assume that because a professional wine writer recommends a wine for drinking it qualifies as IGW. Some wine columnists consistently recommend unobtainable wines. You might read the critic's endorsement, and go to several merchants, only to have them tell you that the wine is only rarely available—not a good sign for a potential IGW trying to make an impression on the market. A prominent New York restaurant critic once mentioned a California Chardonnay we happened to carry. Avid readers bought our entire stock in a single day. Because the vineyard was a small boutique operation, we had no hope of replenishing our supply. Latecomers could only console themselves with the admonition to get up earlier the next time they wanted a fashionable wine. By all means, avail yourself of critics' suggestions, especially if you find your own taste confirming a particular critic's observations. But don't assume that a critic's imprimatur will elevate wine to the ranks of IGW—or even make the wine easily available for purchase.

Buying Rule: Don't Buy from Someone You Don't Trust

FRAUD AND FORGERY are nothing new to the wine trade, and trust me, they're here to stay.

A plague of ersatz clarets, phony Chablis, and fake champagne motivated the French government to form the Institut National des Appellations d'Origine, an organization dedicated to the strict definition of both wine regions and the types of winemaking techniques available to the growers within that region. For example, in some regions watering the vines is forbidden; more commonly, so is the addition of extra sugar.

While it's easy to know when some wines are lower quality, such as wines packaged in jugs, it can be difficult to tell when a supposedly fine wine is really the vintage of a swindler. What other product is sold with the understanding that it won't be usable for 10 years? Regard bargain offers of fine wine with extreme skepticism.

Regard bargain offers of fine wine with extreme skepticism.

A number of years ago, for example, a fraud was perpetrated involving the sale of imitation Château Mouton-Rothschild. Among agents of the Bureau of Alcohol, Tobacco, and Firearms (ATF), and members of the wine trade, the incident is known as the "Great Wine Sting." The scam began in California, where a gentleman named Louis Feliciano, working in his Sausalito apartment, filled several thousand Bordeaux-style bottles with cheap red wine he had purchased in bulk. An unwitting printer supplied him with custom-made "wallpaper" featuring sharply detailed reproductions of the Mouton-Rothschild label. Feliciano scissored the labels out of the pattern and glued them to the bottles. Voilà! Château Mouton-Rothschild, at a fraction of the real wine's cost.

The con artist shipped about 40 cases of the bogus Mouton to a house he owned in Parlin, New Jersey. Operating with a local accomplice, a computer salesman named John Robinson, he began approaching New York wine merchants with a deal he thought they couldn't refuse: 1975 Mouton for $250 to $300 per case, an absurdly low price for the hard-to-get vintage.

Dealers smelled something suspicious, because by the time Feliciano and Robinson approached me the offer was for

10,000 bottles at $8 apiece, less than a fifth of the going rate at the time. The pair—who had earned a place among "America's Dumbest Criminals"—also ran ads in the *New York Times* offering "imitation" Mouton for sale, although I didn't know that at the time. I accepted a sample bottle of the bargain first-growth and sent it to the Buckingham Corporation, the U.S. importer of Mouton. Buckingham immediately identified the wine as a fraud. With ATF agents posing as interested investors, I set up a second meeting with Feliciano. The agents purchased 11 cases of the counterfeit Mouton from Feliciano; they also bought a batch from Robinson at a second sale. Both men were arrested; all of the fraudulent wine was recovered and destroyed. Feliciano and Robinson were charged with selling alcoholic beverages without a wholesaler's tax stamp.

It wasn't the appearance of the wine that tipped me off, but rather the price. The reproduction of the labels was unnervingly authentic-looking (when Feliciano was arrested he still owed the printer $3,000 for his "wallpaper").

Current laws forbidding (or restricting) resale of fine wine between collectors further encourage fraud. Collectors quite naturally feel that they ought to have the right to do with their wine as they please, including selling it to another collector, so these types of forbidden transactions take place all the time. Wine lovers engaging in such transactions should insist upon an appraisal from a bona fide wine expert before committing to such a purchase. If what's in the bottle turns out not to be what's on the label, you have no legal recourse. By the way, I still have some bottles of the fake Mouton. Once in a while, to demonstrate the seriousness of the problem, I invite a dinner guest to attempt to distinguish between the counterfeit and the real thing. People guess correctly about 50 percent of the time—not very good odds for investment purchases.

Buying Rule: Buy Wines Only in Larger Bottles and Cases

THOUGH INDIVIDUAL BOTTLES of wine can sell, a good rule of thumb is not to buy them that way. The market for single bottles of fine wine is small (and the operative word here is *fine*, not *rare*). Just peruse the pages of any wine-auction catalog. A dozen standardized bottles of fine wine (750 ml each), sold individually, do not collectively equal the selling price of a single intact case of the same wine in the same vintage—and there's the added difficulty of selling one bottle at a time. Wine in its original wood case often receives a premium of an additional 10 to 15 percent, just as a rare stamp still attached to an envelope that is canceled with the words "First Day of Issue" has more value than one torn from the corner of an anonymous envelope.

Additionally, wine in its original case is more likely to have been stored properly. Storage is important when it comes to wine in general, but crucial to IGW (see Chapter 11, "Protecting Your Investment").

In general, buy cases, and try to buy at least two cases of everything, one for keeping in the original case, and one for potential drinking and trading. The exception to the case-only rule is with magnums and other oversize bottles. Not only does wine age slower in large bottles, but the bottles themselves exert an unusual attraction. A cellar of magnums, double magnums, and imperials has a weird sort of magical appeal, like stumbling into a cave of sleeping giants. The market corroborates this phenomenon. In 1968, a friend of mine purchased a double magnum of 1961 Pétrus for $400, a fortune in the late '60s. People thought he had parted ways with his senses—until he sold it in 1972 for $13,000.

Bottle sizes run as follows:

	(in liters)
Half-bottle	0.375
Bottle	0.750
Magnum	1.5
Double Magnum	3
Jeroboam (Burgundy)	3
Rehoboam	5–6
Jeroboam	6
Imperial	8
Methuselah	8
Salmanazar	9
Sovereign	26

Vineyards produce oversize bottles in very limited quantities. The larger the bottle, the smaller its production. Bottles larger than magnums are often inconvenient to store because the size of the wine's case doesn't match that of the standard-bottle case. But the return on large bottles, if you can find them, makes it all worthwhile.

Wine also comes in half-bottles, but you shouldn't buy it that way. Half-bottles age faster than regular bottles. The market for them is primarily the restaurant trade and the resale value of two halves rarely equals that of a whole.

Buying Rule: Buy Futures

Some IGW, especially in good years, is only available as futures. Buying futures means that you contract with your wine merchant to pay for cases of wine up front that will be delivered to you at some point in the future, usually one or two years from the time of the contract. Futures offer special opportunities and special risks, which I discuss in Chapter 5; for the moment, just remember that if you want to buy right away, you may have to commit yourself to buying futures.

Buying Rule: Keep a Cellar Log

Keep a complete log of your wines. The log should include the following:

- When and where you bought your wines, including receipts.
- The purchase price.
- Provenance (history) of wines with previous owners.
- Tasting notes.
- A record of futures purchases, including the scheduled date of delivery.
- Location of the wine in your cellar.

All of this information should be within easy reach. The information associated with a beginner's cellar is easily recollected. Most of my clients recall exactly when they bought their first case of wine, including where they bought it and how much they paid. Very few can answer the same questions for the 20th or 100th case. Even a modest investment in wine every year will soon build a substantial cellar, making the last requirement critical, especially for insurance purposes. For example, William F. Buckley, Jr., lost the labels on hundreds of bottles of wine when a storm flooded his cellar. Unfortunately, he hadn't recorded the location of each of his wines so he was suddenly confronted with a cellar of anonymous Bordeaux. He could, with certainty, tell you the names of wines he owned, but he'd be damned if he knew where to find them. The only way he could find out what he had was to check the wine and vintage printed on the corks of the bottles.

Buying Rule: Diversify

No broker puts all his chips on one stock and no wine lover/investor worth his salt will, either. Diversity is not simply a rule. It represents an attitude toward your entire investment, a commitment to expand your range beyond what is easy or familiar.

Buying Rule: Develop a Sense of Timely Buying

The wine trade, like any other investment market, has its cycles of high and low prices. Awareness and anticipation of these cycles will help you buy and sell your IGW at the most advantageous moments. Unfortunately, as in the stock market, there are no guaranteed formulas to predict the exact instant that a boom market peaks, or when a long decline is about to turn upward. However, as in the stock market, there is always an ample supply of gossip, rumor, and genuine hard information bruited about. As you follow some of my suggestions for obtaining information, you should become more adept at separating the wheat from the chaff. Try to gauge current interest in, and prices of, wine by the articles you read, the talk you hear, and the general word on wine at the time. In other words, keep your ear to the ground.

Buying Rule: Think of Your Investments over the Long Term

BIDE YOUR TIME. Wine investing is a long-range commitment. Sometimes you can buy a case and sell it a year later for a large profit, but this is not typical. Usually you have to keep your wine for at least five years to show any return. The highest returns, with the exception of a few superstar wines, come to those wine lovers willing to wait between 8 and 20 years. The scarcer a wine becomes, the more its value increases. As time passes, the number of remaining bottles in a vintage shrinks, and even inferior vintages make remarkable gains in price.

Develop your portfolio of fine wine with the same patience you give to other long-range investments—with an eye to your distant future and that of your children.

Buying Rule: Watch for Market Breaks

MARKET BREAKS ARE periods when prices head downward, sometimes precipitously. In the decades of America's involvement with fine wine there have been a number of them. The first took place from 1962 to 1963; the second from 1973 to 1974. There was also a break in January 1998. Market breaks represent periods of opportunity and danger; they occur in all areas of collectibles and serve to correct overinflated prices.

Since this book isn't concerned with teaching you to become an adept short-term speculator, there are only two pieces of advice you need to know concerning market breaks:

1. Don't allow panic at falling prices to force you into selling your wine; markets always recover and prices eventually rebound.
2. Market breaks make lots of good IGW available at bargain prices, usually from frightened speculators who begin to sense a bursting bubble and as a consequence dump their wine onto a saturated market.

The major breaks in the American market have been preceded by price increases (not unlike those of today). I remember the period right before the break in the '60s. Prices for the 1961 Bordeaux vintage were going through the roof. Expensive wines of the period ($3.99 per bottle) suddenly cost $7 to $8, the equivalent of $50 or $60 at today's prices. When second growths (normally a lot less costly than first growths) shattered the $5 mark, I thought the market was going insane. Then in 1962 and 1963, the wine market took a swan dive that looked like it would never end. The price for a case of 1961 Château Latour tumbled from $120 to $80 in three months (plus a 10 percent discount if you paid your bill within 48 hours). Because I was just a budding wine lover in 1962, and not a keenly aware, hardheaded realist, I didn't buy any 1961 Latour. Today these cases are worth $15,000 apiece. It pains me still.

High prices also heralded the break. A case of 1966 Pétrus half-bottles shot up to $1,500, then dropped within a couple of months to $700. The '70s break showed what happens when people buy blindly. The psychological optimism of 1970–73 lured speculators into the market who bid up the prices of 1971s (an inconsistent vintage) and 1972s (a dreadful one, but even more expensive than 1971) without asking themselves if the wines were really worth it. In April 1973 a friend of mine bought 100 cases of Brane-Cantenac for $112 a case; the price began to drop almost immediately. Instead of battening down the hatches, he desperately began seeking a buyer. Three months later he unloaded the wine—for $22 a case.

In December 1986, the market for red Burgundies experienced a break. In January 1998, prices for high-end Bordeaux vintage wines from 1982, 1986, 1989, and 1990 fell. For example, Château Latour 1990 fell from a December 1997 high of $9,200 a case to $5,750 per case.

During such a time, I advise you to hang on to your previous purchases and keep your eyes open for steals.

Buying Rule: Don't Buy When Prices Are Excessively High

HOW, YOU ASK, am I supposed to know when prices are out of line? One way is to check the auction calendar that runs in the *Wine Spectator.* This carries average prices at auction for investment grade wine, and if you keep up with it you'll become a price savant.

Another way is to ask your wine merchant. Simply because you call a temporary halt to your IGW purchases of the most recent vintage doesn't mean that you've stopped buying wine altogether, and any merchant who's willing to sell you expensive wine ought to have the courage to tell you when it's too expensive.

A number of times in the last three decades—in 1971 and in 1983—I've told my clients that prices for French IGW were too high, and that they ought to shift their wine dollars into other areas. The effects of inflation prompted the first instance; speculation the second.

The wine trade, like any other investment market, has its cycles of high and low prices. Awareness and anticipation of these cycles will help you buy and sell your IGW at the most advantageous moments.

Wine, like other collectibles, increases in value with inflation. In 1971, I made a trip to France for the express purpose of sitting down with Bordeaux shippers and suppliers. We needed a strategy to cope with the runaway inflation for Bordeaux wines then plaguing the American market (an ambitious task, I admit, but we wine merchants are always willing to try). In 1970, America was the major export market for Bordeaux. Sales of these wines to the United States had doubled between 1969 and 1970 (almost one third of all the wines sold in America were French). The demand for the relatively meager supply of high-end French wine pushed prices to astronomical levels. I felt that unless something was done to halt the price upsurge, Bordeaux would soon become unreasonably expensive, pricing itself out of the market. In fact, as a result of the French trade's refusal to confront the problem, that is precisely what happened.

By the end of 1971, I was recommending that investors pass over Bordeaux. The price had inflated beyond reason. I suggested lesser-known names and brands, wines still priced under $100 per case.

Remember, if a wine's purchase price is so high that it cannot reasonably appreciate over the coming years, it's not IGW. The principle holds true regardless of the reason for the increase; whether it's caused by inflation, as was the case in 1971, or because of speculation.

Have the Right Attitude

Make your investments pay for your drinking wines. This rule is just as true as it was when I wrote it years ago—and you can make it happen.

Important Points

- Don't consider a wine's taste the only measure of its value.
- Buy wines only in good vintage years.
- Just because you are introduced to a wine in a particularly lovely setting doesn't necessarily make it an IGW.
- Just because a professional wine writer recommends a wine doesn't mean it's an IGW.
- Don't buy wine from someone you don't trust.
- Buy wines only in larger bottles or cases. Wine in large bottles lasts longer; wines in cases are worth 10 percent more on the auction market.
- Buy some wine futures. This will allow you to obtain wine you couldn't ordinarily get.
- Keep a cellar log of all the wines you store. Include everything from provenance to price to location in your cellar.

- Diversify your portfolio. In other words, don't put all your wines in one basket.
- Develop a sense of timely buying. The wine market has cycles of highs and lows when it is more or less advantageous to buy. Watch these cycles carefully and buy at the right moment.
- Think of your IGW in the long term. Wine doesn't yield big profits quickly. It usually takes years.
- Don't buy when prices are very high.

Chapter Four

Auctions

When Andrew Lloyd Webber sold his wine collection for millions at a wine auction at Sotheby's in May 1997, everyone thought it phenomenal. But that September 18 and 19, Christie's in London conducted the greatest auction sale of all time, selling a 19,000-bottle cellar for an anonymous donor for an astonishing $11.3 million. It was said that the donor hovered in the wings while a rapt auction audience observed wine history being made. Indeed, while the largest overall, the Christie's auction also boasted some individual super sellers, including $114,614 for a jeroboam of Château Mouton-Rothschild 1945, an imperial of Château Cheval Blanc 1947 for $109,324, and a bottle of Château La Mission-Haut Brion 1945 for $45,760.

Paddle Fever

THE BUYER—PADDLE 4002 (so named because paddles with numbers are used so the auctioneer can see bidders more easily)—spent an equally shocking $2.4 million over the two-day auction. Auctions are the most popular places for buying wine. As you can see from the spectacular profits in the previous examples, it is easy to get caught up and spend far more than you should. I have done it myself. And so have many others. The publisher of the *Wine Spectator*, Marvin Shanken, tells of a hair-raising and semi-demented bidding war that he got into with the fabulously wealthy Malcolm Forbes for a bottle of 1787 Château Lafite that was owned by Thomas Jefferson. Shanken was prepared to spend $30,000. But suffering a severe case of what insiders call "paddle fever," Shanken bid up to $150,000 before his sanity returned. Happily, Forbes went to $156,450 and the shocked Shanken kept his paddle down.

Learn How an Auction Works First

ONE OF THE best ways to ensure that you keep your cool is to attend an auction where you do nothing but observe and get the feel of things. You must also educate yourself on auction practices and become totally conversant with wine prices before you make a wet run—and don't bid too much. Auctions ordinarily publish estimated price information in their catalogs (which each year seem to get glossier and glossier) and provide other information, such as details on lots—or groups of wine—

bottlings, fill levels (called *ullage*), and additions to the "hammer" price (the price before the auctioneer's commission and other charges such as value-added tax, any excise taxes that may be payable, as well as delivery charges). You can also get price information from retail merchants, who usually charge more than auctions—except when there is an outbreak of the aforementioned paddle fever.

Auctions are also a good place to sell wine (see Chapter 12, "Liquidating Your Investment").

The History of Wine Auctions

WINE AUCTIONS ARE, of course, not new. They go back at least as far as Roman times, when buyers used to bid on wine in barrels and then haul them away.

Like other salable items, as transportation and communication improved, selling wine became more competitive. Plus producers could ship it to the buyers directly instead of requiring that buyers come to them.

For centuries, wine was sold by the cask or barrel. But in the mid-17th century, the bottle and cork came along. Until this time, wine was a short-haul item: Young wines (those under four years of age) had to be drunk young. However, bottling allowed the same wines to be bottle-aged; indeed, some could remain in the bottle 100 years or more and still be good to drink. Wine went from a short-term to a long-term commodity and became a valued collectible.

Once it achieved this status, the sky was the limit. Certain vineyards, particularly those in Bordeaux, France, produced wine that had measurable value, and like any other collectible it could therefore be put up for sale. Auctions were

Barrels of Bordeaux at Château
Margaux, Médoc, France.

A bottle of 1988 red at Château Haut-Brion, Pessac, Gironde, France.

great places for this because they gathered interested buyers in one place and guaranteed the highest possible prices.

A Giant Step Forward

AUCTIONS TOOK A giant step forward in the 1960s when Christie's and Sotheby's, famed for dealing in fine art, established auctions that dealt not only in older wines but younger ones as well.

There are a number of famous auctions. In Burgundy, for example, every third Sunday in November, the Hospices de Beaune auctions off barrels of wine that area châteaux have donated. While the impulse is essentially charitable, this particular auction serves as the first indication of what the prices of Burgundy wines of that vintage are going to be.

This auction has been very successful and garnered lots of publicity. A number of other French cities, as well as ones in California, have mined it successfully.

Germany also has auctions, such as Die Gloriuche Tage, run by Riesling producers and held at an abbey at the heart of the Rheingau.

There are also famous auctions in South Africa, like the one at Nederburg, which started in 1965. The Heublein distillers held the first U.S. wine auction in Chicago in 1969.

America also hosts many charity auctions, which were triggered by much stricter wine-selling laws of the past and a variety of tax advantages. Unlike Hospices de Beaune, the prices at American charitable auctions are quite high and don't reflect true marketplace prices.

The biggest American auction houses are Butterfield and Butterfield, which is based in San Francisco, and the Chicago

Wine Company. Such magazines as *Wine Spectator* and *Decanter* carry listings of scheduled auctions. Perhaps the hub of the auction trade is in London, where Christie's and Sotheby's slug it out like modern-day dinosaurs.

Competition: Private Collectors and Trade

WHEN YOU GO to an auction to bid for wine—and anyone can attend free of charge—you will be up against other private investors and members of the wine trade. Some of these will be buying for investment, but there are a variety of other reasons, including drinking, stocking restaurant wine cellars, and purchasing for private clients.

People in the trade do most of the buying. While no one has done a definitive study, Christie's conducted a survey in 1992 to get a profile of its suppliers and customers from both the United Kingdom and elsewhere, according to author Jancis Robinson in the *Encyclopedia of Wine.* At its main branch on King Street, London, Christie's found that private buyers made up 76 percent of its trade by number, although they accounted for only 55 percent of purchases by value. Trade buyers, who made up 24 percent of the total clientele, thus bought 45 percent of the lots by value. Those numbers sound about right for the United States as well.

Who Sells to Auctions?

THE SOURCE FOR wine sold at auction also varies. Restaurateurs may auction wine to thin out heavily stocked shelves;

private collectors may need to liquidate their cellars (note, however, that it takes two to three months to receive payment from the auction house); other collectors may want to finance new wine purchases; executors may be disposing of an estate's assets, and speculators may be in it to cash in.

Private Collectors

MOST OF THE wine at auction will be consigned by private collectors—some 75 percent of it, generally. Most of the wine will be red—in general 80 to 90 percent—because its longevity makes it such a great IGW. Red is also popular because its value, if it is from Bordeaux, is relatively easy to determine. The reputation and value of wine from this area has been well established over the years. The key is the classification of Bordeaux wines by the French government, a system that dates back to 1855, a kind of *Consumer Reports* rating of the wines. The rating system proclaimed certain châteaux as having produced the best wines. These wines were dubbed "first growths" or "*premiere cru*," and in 1855, they included Châteaux Latour, Lafite, Margaux, and Haut-Brion. The surprising thing is that these châteaux have stayed preeminent since that long-ago date. In fact, the only change to the original classification was the 1973 elevation of the Chateâu Mouton-Rothschild to first-growth status.

A number of other châteaux are also prominent in buyers' minds. For example there is Ausone, Cheval Blanc, and Château Pétrus. The latter wine is not a first growth, or even classified, but consistently draws high bids and is regarded as an excellent wine.

There are also the so-called "super seconds," a group of wines that generally rated behind the first growths but are consistently good and have good sales records.

Also popular at auctions are port wine and champagne.

Other Factors

Besides longevity, a variety of other factors will make wine more or less valuable at an auction. Following are key considerations:

Celebrity

Again, when it comes to wine, mystique matters. At an auction, that means celebrity. When a famous name is attached to a wine consignment, the price invariably heads one way—up. The Andrew Lloyd Webber auction is one example of this; it is estimated to have sold for 300 percent more than it ordinarily would have without Webber's named attached. And there are many other examples. How much, for example, do you think a consignment of wine from the estate of Frank Sinatra would sell for compared to the same consignment from someone who is not a celebrity?

At root, celebrity is meaningless in terms of wine's taste or quality. All it may mean is that the buyer has the same taste as the celebrity. But, again, it is far from meaningless at an auction.

Provenance

A wine's provenance is its storage history and ownership, and it can make a big difference in price. Ideally, the wine would be bought upon immediate "release" (when it's shipped from the winery) and then stored in perfect conditions until it's put up for auction. If, on the other hand, it does not have consistent ownership or there are some vague storage conditions, price will be lower. This is likely the reason for the mysterious price differences at auction between cases from the same consignment. As author Peter D. Meltzer explained in a March 31, 1998, article in the *Wine Spectator:* Ever wonder why "one case of Lafite Rothschild 1961 commands $6,500 at sale, while another case from the same consignment fetches only $3,500? . . . The answer lies in 'provenance,' which comes from the French word *provenir* (meaning to 'come forth'), and literally means 'origin.' For fine wine, it refers to the history of a bottle's ownership, whereabouts, and storage conditions. This information can make a big difference in a wine's auction value, because the better the provenance, the more assurance there is of its quality and authenticity."

> One of the best ways to ensure that you keep your cool is to attend an auction where you do nothing but observe and get the feel of things.

I have run into this on many occasions, and though I haven't checked out every case, I'd bet provenance is the reason for the price discrepancy.

Occasionally, the provenance is "pristine," as they say in the wine trade. It has been stored at, say, a château in France and is consigned directly to the auction house, so it can be assumed that the wine is in excellent condition. It's not a common happening, but when it occurs the prices rise apace.

For example, in December of 1997, at Zachy's–Christie's auction, a small consignment that had been shipped directly from the Château Haut-Brion was offered. Bidding was fevered, as aggressive bidders vied for the wine. A jeroboam of Haut-Brion 1961 sold for $12,650, much more than it normally would have. Six bottles of the same château's Blanc 1989 went for $2,300, which was 68 percent above the 1997 Third Quarter Auction Index compiled by *Wine Spectator*, which charts average auction prices for various wines.

Ullage

As the years go by, wine inside the bottle evaporates to varying degrees (sometimes hardly at all). When an auction house puts Bordeaux wine up for sale, this is one of the things it will describe, using the term *ullage*, or how well the bottles are filled. Various terms are used to describe ullage, corresponding to points on the height of the bottle. For example, in the catalogue of Acker, Merrall and Condit of New York City there is this description of 11 bottles of Château Les Templiers Vintage 1961: "levels of five base neck, six top shoulder," meaning that in five of the bottles the wine only goes up to what is known as the "base neck" (or "bottom neck") of the bottle, while the others are to "top shoulder."

Ullage can be revelatory in terms of the condition of the wine. Some evaporation is natural, but if there is an excessive amount based on the age of the wine—say it's "low shoulder," well below the neck—it probably means that there was air leakage through the cork, not only allowing oxygen but also microbes, which can adversely affect the taste.

Conversely, if a wine has a normal evaporation it would usually indicate that its taste has survived the test of time.

Following are the terms used to describe ullage, and what they likely indicate (see the Figure 4-1):

> **Into neck:** Normal level for young wines. In wines over 10 years of age, this level suggests excellent provenance. It's a term rarely used, except to emphasize a particularly good fill level when other fill levels in the same lot are less than perfect. If the wine is young, a normal fill level is into the neck of the bottle. If the wine is old, say 10 years or more, it's a sign that the wine is in good condition.

Into neck
Bottom neck
Top/Upper-shoulder
Mid-shoulder
Low-shoulder and below
1992

Bottom neck: A common fill level at which many châteaux release their wine. For wines of any age, this level suggests excellent provenance.

Top/Upper-shoulder: Again, a common fill level at which many châteaux release their wine. For wines of any age, this level also suggests excellent provenance. If the wine is over 20 years old, the fill level should be to the top shoulder.

Mid-shoulder: May suggest either easing of the cork or inconsistent storage conditions. Not abnormal for wines 30 or more years of age. As additional indicators of risk, definitely inspect clarity and color of the wine in the bottle, as well as condition of the cork. If the wine is down around the mid-shoulder level, it's an indication that the cork may be letting go. On the other hand, if the wine is more than 30 years old, that may be normal for its age. If the wine is below mid-shoulder, it may indicate a serious problem. But if the wine is very old and unusual, it may still be highly drinkable.

Low-shoulder and below: Suggests poor provenance. Definitely a risk and generally not salable, with exception given to rare bottling and/or labels. Not recommended for consumption.

Label Condition

If labels are torn or absent, this may also lower the value of wine, because it may indicate the wine was stored in substandard conditions.

Burgundy's Ullage

BECAUSE THE SHAPE of Burgundy bottles do not allow for measuring à la Bordeaux bottles (there is no shoulder), levels are described by means of inches below cork. Generally, Burgundy wines with 1½ inches or more of fill level are considered normal for wines younger than 10 years of age. Wines of 15 or more years of age with fill levels of between 1½ and 3 inches are generally considered to be of sound provenance, though consideration should be given to the clarity and color of the wine, as well as the cork's condition. Burgundy bottles with fill levels lower than 3 inches may be at risk of having been damaged or could be undrinkable, and therefore may be unsalable.

It should be noted that some Burgundian producers tend to overfill their bottles during the bottling process, which may cause a few drops of wine to become trapped between the capsule and the cork. This should not be confused with ullage.

WOODEN CASES

When wine at auction comes in its original cases, this is taken as another sign of solid provenance and it can raise its price by 10 to 15 percent. However, says Michael Davis of Chicago's Davis & Co., "It is just as easy for a wine to deteriorate in wood as cardboard. The same goes for stained or torn labels."

I don't usually recommend buying IGW that's not in a case. My assumption when I see individual bottles of wine for sale is that they have been through the equivalent of wine hell. Auction houses will accept single-bottle consignments of over $500 and occasionally $1,000. (Larger individual bottles—magnums or bigger—may be okay. See Chapter 3.)

Seepage

Another possible sign of poor provenance is seepage (drips of wine that flow past the cork and down the side of the bottle). Another name for it is "legs."

If it's a standard bottle, seepage is something to be concerned about. In larger bottles—magnums and up—it's usually not a problem because this may be just a sign that the cork has taken a while to adjust to the width of the neck.

Points

A wine's point score is, of course, crucial in selling it at auction and anywhere else. If Robert M. Parker, Jr., or other critics have bombed the wine, better think twice before investing in it.

Point scores are easy to come by. The *Wine Spectator* publishes its own scores, as does Parker's publication, the *Wine Advocate*, but you can also get Parker's ratings from newspapers and magazines that use them in their ads.

Some auction houses will open a few bottles of a lot prior to sale for tasting, but others will not. Of course, opening several bottles of, say 27 lots (which may contain 10 or 11 cases each), is not a representative sample. But that's all they'll do.

Buyer Beware!

My bottom-line feeling on wine sold at auction is that any wine of a vintage prior to 1985 or so should be regarded with suspicion, unless the provenance is impeccable, as is generally the case with wine coming directly from the château or from one rock-solid individual, say, St. Francis of Assisi.

As the years go by, wine inside the bottle evaporates to varying degrees (sometimes hardly at all). When an auction house puts Bordeaux wine up for sale, this is one of the things it will describe, using the term *ullage,* or how well the bottles are filled.

Of course, the auction house will do everything it can to make sure the provenance is good before taking the wine on consignment. Not to do so could possibly sully its reputation.

But the plain fact is that collectors' awareness of what constitutes good storage did not really solidify until the mid- to late 1980s. So a lot of wine was poorly stored.

I have been burned myself a number of times. For example, I once purchased three cases of wine from Butterfield and Butterfield. One arrived, the other two were lost, and I was not compensated.

Another time I purchased eight cases from Sotheby's. Among them were 1982s that were overcooked and awful. The Potensac 1982 was barely drinkable. The Sociando Mallet was horrible.

I once bought a few bottles of Romanee Conti from Christie's in London. The wines arrived with *floating corks* (bits of cork floating inside the bottle).

Typical Conditions of Sale by Auctioneer

FOLLOWING ARE THE terms of a typical auction agreement, which are usually full of legalese.

1. Every attempt has been made to describe all property as accurately as possible. However, XYZ Auction Company and Seller are not responsible for the accuracy of catalogue descriptions, including but not limited to vintage, provenance, authenticity, quality, and condition as may be described in this catalogue. Any and all material relating to the property in the catalogue or salesroom or contained in advertisements or promotional materials are merely statements of opinion and can at no time be construed as warranties or representations of fact or assumptions of any liability on the part of XYZ Auction Company.

2. The Buyer accepts all purchases "as is." Notwithstanding any other terms of these Conditions of Sale, should XYZ Auction Company receive any written claims within 15 calendar days of the auction that any property is with a shortage, ullaged, or otherwise out of condition, or that any statement in the catalogue is without basis, then XYZ Auction Company will deem such dispute as between Seller and Buyer. XYZ Auction Company will judge any claims through inspection of the property or by any other just means, and may cancel the sale and refund the purchase price. At all times the decision of XYZ Auction Company will be final and binding on all parties.

Auction Talk

As part of educating yourself about auctions, it's good to familiarize yourself with some common terms.

Buyer's Premium: This is a fee added to the sale price, usually 10 to 15 percent, depending on the auction house.

Seller's Premium: A fee that the seller pays to the auction house. It ranges from 10 to 20 percent of the final price.

Hammer Price: Final price of the wine. It does not include the buyer's premium.

Lot: One or more cases of wine sold together.

Parcel: Refers to multiple lots of the same wine. Buying a single parcel gives the buyer the right to buy one or more lots at the same price.

Reserve: This is the price below which the auction house and seller have agreed the lot cannot be sold. If the wine does not meet its reserve it is "bought in" or "passed," which means no sale.

3. The term "final bid" as used herein shall refer to the price at which any lot is knocked down to the Buyer. The purchase price, due from the Buyer, shall be the aggregate of the final bid and a premium of 15 percent of the final bid, together

with any applicable sales or use tax. The complete purchase price will be due by return mail upon receipt of the invoice. No property will be released to the Buyer until XYZ Auction Company receives full payment for lots purchased along with any applicable state and local taxes which XYZ Auction Company may be required by law to collect. Any applicable handling fees must also be received prior to the release of the property.

4. Bidder warrants that he/she is at least 21 years of age and is purchasing the wines for personal use.

5. XYZ Auction Company reserves the right to amend the description of any lot by means of an announcement or notice in the salesroom, or to withdraw any lot at any time.

6. Unless otherwise indicated, it may be assumed that a reserve, or confidential minimum selling price, has been established on all lots. Should bidding not meet the reserve price, XYZ Auction Company may enforce the reserve by bidding on behalf of the Seller.

7. The highest bid accepted by the Auctioneer shall be the Buyer, who will assume full risk and responsibility of the lot upon the fall of the Auctioneer's hammer. The Auctioneer may refuse any bid and advance the bidding at his discretion. If, during the auction, the Auctioneer considers that any dispute has arisen between any bidders, such dispute will be resolved by the Auction Director. The Auctioneer may determine to open any lot for rebidding at any time during the auction. In the event of any dispute during or after the auction, the records of the Auctioneer will be final, and the decision of XYZ Auction Company will be final and binding on all parties.

8. Bids submitted to XYZ Auction Company are processed and executed as a service and convenience to bidders and are executed in the order in which they are received. Neither XYZ Auction Company nor its staff shall be responsible for any failure to execute such bids or any error relating to same.

> If labels are torn or absent, this may also lower the value of wine, because it may indicate the wine was stored in substandard conditions.

9. Should any buyer fail to fully comply with these Conditions of Sale, XYZ Auction Company may hold the Buyer liable for the purchase price or resell the property after the reasonable notice is given to the Buyer.

10. The rights and obligations of all parties shall be governed by the laws of the State.

11. Payment: Remittance must be made in United States currency, with checks drawn on United States banks. We also accept VISA and MasterCard. Invoices will be mailed immediately after the auction. In the event that the successful bidder is a retail licensee, purchases will be processed through an appropriately licensed wholesaler. Should a wholesaler be required for legal importation into the Buyer's state, a special handling charge of $25.00 will be applicable and due from the purchaser. Please note that any client whose check is returned for any reason will be subject to a $25.00 processing fee.

12. Consignors may at no time bid on their own wine.

Typical Auction House Policy on Collecting Money and Shipping Wine

BIDDERS SHOULD BE aware of limitations and restrictions imposed by various states regarding importation of alcoholic beverages that have been purchased at auction and brought into that state's jurisdiction from another state (for more details, see Chatper 6, "Other Ways to Buy Wine"). It is the sole responsibility of the purchaser to investigate, apply, obtain, route, and comply with all special permit or license requirements prior to collection or shipment of wines purchased at XYZ Auction Company. XYZ Auction Company assumes no obligation or responsibility for obtaining permits or licenses on behalf of the purchaser prior to shipment. Bidders are urged to familiarize themselves with their respective states' importation statutes prior to bidding at auction to determine if, when, and how wines may be delivered from the State of [state Auctioneer is in], while remaining in compliance with existing statutes.

Typical Auction House Policy on Wine Pickup, Delivery, and Taxes

COMPLIMENTARY PICKUP IS available at XYZ Auction Company by appointment only. Please schedule your pickup by contacting the Auction Department at (555) 555-5555 at least 48 hours in advance. Wines will not be released until payment has been received and funds have been cleared. If you are paying by personal check, please allow five business days prior to release of goods.

Local Delivery

XYZ Auction Company will arrange free delivery (within a certain radius) and at a cost of $5.95 per package. Delivery can usually be made within three business days of your request at a prearranged time. All wines are insured at the hammer price while in transit. Delivery within the State is subject to taxation [depending on your state's laws] unless a resale certificate is presented by the holder of the State Liquor Authority license to XYZ Auction Company prior to purchase. Remittance for delivery charges must be paid in advance.

Taxes

Shipment will be at the purchaser's expense and must be prepaid or sent freight collect. Shipping arrangements for your purchase can be made once payment has been received and funds have been deposited into our account. Please allow three business days' notice when arranging shipment within the continental United States, and seven business days for states and territories outside the continental United States, as well as for international shipments, which may require customs documentation or special routing attention. Please remember to complete the Shipping Instruction Form, which will accompany your invoice, and return it to XYZ Auction Company to expedite your request.

We offer various methods of shipment including, but not limited to: UPS, Airborne Express, various air freight carriers, seasonal common carriers to limited destinations, and temperature-controlled freight service. In all instances, we try to achieve the safest, most efficient, and cost-effective method of shipment on behalf of the purchaser. A handling and packing fee of $7.00 per lot will be charged, and service charges on all shipments will not exceed 10 percent. Wines are insured at a nominal charge, though wines being shipped via UPS cannot be insured. Any loss or damage resulting from shipping wines via UPS will be the sole responsibility and at the risk of the purchaser. XYZ Auction Company will not be held responsible for any deterioration of wines occurring while in transit.

> I don't recommend buying IGW that's not in a case. My assumption when I see individual bottles of wine for sale is that they have been through the equivalent of wine hell.

Wines shipped within the State are [or are not] subject to taxation. Holders of State Liquor Authority Licenses may be exempt from taxation and should present the required documents to XYZ Auction Company prior to purchase. Wines shipped outside the State are [or are not] exempt from State taxation provided delivery is made by a registered ICC-licensed carrier. Taxation is determined by the governing body of the final destination of the shipment. Successful bidders are required to comply with their respective states' regulations regarding importation of alcoholic beverages. Please contact [name of person] of XYZ Auction Company to arrange shipment or request a shipping quotation.

Important Points

- The best way to learn about auctions is to attend one (they're free) and simply observe.
- Most auction buyers work in the wine trade.

- "First growths" is a term coined by French wine brokers in 1855 (as part of the Official Classification of 1855). It refers to the top wines (also known as *premiers crus*) in Bordeaux, France. They are generally regarded as the best wines in the world.
- When a person is famous, his or her wine collection will almost surely rise in value.
- Provenance is the history of the wine—how it's been stored—and is the single most important selling asset in auctions. "Pristine" provenance, where the wine has been stored at the château, is the best possible provenance.
- Ullage (how far up the bottle is filled) is the single most important detail related to provenance.
- As a rule, don't buy single bottles of wine. As mentioned here and in Chapter 3, cases are best.
- Before buying a wine, make sure you know its point score. A point score that's too low can make it difficult to sell.
- The price you pay for wine at an auction will be hiked up by the 15 percent commission the auction house adds, as well as sales tax.

Chapter Five

Wine Futures

The way a wine future works is simple. You pay a wine merchant a certain price for this year's harvest (usually Bordeaux, but some other areas also offer futures), which will not be bottled for 18 months to 2 years. At the release of the wine, prices will be established—high, low, or in-between—depending on the winery's evaluation of the vintage. If the prices are higher than what you paid, then you've saved yourself some money. For example, if you bought, say, Pomerol futures in the Bordeaux area of France at $200 a case (prices are always set by the case) and the vineyard release prices are $400, you'd be the immediate recipient of a $200 profit, because you paid $200 instead of $400.

Get the Wine You Like

SAVING MONEY IS not the only reason people buy futures. Another is to be sure to obtain the particular wine they crave. For example, in the Pomerol district, some vineyards have such tiny productions that buying futures is the only way to guarantee you'll get what you want. Indeed, if you want wine from the small châteaux, such as Lafleur, Gombaud-Guillot, Bon Pasteur, Le Pin, Clinet, La Conseillante, and L'Evangile, which do not produce large numbers of cases—under 5,000 per year—buying futures will be your only option.

Bottled As You Like It

ANOTHER GREAT ADVANTAGE of buying futures is that you can usually get them bottled in any size you wish. Just ask your wine merchant to have it done. Nonstandard bottle size can be handy. For example, you may want to order half-bottles if you are buying strictly for drinking—half-bottles are an excellent drinking size. Or, you may want to order magnums if you are storing the wine as an investment—because magnums keep better than standard-size bottles. Or you may want to order an Imperial for a friend who has a secret longing for a hernia operation.

Take Care

WHILE BUYING FUTURES can be a very positive thing, it can also have its drawbacks: It's not hard to lose money. There are a number of potential pitfalls.

One major problem occurs when a château sets its prices lower than what you paid the wine merchant. For example, vintage prices in Bordeaux in 1986 and 1990 were set lower than in 1985 and 1989. So anyone who bought the 1986 and 1990 vintages immediately lost money in the short term. And the prices on those vintages rose slowly, not following significant price rises that are typical of IGW. In fact, many wines, even first growths, will not increase in price more than 25 to 30 percent between the time they're offered as futures and the time they're released for sale. In those cases, it hardly makes sense to buy futures in IGW for the short term, because you could earn that percentage through some other investment vehicle, such as mutual funds or stocks, and not have to cope with storage and the like. On the other hand, in the long run the prices could rise significantly, causing the investment to be well worth your while.

To add tasting insult to fiscal injury, you can also end up with a mediocre wine. "I bought futures in 1994," says one man who prefers to remain unnamed, "and from an investment of $10,000 I reaped a big $110!"

Lowering Your Risk

TO LOWER YOUR risk, I heartily suggest that you follow a series of careful strategies. "When you get into the futures area," says one wine insider, "consider it a ride down the Colorado River. The best thing you can get is a good guide."

The best guide to lead you through the futures rapids is a savvy—and solvent—wine merchant. This is by far the most important step you can take, because if the merchant is good, you will avoid other problems.

For one thing, working with an experienced wine merchant enables you to buy IGW in the first place. The wineries and châteaux commonly give merchants preferred access to the wine because they want repeat business.

This "pull," as it were, can be more important because as a vintage's quality becomes evident, the more obvious it becomes that the supply will be finite; that is, people will start to drink it out of existence. Good merchants will not only have access to these wines, but they will have an exact idea of how many cases they can sell futures of with a certainty that they'll deliver. My own sales figures are evidence that wine buyers are concerned about access to wines from good vintages. Almost a whopping 65 percent of my futures sales are to out-of-state customers. Some of these sales involve a great deal of inconvenience to the clients, who have to acquire the requisite permits from the alcohol and beverage authorities in their home states before I can legally ship their wine (see Chapter 6, "Other Ways to Buy Wine").

IGW is generally available in good vintage years, and that's where you—and your wine merchant—should focus. But that doesn't mean you can't get IGW from other vintages, even mediocre ones. It may be like digging for gold, but if you—or more particularly, your wine merchant—know where to look, you can unearth the treasure.

Nondelivery

A GOOD MERCHANT will also help you avoid problems with nondelivery.

When you agree to buy futures, you sign a contract with a wine merchant and give a down payment, with the balance due within, say, 30 or 60 days. But that contract—like any contract—is only as good as your merchant. How do you know you will receive your wine? When the time comes to deliver the wine, what's to prevent the merchant from defaulting? They do, for a variety of reasons.

"When you get into the futures area," says one wine insider, "consider it a ride down the Colorado River. The best thing you can get is a good guide."

Sometimes, a merchant will, in effect, gamble with a client's money. That is, the merchant takes the money for the futures then fails to get a commitment from his supplier for the wine. This problem reared its head starting with the 1982 vintage in Bordeaux. Before this, a merchant who got into trouble with futures by not getting a commitment on the wine could always plead his case with the château, hoping for an extra allotment. But in 1982, I knew of more than one merchant who had too many irons in the fire. One merchant ended up in the unenviable position of owing a client a hundred cases of Pétrus. The futures purchase was $60,000; the worth of the wine at the time of delivery was an eye-popping, stomach-squeezing $300,000. The futures client, who was also known to me as a canny investor, sent the merchant a letter offering to simply take the money instead of the wine. Generous terms. The wine dealer desperately called everybody in the trade who owed him a favor; he managed to locate a total of 15 cases of uncommitted Pétrus, far fewer than what he needed. He's still in business today, but God only knows what sort of deal he cut with the devil to extricate himself.

Sometimes a wine merchant gets in way over his head and goes bankrupt. He signs up futures, his fiscal philosophy being to rob Peter to pay Paul, but it doesn't work, and his creditors—one of whom is you—end up getting pennies on the dollar.

Sometimes, nondelivery is not the wine merchant's fault. Say a shipper goes bankrupt. Or shippers short the merchant and this includes your order. I had this happen to me. One whole shipment, direct from a château, disappeared. An examination of the shipping documents, sent to me from France, showed the ship's registry as South Molucca. Someone had a hell of a party at my expense. On another occasion a salesman from an unfamiliar wholesaler talked me into using his boss as my supplier for my futures sales. I paid the company 30 percent of the total value of my order. When the futures prices of the particular vintage began escalating, the owner of the wholesale business decided he wouldn't make enough profit. He fired his salesman and denied I'd ever contracted for the wine.

Though I don't want to appear too saintly, the bottom line for my futures customers is that they would not have received the futures—cases of Léoville-Las-Cases and Cos d'Estournel—if I hadn't found other sources (at practically triple my original wholesale price) and delivered as promised.

Check the Merchant

EVEN IF THE merchant appears as trustworthy as the Pope, a discerning futures buyer should investigate him or her in a variety of ways.

First, ask about the merchant's experience in futures, and check his or her delivery record. If a large amount of money is involved, have your banker check out the merchant's solvency with Dun & Bradstreet. They offer a variety of financial reports, but you can get a basic one for $75 by calling (800) TRY-1-DNB. Such reports provide information as to how merchants pay their bills, and thereby indicate if a merchant is healthy, fiscally speaking.

Another good idea is to get a written statement of the merchant's policy regarding nondeliverable wines. You should get a guarantee that should the wine fail to be delivered, you will be paid fair market value established by current retail or wholesale lists. Keep accurate records, with receipts, of all your futures purchases. All merchants may experience a shortage of wines for reasons beyond their control. What's important is that you find a trustworthy merchant who will indemnify you. When a wholesaler left me unable to deliver two cases of 1982 Certan de May, I offered my client two options: I would guarantee to obtain the wine for him at a later date (not a bad deal, since he wouldn't have to worry about storing it in the interim) or I'd pay him the market value of his purchase. The second option, though justified, is not standard practice. He opted for the money. I wrote him a check for $1,500, no questions asked. (Maybe I am a saint!)

Problems with unreliable merchants have not been as common since the hectic mid-'80s, but in addition to the previous suggestions, you should still ask the merchant for written proof that he has a commitment from his shipper to receive the wine.

Speculators

ANOTHER THING THAT can militate against your getting the wine is the interference of speculators. Speculators buy enormous amounts of hard-to-get IGW futures in 50- and 100-case lots—the ones on the number one IGW list. By delivery time, the wines are sold out or available only at astronomical prices. Wine is not a commodity that can be generated by simply starting up production again. Once the vintage is off the vines and into the bottles, that's it. In the meantime, the price has risen from say, $600 to $2,400 per case.

A vintage that causes a lot of speculative activity poses an additional danger to wine buyers in that it attracts all sorts of con men and tricksters. Desperate buyers will listen to anyone who claims he has access to unobtainable wines. A Swiss group sold many millions of dollars' worth of the 1982 Bordeaux and then disappeared before making delivery. In Chicago, a wine merchant paid $1.5 million to a wholesaler, but his clients never saw their wine. He was the victim of an unscrupulous Frenchman who went around the United States collecting money for wines he had no intention of delivering. In San Francisco, a wine shop closed after selling $100,000 in futures sales on which delivery proved impossible.

> Even if the merchant appears as trustworthy as the Pope, a discerning futures buyer should investigate him or her in a variety of ways.

Lawsuits may sometimes offer a remedy (the San Francisco clients recouped some of their loss by suing the importer, whom the bankrupt merchant had already paid for their wines), but legal action isn't practical most of the time. The best defense against such an occurrence, in addition to taking the steps suggested here, is to thoroughly check the reputation of your merchant. Ask for the names of other clients who have bought futures from him or her, and ask the opinion of other futures investors.

A mind-blowing scenario is to imagine you're spending, say, $10,000 on futures for three cases of Pétrus. As the months go buy, you see your futures selection rise in value. As the delivery date approaches, you eagerly cross the days off your calendar.

Finally, the happy morning arrives. But much to your chagrin, your merchant explains that he goofed up your order; your wine, much to his regret, isn't available. What would you do? Would you be content if he simply offered to refund your money? Wouldn't you want the market value of your wine? But the kicker is that, at present, nothing obligates merchants to pay the market value of the wine, except their interest in assuaging a justifiably disgruntled customer. I believe that question will have to be settled in court.

> Wine is not a commodity that can be generated by simply starting up production again. Once the vintage is off the vines and into the bottles, that's it.

In summary, my advice concerning futures investment centers around five basic rules:

Rule Number 1: Use a reliable wine merchant, one with a history of dealing with producers and wholesalers, and who knows what he or she can realistically expect for his allotment of wines.

Rule Number 2: Check the merchant's fiscal and delivery track record. If it seems at all shaky, look for another merchant. Ask for a written statement regarding his or her policy on undelivered wine. Will the merchant offer an alternative wine of the same vintage? The original wine at a later date? Or a cash refund of your futures, at present market value?

Rule Number 3: Keep accurate records of purchases, including receipts that document your delivery times.

Rule Number 4: Try to negotiate a partial down payment. If your purchase is over $5,000, I recommend a down payment of 20 to 30 percent. Whenever and wherever possible, pay as little as necessary up front.

Rule Number 5: Buy futures as you would bottled wine: good wine in good years.

Important Points

- Wine merchants sell futures.
- Buying futures may be the only way you can get certain wines.
- You can break even (not a desirable investment goal!) or lose money from futures if:

    The winery sets prices lower than what you paid.

    The merchant doesn't deliver as promised.

- Before contracting with a wine merchant you should:

    Check out the merchant's track record thoroughly.

    Get a written statement of his or her policy on futures.

    Try to negotiate a partial payment.

- Buy only good wine, either from good vintages or because your merchant recommends it.
- Beware of con men, particularly during times of wine scarcity.
- If you buy futures, you can usually get the wine bottled as you like it.

Chapter Six

Other Ways to Buy Wine

BESIDES FUTURES AND auctions, there are two other ways to buy wine. One way is through a retail wine shop, and the other is by mail order. Purchasing through mail order (as detailed later in this chapter) is not something that can be done easily in all U.S. states. Some states impose pretty heavy restrictions.

Retail Shops

BUYING FROM A retail shop—I say with total objectivity, of course!—has some advantages over other ways.

For one thing, it's very convenient. You walk into the store and buy the wine—and that's it.

For another thing, it can be cheaper than buying at auction because the retailer does not charge the same extra fees that auction houses do. You can subtract the 10 to 25 percent off the auction price right from the start.

Another thing: If you have a complaint about the wine, chances are you can get some sort of satisfaction from an established dealer. Smart dealers will put things right because they know the power of "word of mouth." Believe me, they won't want negative word of mouth (about their establishment) polluting the atmosphere.

One other positive aspect of buying from a retail shop is that you develop a relationship with a merchant. This can and should naturally involve him acting as your wine guru, giving you advice on what wines to drink as well as what to buy.

Make the Most of Buying Retail

To get the most out of buying at a retail shop, I have a number of suggestions that will make for a more informed, profitable, and enjoyable experience.

1. Put yourself on the mailing lists of several wine shops, particularly ones that have flyers or bulletins that talk about wine and provide lists for comparing prices.

2. Try to shop at one place, even if you pay a little more, so you establish a relationship with a knowledgeable dealer.

3. Before buying any wine, read up on it. Also discuss your purchase with the dealer beforehand.

4. Note how the shop you choose stores the wine it sells. Most wines should be stored on their side so the cork stays wet. Wine can survive upright, but there is a point of diminishing return.

5. If possible, taste wine before you buy it. Many wine stores have tasting bars.

6. If you are buying an IGW, inspect it for ullage (fill level) just as you would wine bought at an auction. (For more on ullage, see Chapter 4, "Auctions.") What does the label look like. Can you see any leakage?

7. Just as you would at an auction, buy the wine by the case. Most stores will give you a 10 percent discount this way.

Direct Mail

BUYING BY DIRECT mail can also be rewarding in more ways than one, but you must take care. Your local library should have guides listing all kinds of mail-order companies that sell wine. Buying wine by mail has gotten more restrictive, and this trend seems on its way to enlarging and deepening. In many states, buying wine by mail order is illegal.

To understand why restrictions on selling wine this way have tightened, we must look at a variety of factors. One is that shipping and handling techniques and practices have been improved. Years ago, if you ordered something by mail you'd have to wait forever for it. Today you can get something overnight.

This has led to much-increased sales. More consumers are ordering wine from small, local wineries—or big retailers.

These are outfits that big wholesalers do not normally deal with because it's just not profitable. The result is that many times consumers can get a better selection through the mail than at a local wine shop or liquor store. It is estimated that direct mail now makes up 5 percent of the $14 billion wine market.

> One other positive aspect of buying from a retail shop is that you develop a relationship with a merchant. This can and should naturally involve him acting as your wine guru, giving you advice on what wines to drink as well as what to buy.

States used to turn a blind eye to interstate wine sales. But as the wine business has grown, more and more states—which have had control of alcohol sales since Prohibition—have taken notice. States are concerned about direct alcohol sales for two major reasons.

One is concern for minors drinking. States don't want underage kids to break the law by purchasing or drinking alcohol, including wine. Of course, as someone pointed out, it's highly unlikely that a kid who wants to drink will steal a credit card, order the wine, then wait for it to come in—risking interception by parents—and then drink him- or herself into a stupor.

The other—and probably more potent—factor is that an increase in direct-mail marketing closes the door on the collection of a lot of state taxes. Indeed, most people think that's the true reason for the crackdown.

Whatever the reason, some states are really getting tough. For example, in a 1995 case in Kentucky—a state where the control of alcohol distribution to minors is a priority (though, ironically, Kentucky is the birthplace of Bourbon whiskey)—a child was able to purchase a small quantity of beer, wine, and whiskey from a Los Angeles retailer. It was shipped to him with no questions asked. But it was discovered, and the resulting media frenzy raised an alarm among a teetotaling public, which resulted in the state legislature passing a law making it a felony to ship alcohol from another state to Kentucky consumers.

Soft States Turning Hard

Even states that have always applied relatively liberal laws are changing their tune and considering repealing what are known as rules of reciprocity. These rules essentially say that states will follow the law of the state from which wine is being shipped, even if that state of origin has more liberal laws regarding direct sales of alcohol than the receiving states. Now, at least 13 states with rules of reciprocity are restructuring them to limit wine quantities shipped to a consumer, and they are only allowing wine to be shipped from wineries.

Fighting Back

It's not as if no one is fighting this crackdown. There's too much at stake. Since convicted felons cannot hold the federal permit required to make and sell wine anyway, the wineries drew a line with Kentucky and chose to take a stand. In May 1996, 40-odd California wineries called a boycott of the entire state. With negotiations and some compromise on both sides (including a promise from Kentucky wholesalers to carry more labels), the parties finally reached an interim agreement. But many people are still lobbying for a complete repeal.

Following is a state-by-state guide to current alcohol mail-order laws. But they could change, and I suggest that before acting on them you call your state's alcohol control board to verify its policy. You will find addresses and telephone numbers in Appendix D, "State Alcohol Control Boards." You can also contact the Wine Institute at (415) 512-0151 or access their Web site at www.wineinstitute.org.

State Wine Regulations

Alabama

You can obtain written permission to ship or receive shipments of alcohol from the Alabama Alcoholic Beverage Control Board at 2715 Gunter Park Drive West, Montgomery, AL 36109. Direct shipments are prohibited without prior approval from the board.

Alaska

A "reasonable" quantity of wine for personal use and consumption is allowed.

Arizona

No direct shipments are allowed.

Arkansas

No direct shipments are allowed.

California

You can obtain a permit to receive as much as 2.4 gallons of wine from another state whose laws are not reciprocal or similar to California's. Permits can be obtained from the Department of

Alcohol Beverage Control, Business Practice Office, 901 Broadway, Sacramento, CA 94818. Two cases of wine per month may be carried in or received from states with reciprocal privileges for private use.

Colorado

Two cases per month can be received from wineries for private use from states that afford Colorado the same privilege. You must, however, buy the wine in person and consign it to your home address. Otherwise, no direct shipments are permitted.

Connecticut

You can carry 4 gallons of wine, tax-free, into the state. Limits for direct shipments are 5 gallons from any state in a two-month period, but only for personal consumption.

Delaware

You may carry in the amount of alcohol exempt from payment of duty under federal law, which is 1 liter. No direct shipments are allowed.

District of Columbia

You may carry in as much as 1 gallon of wine from another state. Direct shipment is limited to 1 quart, however.

Florida

Permits allow wine to be shipped from other countries when you have purchased it personally, but the state requires a payment of excise taxes. You can obtain a permit application from the Director of Alcoholic Beverages, Licensing and Records, 1940 N. Monroe St., Tallahassee, FL 32399. One tax-free gallon of wine may be carried in from another state, but otherwise, no direct shipments are permitted.

Georgia

State excise taxes are required when carrying in more than ½ gallon of wine. No direct shipments are permitted.

Hawaii

Up to 1 gallon of wine may be carried in from another state. Permits for direct shipments can be obtained for a $10 fee from the Liquor Commission of the City and County of Honolulu, 711 Kapiolani Blvd., Honolulu, HI 96813. Limits with the permit are 5 gallons per year and 3.2 gallons if it is an unsolicited gift.

Idaho

Idaho allows up to 2 cases of wine a month for personal use without imposing fees or taxes if the wine comes from another reciprocal state.

Illinois

You can receive direct as many as 2 cases of wine a year with up to 9 liters per case if it comes from another reciprocal state. It is possible to receive more than 1 gallon a year with either an importing distributor's license or written permission from the Illinois Liquor Control Commission, 100 W. Randolf St., Suite 5-300, Chicago, IL 60601. Otherwise, one may only receive as much as 1 gallon a year from direct shipment.

Indiana

One quart of wine may be carried into the state. No direct shipments are allowed.

Iowa

You are allowed up to 18 liters of wine per month from a reciprocal state.

Kansas

No direct shipments are permitted.

Kentucky

Residents traveling out of state can ship up to 2 cases of wine back home. Otherwise, no direct shipments are permitted. The first offense brings a warning, but a single repeated offense can bring felony charges.

Louisiana

No direct shipments are allowed.

Maine

Allows shipments from states with the same rules of reciprocity, but with some additional requirements. Limited quantities can be shipped from any state by obtaining a $10 permit every time you plan to receive a shipment. For a permit application, write to the Alcoholic Beverages and Lottery Operations Bureau at 8 State House Station, Augusta, ME 04333.

MARYLAND

One quart at a time may be carried in tax-free. No more than 2 quarts are allowed per month, however. Direct shipments are not permitted.

MASSACHUSETTS

Special permits allow you to import wine from other states. They can be obtained by contacting the Alcoholic Beverage Control Commission, 100 Cambridge St., Boston, MA 02202.

MICHIGAN

Direct shipping is allowable for up to 9 quarts of wine at 21 percent alcohol by volume.

MINNESOTA

The limit is 2 cases per year, up to 9 liters per case, with a reciprocal state.

MISSISSIPPI

No direct shipments are allowed.

Missouri

Direct shipments may be obtained from states with reciprocal agreements, not to exceed 2 cases per year, 9 liters in each case.

Montana

Whether from another state or another country, 3 gallons of wine may be carried in. No direct shipments are permitted.

New Hampshire

Up to 3 quarts may be carried in without a permit, but up to 3 gallons of wine are allowed with a permit from the State Liquor Commission, P.O. Box 503, Concord, NH 03302. No direct shipments.

Nebraska

Direct shipments may be received from other states, but only up to 1 case per month.

Nevada

The amount of alcohol exempt from federal duty can be carried in. You may receive up to 1 gallon per month by direct mail from another state.

New Jersey

One gallon of wine per day may be carried in; this limit rises if taxes are paid and a permit is obtained from the Division of

Alcoholic Beverage Control, CN-087, Trenton, NJ 08625. The same division can provide you with a permit to receive shipments directly from a licensed producer.

New Mexico

A "reasonable" amount of wine for private use and consumption may be carried into the state. Two cases of wine per month for private use may be permitted if shipped from another state that gives New Mexico the same privilege.

New York

No direct shipments are allowed.

North Carolina

As much as 20 liters of table wine and 4 liters of dessert wine can be carried into the state. Direct shipments are not permitted.

North Dakota

No direct shipments are allowed.

Ohio

You can carry in up to 15 gallons of wine every three months if you pay the proper fees and taxes and get a permit from the Ohio Department of Liquor Control, 2323 W. Fifth Ave., Columbus, OH 43204. No direct shipments are allowed.

Oklahoma

As much as 1 quart of wine may be carried in or received tax-free.

> Buying wine by mail has gotten more restrictive, and this trend seems on its way to enlarging and deepening. In many states, buying wine by mail order is illegal.

Oregon

If the state shipping to Oregon allows its residents to receive shipments from Oregon without state taxes, fees, or charges, then the Oregon recipient may get up to 2 cases of wine a month without any taxes, fees, or charges.

Pennsylvania

Some military personnel may carry in as much as 1 gallon of wine. Direct shipments are possible if proper taxes and a service charge of 25 cents on each gallon are paid and a permit is obtained from the Liquor Control Board, Bureau of Licensing, Northwest Office Building, Harrisburg, PA 17124. Tax payments must be made in advance of delivery.

Puerto Rico

If you are 18 years or older, you may bring up to 1 liter every 30 days from any state. Up to 3 liters more may be brought if the proper taxes are paid.

Rhode Island

As much as 3 gallons of wine may be carried in or shipped directly, tax-free, from any state. Paying appropriate charges and taxes allows for still more quantities if you first obtain permission from the Department of Business Regulation of the Division of Taxation, 1 Capitol Hill, Sales and Excise Office, Providence, RI 02908.

South Carolina

Up to 1 gallon of wine may be carried in. An arrangement for a special order through a wholesaler is allowed, but otherwise, no direct shipments are allowed.

South Dakota

As much as 1 gallon may be carried into the state. Direct shipments are not permitted.

Tennessee

No direct shipments.

Texas

As much as 3 gallons of wine may be carried in once every 30 days with payment of taxes. No direct shipments are permitted.

Utah

If you intend to move to Utah with stock that has not been purchased at an in-state store, all taxes and markups must be paid and permission obtained from the Department of Alcoholic Beverage Control, P.O. Box 30408, Salt Lake City, UT 84130. No direct shipments.

Vermont

Up to 6 gallons of table wine and 8 quarts of dessert wine may be carried in. Direct shipments require a tax payment and a permit from the Vermont Department of Liquor Control, Green Mountain Drive, Montpellier, VT 05602.

Virginia

Quantities of wine less than 1 gallon or 4 liters may be carried in without a permit. Permits for greater quantities can be obtained from the Alcoholic Beverage Control Commission, P.O. Box 27491, Richmond, VA 23261. No direct shipments are allowed.

Washington

As much as 2 liters may be carried in tax-free per month. You can bring in more ("reasonable quantities") by paying taxes and markups and getting written permission from the Washington State Liquor Control Board, Liquor Purchasing Agent, 1025 E. Union Ave., Olympia, WA 98504. No more than 2 cases of wine a year, purchased from wineries in states with reciprocal agreements, may be shipped in directly.

West Virginia

Residents may receive as many as 2 cases of wine per month, not containing any more than 9 liters per case, from states with reciprocal arrangements.

Wisconsin

Allows 9 liters of wine in a year from wineries in states with reciprocal agreements.

Wyoming

As much as 3 liters of wine can be carried in or shipped directly, tax-free.

Important Points

- In addition to futures and auctions, you can also buy wine from retail stores and through the mail, however, each state has different laws. Be sure to check the laws of your state before purchasing through the mail.
- Selling from one individual to another is illegal.

Chapter Seven

French Investment Grade Wine: Bordeaux, Burgundy, Rhône Valley, and Elsewhere

When I wrote *Liquid Assets* in 1987, the world was a different place. But one thing, which I have emphasized (perhaps ad nauseum) in this book, is that in general, Bordeaux, France, still leads the way when it comes to investment grade wines. Its geographical neighbors, Burgundy, Sauternes, the Rhône Valley, and Champagne also produce some noteworthy IGW. What follows is a look at some of the leading châteaux in these areas. You should get a sense of who they are, and where they are—which might help you determine where they're going—as well as IGW they produce.

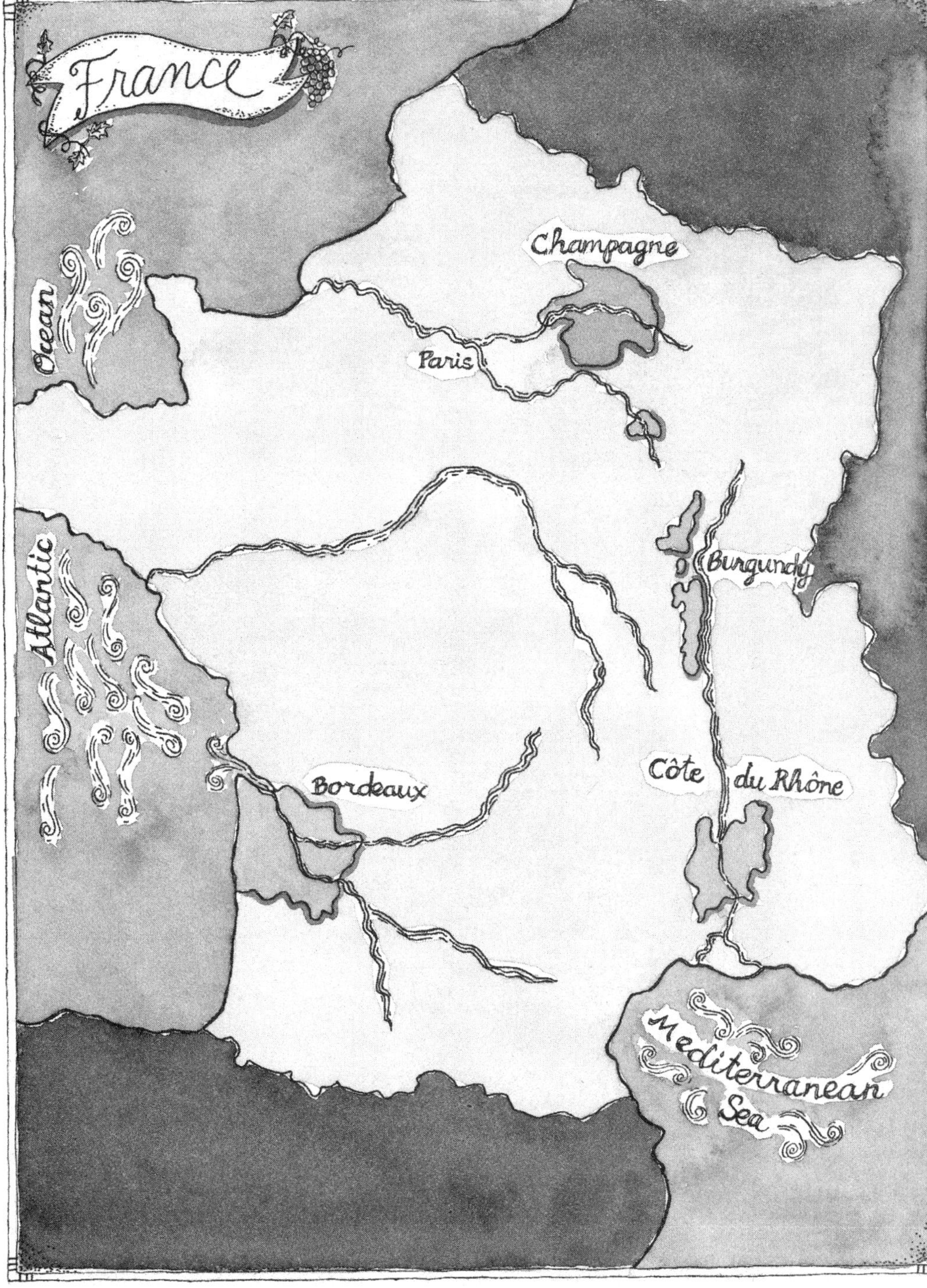
France
Champagne
Paris
Ocean
Atlantic
Burgundy
Côte
du Rhône
Bordeaux
Mediterranean
Sea

Bordeaux: Origin of the Best Red Wine in the World

BECAUSE IT HAS such a revered name in wine, many people think Bordeaux produces more wine than any other country in the world. Actually, that distinction goes to Italy. But Bordeaux leads in another way besides the excellence of its wines: It is the winemaking methods of France, mainly Bordeaux, that other areas, such as California, have used as a model to produce IGW.

Small wonder that Bordeaux has the capacity to produce excellent wines. Bordeaux châteaux have more than a little experience. It is said that the Greeks first introduced winemaking to France in the 5th century B.C., and although it did not become operational until the third century A.D., that's still a hell of a long time to be able to practice your craft.

Good Soil

The soil varies depending on where you are in the region, but it is generally very good for grape growing—though different grapes do better in different types of soil.

Amazingly, the greatest grape-producing area of Bordeaux, the Médoc region in the north, didn't even exist until the mid-17th century—it was marshland. Happily, though, the French had started trading heavily with the Dutch and the people there, who dealt with the same soggy soil conditions in Holland, had the expertise to drain it off. Rather than lush bottomland, the soil below the marsh was gravelly—just the kind of soil grapes thrive in. Indeed, Thomas Jefferson and others have observed that grapes are much more suited for making

Cristal Champagne in the cellars of Louis Roederer, Reims, France.

Château Petit Village, Pomerol, Gironde, France.

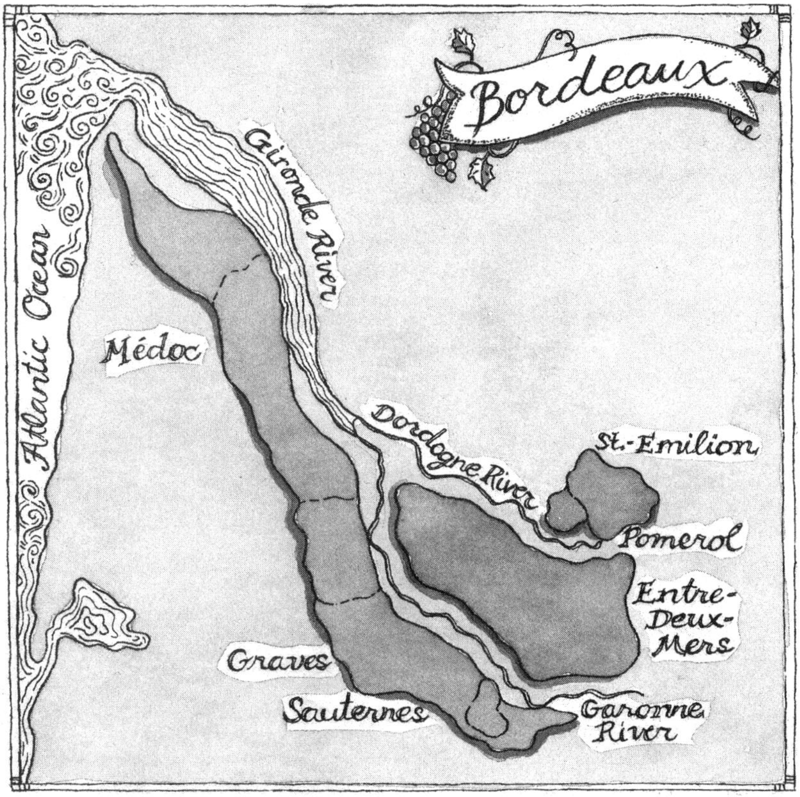

great wine when they have to struggle, just as adversity often makes people stronger and better at what they do.

Bordeaux produces two types of wine, red and white—roughly 75 percent red and the rest white. The area is divided into two winemaking districts when it comes to the top red wines.

Geography

Bordeaux borders on the Gironde estuary and the Dordogne and Garonne Rivers, which feed into it. It is roughly divided into a "left bank" and "right bank" with Graves and Médoc on the left, and Pomerol and Saint-Emilion on the other side.

These two banks make up the two winemaking districts. In between these two areas lies the huge district of Entre Deux-Mers, which means "between the two seas." The vineyards of Bordeaux are very flat and low, rising only a couple of yards or so above sea level.

In Bordeaux there are 54 "appellations" or named châteaux, but Bordeaux Appellation Contrôlée are by far the most important. The others are infrequently seen outside Bordeaux.

Most of the great red wines come from the Haut Médoc area, while châteaux in Graves, which is south of the river Garonne, produce many white wines. Soil-wise, most of the great wines come from well-drained, gravelly soil, such as that found in Médoc and Graves and also more calcareous terrain such as that found in part of Ste. Croix-du-Mont.

Climate

The climate of Bordeaux, obviously, is well suited to making wine.

While the inland areas of France can have some nasty, cold winters, Bordeaux usually does not. Its temperatures are moderated by its proximity to the Atlantic Ocean and the estuary.

Of course, Nature sometimes wreaks havoc. In 1956, there was a meteorological bloodbath. In February, the temperature plummeted to below zero and killed a good part of the grape crop. Again, in April 1991 the crop was greatly reduced by a killing frost.

In spring there is plenty of rain, the temperatures are mild, and the grapes ripen gradually. However, rain can also be a threat. It creates conditions conducive to mold formation, bringing such pests as the Millerandage and Coulure fungi. Merlot grapes—a grape that is often used to soften the taste of wine—are particularly vulnerable.

Appellation d'Origine Contrôlée: Control Laws

ALL FINE WINE made in France is subject to the Appellation d'Origine Contrôlée, which in English means "control laws." They are established by the government and signify that wines so labeled are legally controlled: The amount of harvest is legally monitored, and the methods of pruning, growing, and fertilizing, as well as vinifying and aging, are also legally controlled.

The purpose of these laws is to ensure that the consumer who purchases wine made under the control of the laws can expect excellent quality. The assumption is that because the winemakers have carefully followed all of the steps dictated by the laws, they will have produced fine wine. For example, if you wanted to make the best possible strawberry

(continues)

June is a critical month in the growth cycle. Flowering has taken place, and the winemakers will watch with anxiety for strong winds and cold rain, which can take a nasty toll. It's a wonder these people live to ripe old ages!

July is usually the driest month, hot but not overbearing.

August, the month just prior to the harvest, which takes place from September to October, is the hottest. The temperature shortcake, you would have to use fresh eggs and flour, fresh, plump strawberries from a certain area, real whipped cream, and you would have to follow all the procedures for mixing and baking to produce a top-quality cake. So, too, is every facet of making wine in France spelled out and controlled. While it may seem like a cumbersome system, it works, in fact, because there is a respectful and professional relationship between officials of the Institut des Appellations d'Origine in Paris who administer the law and the technical experts from each wine region.

Not that the laws are all the same. They aren't. Instead, they are adapted to get the best possible results from each particular area. For example, the laws for Château Lafite would be different than those for Château Pétrus, because different growing conditions apply.

So, although the control law is adapted to each specific area, the following general fields are taken into account:

averages 79 degrees. Happily, the forests of Landes help moderate the temperatures. August is normally the sunniest month, the grapes ripening steadily as the vineyards experience an occasional rainfall. Overall, Bordeaux gets 2,000 hours of sunshine a year.

But sometimes Mother Nature doesn't follow form. In 1989 and 1990, for example, August was so hot that the grapes stopped ripening.

Area: The composition of the soil of a particular area is analyzed to see if it is suitable for a particular grape variety. If it is, the area is marked out and the grape may be grown there.

Grapevines: Only certain vines may be grown in a particular area because the same vine under different skies and in different soils will produce different grapes, which may or may not be suitable for the wine being produced.

Minimum Alcoholic Content: When fermentation takes place, sugar turns into alcohol. (See Appendix A "How Wine Is Made.") Because the control laws set minimum alcohol-content levels, wine grapes must have a minimum sugar content, so that after fermentation, the wine will contain (at least) the minimum alcohol content set by the laws. If a vineyard owner gets greedy and overproduces, the resulting grapes can have too little sugar and be deemed unfit for wine production.

(continues)

The final threat that the winemaker worries about is excessive rainfall around harvest time, particularly in a vintage where full ripeness has not yet been achieved. Excessive rain at this critical time can swell grapes and dilute their taste.

The winemaker also needs great courage. Sometimes late in the growing season, if the grapes have not ripened to the point he would like, he must make a decision: to pick or not to

Harvest Size: This means that the amount of grapes grown must be such that they do not overburden the soil or produce a large crop that would also be of lesser quality.

Specific Viticultural Techniques: This includes fertilizing, pruning, and the like. Pruning is particularly watched because it can be done in such a way as to produce huge crops, which would also be considered inferior.

Vinicultural Techniques: Winemaking techniques must also follow the law.

pick. And if the timing is wrong, rains or some other undesirable meteorological event can reduce—or even destroy—a crop.

Châteaux that produce sweet wine, many of which are clustered on either side of the River Garonne—welcome moisture. Morning mists encourage the growth of noble rot, which produces grapes used to make very sweet wine. The grapes are permitted to grow on the vine slightly longer than most grapes so they become overripe. The noble rot, a thin mold that grows on the skins, makes the skins porous, allowing water to escape and the sugar to concentrate, resulting in very sweet grapes. Of course, there is a form of fungus, known as gray rot, which just rots the fruit completely.

Scourges of the Past

Bordeaux has had some bad memories. It was subject to three great scourges in the 19th century that seriously harmed the vineyards.

In the 1850s, powdery mildew arrived. It attacked both leaves and grapes, splitting the grapes and making the leaves dry up. The answer to the problem was discovered quickly (see the section on Château Ducru-Beaucaillou later in this chapter). But the mildew, also known as öidium, had already ravaged vineyards. As a result there was a wine shortage, prices spurted upward and have never really dropped to levels equaling what they were before the infestation.

In 1869, the phylloxera louse made its debut in the Gironde, but did not cause significant damage in the Médoc region until 10 years later. The louse's potential to do harm is Götterdämmerung-like. Unlike öidium, which attacks grapes and leaves and lasts one growing season, phylloxera destroys the vine itself. Replacement vines need four or five years to start producing, so you can see the nature of the threat.

The phylloxera louse has been an unwelcome émigré from America. It was an American viticulturist named Leo Laliman who came up with the solution to the problem—and rapidly, in 1871—but he was the proverbial wolf howling in the wilderness. Then, when nothing else worked—by 1882, with almost 98 percent of the vineyards infested—the French let Laliman try his curative, which was to graft a European vine to an American vine. It worked, but it took some châteaux a long time to do the grafting. Indeed, Château Latour did not do it until 1901; it was two decades before the grafted vines fully replaced the existing ones.

The final scourge is known as downy mildew, or Peronospera. It assaulted the south of France in 1882. But it just attacked the leaves, and applying copper sulfate soon solved the problem.

Winemaking in Bordeaux

The way wine is made in Bordeaux changed considerably in the 1970s, under the guidance of scientists at Bordeaux University. Nevertheless, the techniques employed to make wine the old and new ways at the top estates still produce some of the finest red, white, and sweet wines in the world. A detailed description of these techniques is given in Appendix A, "How Wine Is Made."

Despite the expertise, the weather, the soil, and all the rest, Bordeaux does not always produce spectacular wines. When there are good years in individual châteaux, they will declare a "vintage" year, a word that designates that the wine of that year is outstanding. In general, when one château has a vintage year, so will the others, because despite microclimates and differences in soil, the same general conditions prevail.

Bordeaux Investment Grade Wines

I compiled the following list of Bordeaux IGW. The two major categories are IGW #1 and IGW #2. They each represent different degrees of risk. The first group is a collection of blue-chip wines. The reputations of these wines, in some cases, is several centuries old. Since they provide the greatest likelihood of return with the least amount of risk, they may be difficult to obtain. They are certainly the most expensive of all the IGW.

Wines in the second group are close to the quality of those in the first group, but they are far more affordable, and almost equal—if not equal—in taste to IGW #1. They are also much easier to obtain. In my view, IGW #2 has the best chance of taking on IGW #1 characteristics—longevity, a solid reputation, and the potential to become scarce—which will eventually move them into the IGW #1 category. And among them may be a gold mine waiting to be tapped, as illustrated by the many examples of wine that over the years shot up in value. Note: All the wines are red, unless otherwise indicated.

My recommendations refer to the years of the vintage only, but this is the way the wine trade talks. To get the specific wine you want, all you need to do is know the name of the château and whether the wine is red or white.

I heartily suggest you do your homework—or winework—before making your selections. That is, listen to what is said about the wine; check out point scores awarded to it by Parker, the *Wine Spectator*, and Clive Coates; check reference books and the Internet; and harvest the knowledge of your wine merchant. Learn what you can about the châteaux and the people involved, because people make wine, not vines, and this can help you in collecting future liquid assets. Once you've gathered all this information, a buying decision will be relatively easy. (Also see Appendix C, "Where to Get More Information.")

IGW #1: Bordeaux

Note that five of the châteaux listed here—Lafite, Latour, Margaux, Mouton-Rothschild, and Haut-Brion—are at the top of what are known as "classified growths." The classified growths were set back in 1855 when French wine brokers rated the best wines Bordeaux had to offer. The first five listed here are rated "premier crus," or "first growths," the crème de la crème of the classified growths.

Château Lafite If you're looking for a wine from a château with legend, history, and reputation behind it, Château Lafite will serve nicely.

Its origins can be traced back to 1234 when it was owned by Gombaud de Lafite. Within a century, the wine was already famous. Madame de Pompadour, mistress of the French King Louis XV, served it in the 18th century. Madame DuBarry, her successor as mistress of King Louis XV, once stated that Bordeaux wines were the favorite of the king, that he would drink no other—and it's highly likely that the wines came from Château Lafite.

Of course some of the château's history is slightly horrific. For instance, in 1794, during the French Revolution, it became public property because its owner, who at the time was the president of the parliament at Guyenne, had kept a date with the guillotine.

Like all Bordeaux châteaux, Château Lafite has changed hands over the years, finally being bought at auction in 1868 by the fabulously wealthy Baron James de Rothschild for what would be well over $2 million today.

Coincidentally—or perhaps not so coincidentally—Rothschild's banking enterprise was located in the Rue Lafitte in Paris.

Château Lafite consists of about 300 acres, half of which are geared to viticulture. The land is in the Haut-Médoc district in the commune of Paulliac. The tree-surrounded château is located on the highest knoll in the Paulliac area, high above the marshland that surrounds it, with a dramatic view of the river and incoming and outgoing ships.

When I first visited Château Lafite in 1981, I got a surprise. Based on the magisterial wines it produced year in and year out, I expected Buckingham Palace. Instead, I was greeted by a faded yellow château, built in the 16th century. Located

Return on Investment—Lafite

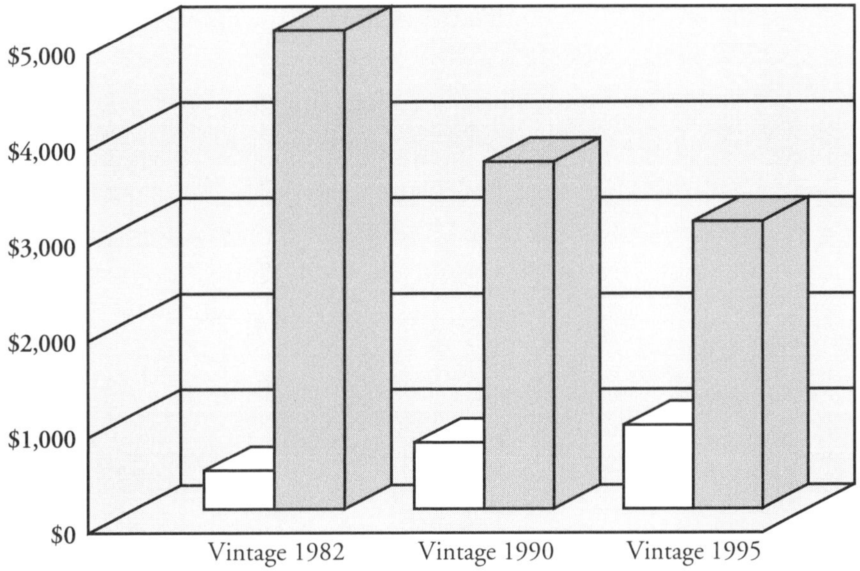

☐ Opening Price/Case:	$400	$700	$900
▩ 1998 Price/Case:	$5,000	$3,600	$3,000

at the center of the vineyard, it was an unostentatious blend of formality and agriculture.

The interior was equally elegant but low-key. Yet the cachet, the mystique, of the wine the château produces came through. Its name is associated with the best in French wine. The interior of the château was designed on a very human scale. A sitting room opens on your right as you enter the house, and there's a small formal dining room. A marble staircase leading to the second-floor bedrooms is about as magisterial as the château gets.

Understatement was the order of the day—in the wine, in the manners of the manager who guided us through the vineyard, and in the dignity of the chais (the buildings where the wine is made). Greatness doesn't have to advertise with neon signs.

These days, every time I drink Lafite, I'm reminded of the earthen floor of its cellar. Lafite's cellar—as in so many other aspects of the château, including the wine—contrasts dramatically with Mouton's. If Mouton's cellar resembles a church, then Lafite's is closer to a medieval crypt, a rough-hewn subterranean room, dimly lit and floored with earth. The château's oldest vintages are displayed behind the iron bars of a small enclosure off to one side—a nice touch.

We visited the estate for the express purpose of having a half-dozen 19th-century bottles recorked—magnums and double magnums from 1865 and 1870. A few years earlier, I'd shared an 1870 Lafite with two friends. At that time I hadn't had very many old wines. After opening the bottle I poured each of us a glass and cried, "Drink up!" When we did, I expected the flavor to fade within a matter of minutes. In fact, it lasted the course of our entire lunch, convincing me that old wines, if properly maintained, have remarkable staying power.

On that trip, four of us—my wife Gloria, my attorney Eric Rosenthal, his wife-to-be, and I—flew to France with the bottles. During takeoff, I rode with the wine belted into the seats on either side of me. After a couple of hours, I began to worry about turbulence, so I carefully set all the bottles in the carpeted legroom space. The stewardess had to coax me up from the floor so I could strap myself in for the approach to Orly!

It was a wonderful trip, the memory of it still with me. At the château I learned they had no more 1865, so we topped off one bottle with wine from 1870. And in a magnanimous gesture of hospitality, the château used a bottle from its own cellar instead of cannibalizing one of my own—at no extra charge. The better part of an entire bottle of 1870 disappeared down the throats of my magnums and double magnums.

Lafite grows a variety of grapes. Though numbers can vary from year to year, the vast majority are Cabernet Sauvignon; the rest are Cabernet Franc and Merlot.

Lafite's wine is lighter than that of other top châteaux such as Latour and Mouton. Also, unlike other châteaux, which usually bottle 21 months or so after harvest, bottling at Lafite rarely occurs less than two years from harvest.

Vintage years: 1959, 1982, 1985, 1988, 1989, and 1990.

Château Latour Château Latour was already famous by the 16th century when the French philosopher Montaigne, who grew grapes himself, discussed it in his famous essays.

The name comes from the word *latour*, which means tower. A tower now stands by its lonesome self at the edge of the vineyard. Once, it was part of a wall that was erected by the people of Médoc in the Middle Ages to defend against pirates.

The greatest legend about Latour is that of buried gold. It is said that during the One Hundred Years War a large amount of gold was tossed into the moat surrounding the château, which was then a fort. While there seemed to be some historical substance to it, efforts to unearth it have remained unsuccessful.

One often associates fine wine with fine old-fashioned methods of making it, but Château Latour has always led the way in modernizing winemaking methods, although not unaccompanied by risk: Making world-class wine does not allow for a great deal of experimentation.

The major change occurred in 1964. Latour changed to stainless steel vats, most of 200-hectoliter capacity, which replaced the existing oak vats and included thermostatically controlled water flow that would cool down the wine if fermentation was making its temperature too high. The wine world watched and waited to see the results and, of course, the quality of the

Return on Investment—Latour

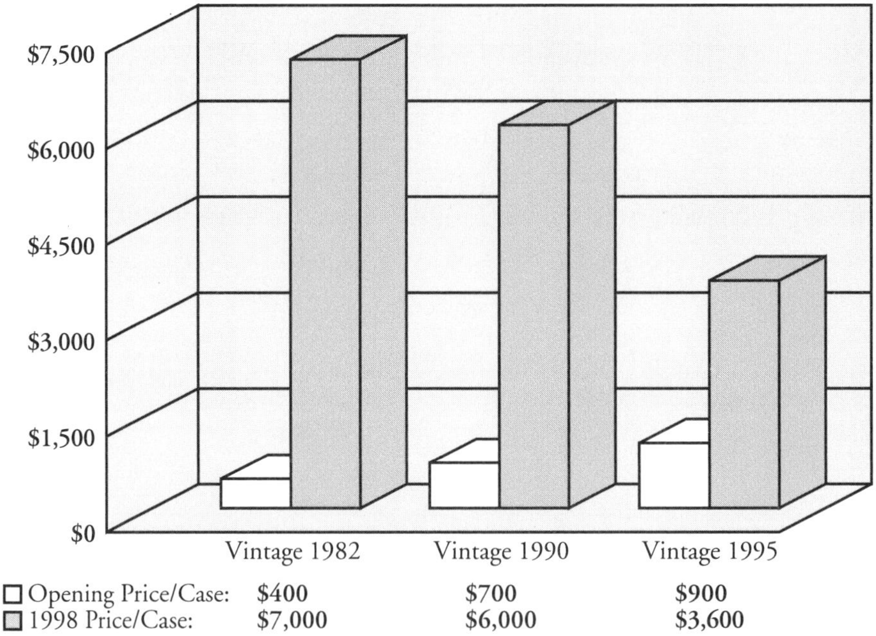

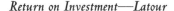

wine was not affected adversely. After a trial period, other châteaux followed suit, all realizing that what wine fermented in was not crucial; controlling the fermentation process was.

The vineyard has also seen steady expansion since 1963 and occupies 148.2 acres in three plots. The land is excellent for wine growing, perhaps the best in Bordeaux.

I first visited Latour in 1971 and, in my opinion, the wine today—30-something years later—is still the same: consistently the darkest, richest, biggest wine in the Médoc. And it's also one of the longest-lived, therefore a great investment. There are a variety of factors that go into its success, not the least of which is the soil. Half of it is comprised of egg-shaped stones. As Alexis Lichine wrote years ago in the *Encyclopedia of Wines and Spirits:* "Strain two pounds of it (the soil) and a pound of stones will remain in your sieve." Lichine said that the plows used to work it have to be sharpened twice a day, and that when oxen were used to draw the plows, the soil had so much density that two animals were required to shoulder the burden.

The soil is basically gravel, which has excellent drainage. In some spots it allows the vines to penetrate some 4 or 5 meters into the earth (a meter is roughly equivalent to a yard). On average, only 60 percent of the harvest is deemed by the winemakers as good enough to be bottled as a grand vin. But in one year, 1974, only one-quarter of the harvest was considered a premier cru.

Vintage years: 1959, 1961, 1970, 1982, 1985, 1989, and 1990.

Château Margaux This is a first-growth château located in the Médoc, and like others in the area, has been around for hundreds of years. In the early 1700s, it was said that the wine declined somewhat, but then the vineyard was much improved by replanting around the middle of that century.

In the early 1970s, I took my son, who was then two, and my daughter, who was seven, on a visit to the lower Médoc. One of the places we visited was Margaux. Margaux is a landmark, a formal, colonnaded edifice. Our first sight of it overwhelmed me—a majestic row of columns at the end of a long drive, like something out of a Hollywood movie. It had power, majesty.

As I drew closer, however, my awe turned to shock: Everything was run-down, beaten up, or in disrepair. A dismal atmosphere of ruin permeated the estate, not at all what one expects from a great château. Later, I tasted the 1970, still in the barrel. The impression of decay persisted, even in the cuverie (the part of the cellar where vinification takes place).

The next time I saw Margaux was in 1981. I was visiting Prieuré Lichine. Alexis Lichine took me over to Margaux while

Return on Investment—Margaux

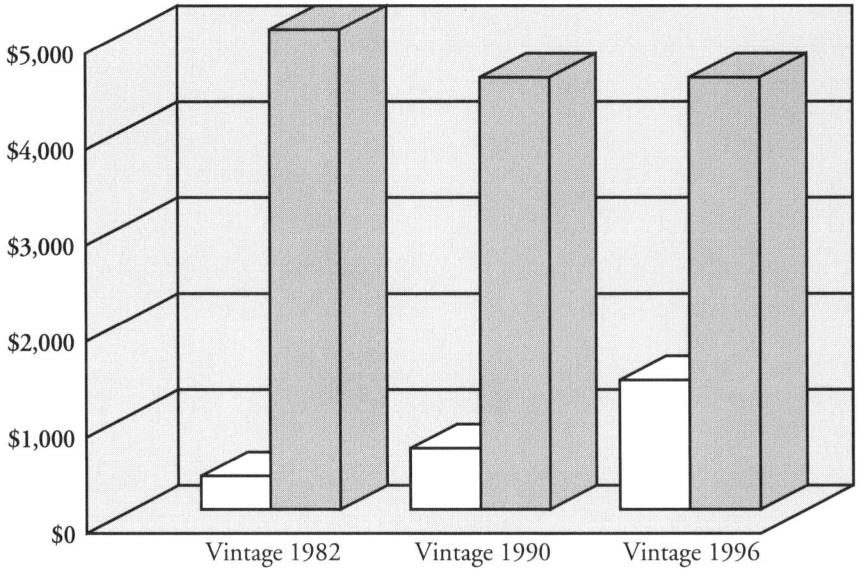

☐ Opening Price/Case:	**$300**	**$600**	**$1,300**
▩ 1998 Price/Case:	**$5,000**	**$4,500**	**$4,500**

it was still in the process of being restored. Since my last visit, Pierre Ginestet had sold the estate. The change was breathtaking. Workers were spreading fresh earth over the vineyards; the château itself had undergone a facelift and the interior now resembled a French salon.

The new owner was André Mentzepoulos, a major shareholder in a French supermarket chain, and he gave the château the attention and investment that first-growth estates deserve.

Besides making some key personnel changes, Mentzepoulos improved the land. He drained it, dredging the stream that ran through it, and replanted almost 200 acres.

The wines themselves had also changed, mirroring the vigor of the new owners. Most of the wines from the early '70s must be carefully examined for evidence of over-lightness.

Margaux is ordinarily a supple wine, but wines from that period seem too light for me. Later wines, on the other hand, beginning with 1978 and 1979, are outstanding examples of the estate's best efforts.

At one point I found myself at Château Pontet-Canet, participating in a horizontal tasting (different wines, same vintage) of Bordeaux wines from 1980. Three wines stood out: Margaux, Latour, and Pichon-Lalande. For the most part, the 1980 was not appreciated in the United States because it wasn't a "star" vintage. Too bad. For only $20 to $25 somebody could have a great experience of a first growth. I sold dozens of cases of 1980 Margaux in New York. Now there's none left.

Margaux has a history of owners with a flair for innovation, although it hasn't always been successful. Pierre Ginestet imposed very strict standards for Margaux's wines in the early '60s.

In 1982, Margaux was one of the vineyards that had problems with "hot" fermentation. This occurs when fermentation proceeds too quickly and the temperature rises beyond the point at which yeast, which aids fermentation, can survive, killing the yeast before fermentation can be completed. (See Appendix A "How Wine Is Made.") The estate lost a good percentage of the vintage. The remaining wine made it into bottles, however, and it tasted good—still does. The following year's 1983 vintage was a star.

I am always amazed at the daring of winemakers. André Mentzepoulos was a prime example. During his tenure at Margaux, it became necessary to replace the fermentation vats. Ignoring the advice of some experts, he installed new oak rather than stainless steel.

The results were good, but Mentzepoulos was not around to enjoy them. He died in 1980, at age 66, before the results could emerge. But his widow, Corinne, took over and has proven herself worthy of the task. In 1981, for example, she undertook a massive cellar expansion. She is attractive, intelligent, and always a star with the media—an important aspect of keeping a wine in the public eye.

Vintage years: 1983, 1985, 1986, 1989, and 1990.

Château Mouton-Rothschild A number of years ago, when I drove up to Château Mouton-Rothschild, I got the feeling that I was approaching a small government building surrounded by a garden; everything precise and in its place. The formal, but not unfriendly, restraint of the employees suggested well-mannered officials rather than vineyard workers. The interior of the château is awash with marble and art; the high ceilings connote stately importance. There's an overwhelming presence of wealth at Mouton-Rothschild—more than at any château I've ever visited.

The château itself is particularly imposing; the manicured lawns, the gardens, cuverie, and cellar rooms create an impression of money, power, prestige, and elegance—all in a space much smaller than other renowned châteaux like Margaux, for example. Proof of that power was Mouton's elevation to first-growth status in 1973, the only château to have achieved that following the original classification of growths in 1855.

Mouton has not been as dedicated to preserving its old wines as its rival Lafite. Interestingly, the bottles of 1869 Mouton that I presently own came from Lafite. Recent years have seen a fashion among collectors of rare bottles for vertical collections—all Mouton vintages from 1945 through the present day. One reason for this is the innovative idea of having a different artist design the label each year. I personally know of only four complete collections, fabulously expensive, because of the difficulty of obtaining bottles in the off years like 1950 and 1951.

Return on Investment—Mouton-Rothschild

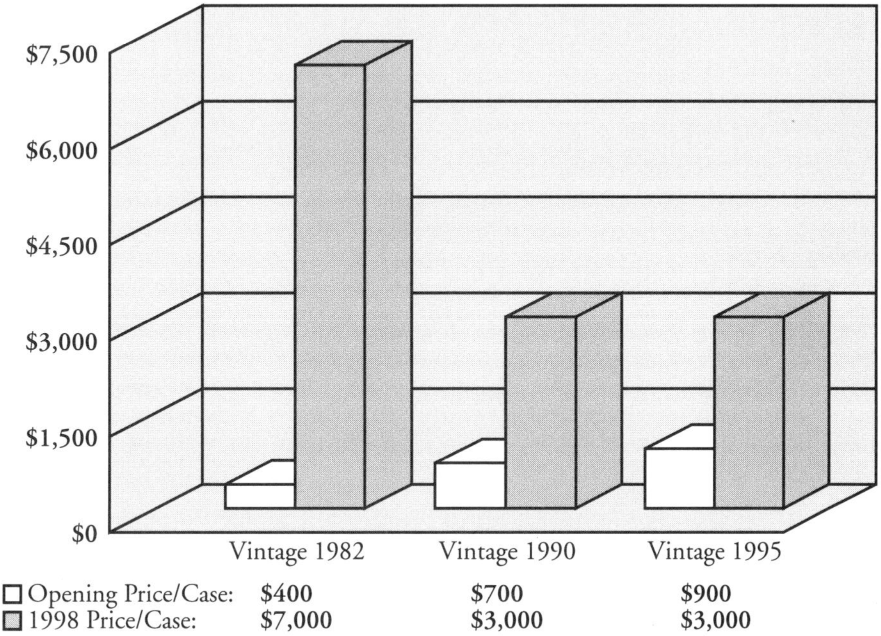

The heart and soul of Mouton-Rothschild was Baron Philip de Rothschild, whose life reads like a heroic novel. He was a dashing figure given to wearing capes, a man of tremendous energy. He died at the age of 86 in 1988, but it was said that until he was 80 he swam a half-mile every day.

He took over the estate that bears his name (Mouton refers to the mound of ground the estate stands on) when he was only 22 years old in 1924, but it was not until 1947 that he actually assumed ownership, buying his brother's and sister's shares.

When he took over, the château consisted of a small gabled villa built in 1880 that, by 1920, was buried in ivy and other vegetation.

Rothschild set about to change things. Over the years he built a magnificent château that was to be much imitated, and also established a museum containing the work of world-class artists, such as Picasso, the subject matter of which all relates to wine.

> Indeed, Thomas Jefferson and others have observed that grapes are much more suited for making great wine when they have to struggle, just as adversity often makes people stronger and better at what they do.

Deep inside he had always suffered and felt indignation because Château Mouton-Rothschild had not been given first-growth status. He thought it was patently unfair. He spent a good portion of his life fighting to get it elevated.

During World War II, Rothschild was imprisoned in a Vichy prison camp for four years. Meanwhile, the Germans kept up the production of his wine, but let the house fall into disrepair.

In 1944, Rothschild escaped from prison and fled to England. His only child, Philippine, survived the war, living in France. But his wife was shipped to Ravensbruck concentration camp, where she died.

Rothschild, like any other château owner, had some years that were less wonderful than others, but he kept working and improving the quality of his vintages. Greatness was his vision—that's what drove him—and he finally made it!

In 1973, his lifelong dream—maybe the most important accomplishment in a life filled with accomplishments (he was a poet, artist, and more)—of getting Château Mouton-Rothschild elevated to first-growth status occurred. The director of the Department of Agriculture signed a special decree, correcting what was really a 100-plus-year-old injustice.

Legend is emphatically part of the wine experience. Today when I drink a glass of Mouton-Rothschild, I can't help but think of the man behind it.

Vintage years: 1961, 1982, 1985, 1986, 1988, 1989, and 1990.

Château Haut-Brion Haut-Brion's cuverie made a strong impression on me when I first visited it in the mid-'60s. The estate had just installed electronically controlled vats of stainless steel. Their methods and equipment struck me as incredibly forward at the time, which raises the question: Why haven't these wines commanded a higher value? All I can surmise is that Haut-Brion's marketing has not kept pace with that of the other châteaux.

Another odd fact is the conspicuous absence of 19th-century wines from this château; I have seen only one Haut-Brion from 1899. Other than that, I have never come across a bottle earlier than the 1920s. At a Christie's auction to celebrate the 50th anniversary of the estate's ownership by the Dillon family, the oldest vintage available was from 1920.

Haut-Brion is the oldest château in Bordeaux, and has long produced wine appreciated by a variety of famous people. For example, Samuel Pepys's diary entry from April 10, 1663, speaks of having a French wine called "'Ho Brion,' that hath a good and most perticular taste that I ever met with." Haut-Brion was also mentioned by literary greats Daniel Defoe, John Dryden, and Jonathan Swift. For the past 25 years, the winery has undergone modernization efforts, which included the stainless steel vats. They were not just any vats, but were designed to be squat rather than tall and cylindrical like those of Château Latour. The designer/winemaker Jean-Bernard Delmas feels that the maceration must have as much contact with the marc as possible, and one should avoid moving the marc around because this can give the wine an herbaceous taste. (See Appendix A, "How Wine Is Made.") Following the installation of the new cuverie, a new *fouloir-egrappier* (a device that removes stalks and

Return on Investment—Haut-Brion

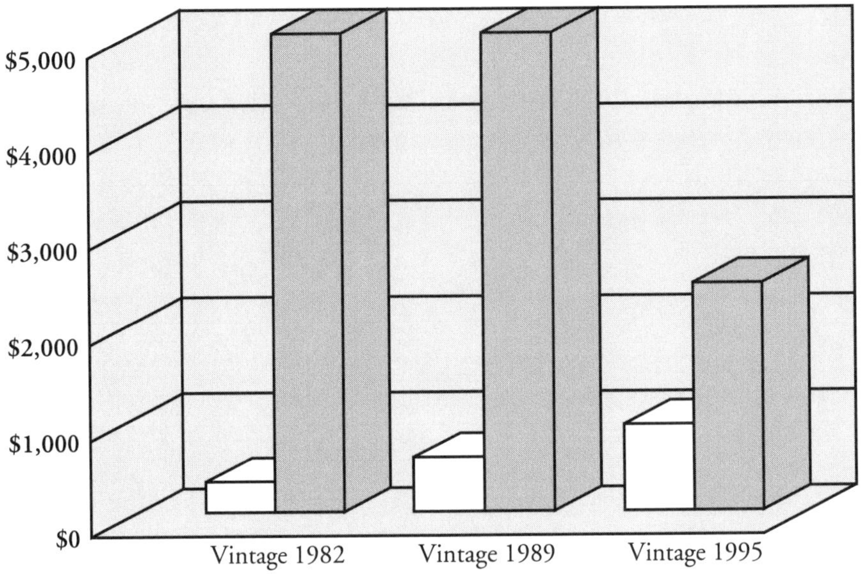

☐ Opening Price/Case:	**$300**	**$600**	**$900**
■ 1998 Price/Case:	**$5,000**	**$5,000**	**$2,400**

opens grape skin) and reception bay were installed in 1970 and, four years later, a large storage cellar.

Haut-Brion is in Pessac, about five miles from the center of the city of Bordeaux. During World War II, the Dillon family gave the château, which looks just like the one on the Haut-Brion label, to the French government to be used as a hospital.

The vineyards are on a mound 27 meters above sea level and, though there are parts of the vineyard where clay is predominant, the main soil is gravel. It is particularly deep—18 meters. There are currently 105 acres of vines, planted in the ratio of 55 percent Cabernet Sauvignon, 20 percent Cabernet Franc, and 25 percent Merlot. The vineyards turn out up to 150 *tonneaux* of grapes (the equivalent of approximately 1,800,000 grapes) per year.

Vintage years: 1982, 1985, 1989, and 1990.

Château Pétrus Château Pétrus is the exception to the rule. It does not produce wine that is even a classified growth, and the château's physical appearance is nothing special. It's small and impeccably maintained, but so are other vineyards in the Pomerol region, an area of Bordeaux noted for the small acreage of its estates. Nevertheless, it still produces the world's most expensive wine and is perceived as a *premier cru*, on a level with Lafite and other top châteaux.

Pétrus reminds me of a baseball player with an exceptional agent, a brilliant negotiator capable of parlaying his client's reputation into a salary of several million dollars a year. Are other players as good? Without a doubt. Are their agents as good? Not likely. Pétrus had the now retired Jean-Pierre Mouiex, who has been the sole *négociant* for Pétrus since 1947, and the rest of the wine world had . . . well, everyone else.

Mouiex is a man of legendary canniness. Before the '60s, Pétrus was not a well-known wine. Over time the wine acquired a cachet that increased in inverse proportion to the size of its production. Through the '70s, the price of Pétrus kept pace with the best of the Médoc vineyards—first $200, then $300, then $400 a case. But in 1982, the château broke away from the pack. Pétrus's opening price was almost contemptuously out of proportion to other Bordeaux vineyards—and instead of discouraging sales, the high price seemed to fuel demand.

Mouiex had some major assistance in helping to start Pétrus on the road to first-growth status, and this was its owner, Madame Edmond Loubat. She always thought of her wine as second to none, a first growth in quality if not in fact.

She recognized the worth of Jean-Pierre Mouiex, and when she died in 1961 she left him one share in the property to ensure that he would have a say in its management. Mouiex has since been succeeded by his son, Christian and his nephew, Jean-Jacques. They run the château today, and quite well.

Return on Investment—Pétrus

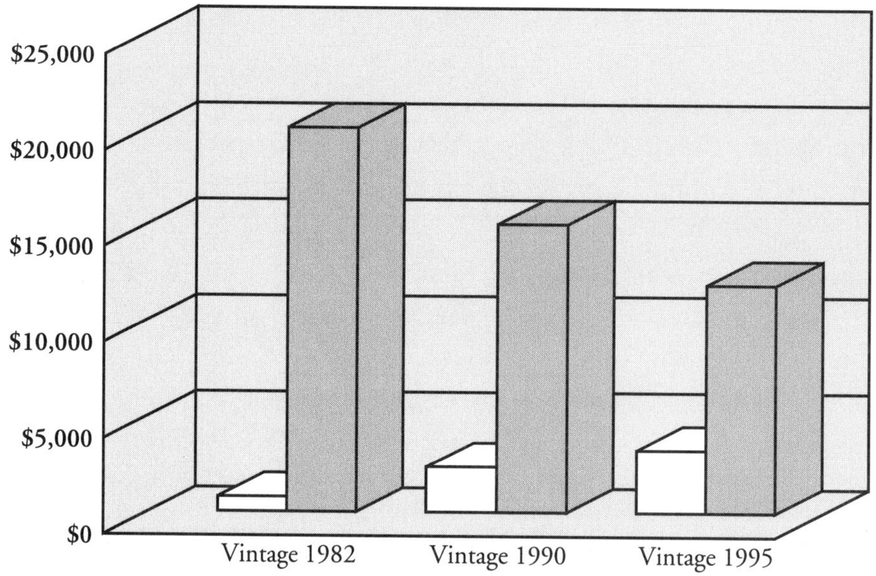

	Vintage 1982	Vintage 1990	Vintage 1995
☐ Opening Price/Case:	$600	$2,400	$3,600
▣ 1998 Price/Case:	$20,000	$15,000	$12,000

There are a number of interesting aspects to the winemaking, not the least of which is the soil. Pétrus soil is clay and has a blue cast to it, probably because of the iron content. Under the clay is a layer of gravel, and beneath this is soil that is as hard as iron, known as *machefer*.

Unlike other châteaux, Pétrus uses 100 percent Merlot grapes, but also grows Cabernet Franc. In years when it reaches perfect ripeness—which is not always the case—a blend is used: 95 percent Merlot, 5 percent Cabernet Franc.

The vines at Pétrus are old, some 80 years old, but they still do the job. In fact when a frost killed two-thirds of them in 1956, Madame Loubat chose to regraft onto the existing rootstock rather than plant new vines.

Perfectionism has been known to become fanaticism during picking time at Pétrus. In certain years, when rain has come at harvest time, helicopters have been utilized to fly over the vineyards, the blast of air from their blades drying the grapes.

In 1992, plastic sheeting was laid on the earth so that moisture couldn't penetrate, and the pickers always wait until the afternoon to pick so that the morning dew that covers the grapes has time to dry.

The wine is known for its concentration (or heavy fruit flavor), with maceration on skins (for up to 25 days), and with between 20 and 30 percent of the stems. (See Appendix A "How Wine Is Made.")

Total wine production is about 4,000 cases, and as spectacular as the wine is, it is equally difficult to find. If you do, you will remember it.

Vintage years: 1961, 1975, 1982, 1985, 1989, and 1990.

Château de Valandraud Never heard of Château de Valandraud in Saint-Emilion? Join the club. But if you haven't, you will. This château is on its way to establishing itself as one of the producers of IGW of the future.

The château did not even exist before 1991. Indeed, as writer Alan Richman points out in the May 1998 issue of *GQ* magazine, "Valandraud is so new it is not mentioned in 'The New Sotheby's Wine Encyclopedia,' published in 1998."

Valandraud is now selling its red wine for about $300 a bottle, but that price is going to head upwards. The owner, Jean-Luc Thunevin, is building a house that has those from Bordeaux (the *Bordelais*) agog. It will feature a gymnasium, indoor swimming pool, and floors of marble costing a small fortune per square foot.

Thunevin has no trouble paying; he just pays out of the profits that his wine has generated.

While the house is *très magnifique*, the vineyard parcels, three small ones in all, that produce the grapes is a former sandy, undistinguished area that is known among locals as "the beach." Thunevin told Richman that he must be a good winemaker because he has no *terroir*, the ideal site and climate that are so valued by French winemakers.

> When there are good years in individual châteaux, they will declare a *vintage* year, a word that designates that the wine of that year is outstanding.

But Thunevin had help in making his wine. He was advised by Michel Rolland, a highly respected enologist, on how to do it, and the result is a wine that is said to be softer and much less tannic (astringent) than standard Bordeaux wines yet boasts the same scents as the great Bordeaux wines of the past—cedar, cassis, and lead pencil.

Wine critic Robert M. Parker, Jr., put Valandraud on the map—the world map. He characterized it as one of the greatest wine discoveries he ever made. Following this praise, Valandraud attracted an avalanche of attention.

Vintage years: 1995 and 1996.

Château Ducru-Beaucaillou Discoveries—some of them great—often happen by accident. For example, the cure for the mildew that plagued grapes was discovered by accident at Château Ducru-Beaucaillou. As it happened, grapes were being stolen, and to ward off the thieves, a man named M. Davis painted the most vulnerable grapes with a bright blue copper–sulfate solution. He hoped the thieves would no longer want those vines.

But he noticed that the grapes painted with sulfur were also immune to mildew attack, and one thing led to another. The cure for mildew was found.

The great wines that come out of this château make it difficult to believe that the château ever had a less-than-perfect record of quality production since it was founded a century and a half ago. But, in fact, the fortunes of the Nathaniel Johnston firm, which had owned the estate since 1866, suffered a decline in the decade before World War II, and Ducru suffered as well. The restoration of the wine to the prestige and glory befitting a second growth began with Francois Borie, who bought the estate in 1941. The estate passed to his son, Jean-Eugene Borie, in 1953, and has seen nothing but an increase in stature and price, especially since the early '70s.

Ducru illustrates what can happen when a dilapidated estate with old vines receives the sort of continuous investment, care, and promotion it deserves. The physical layout of Ducru is magisterial; the château suggests the sort of aristocratic wine associated with Borie's northern neighbors, Lafite and Latour. For more than 40 years, Borie has diligently pursued a standard of winemaking to match this expectation, with the price reward that such dedication brings.

Ducru is hardly undiscovered wine. Wine lovers expect great wines from this estate and seem willing to pay almost first-growth prices for good vintages.

Vintage years: 1982, 1985, 1986, 1988, 1989, and 1990.

Château Pichon-Lalande Pichon reminds me of Château Margaux in that an improvement in the quality of the wine coincided with an upgrading of the vineyard and its equipment. Madame de Lencquesaing and her children own the estate, and she worked hard to promote Pichon's wines. Also, like Margaux, she at one time used the legendary Professor Emile Peynaud as a consulting enologist.

In the spring of 1983, Mme. de Lencquesaing arrived unannounced in my New York shop. She sputtered and fumed about Robert M. Parker, Jr., who had condemned her 1982 Pichon without ever visiting the château. Instead he had telephoned the cellar master, who quite candidly admitted that they were having problems with a hot fermentation. Rather

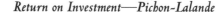

Return on Investment—Pichon-Lalande

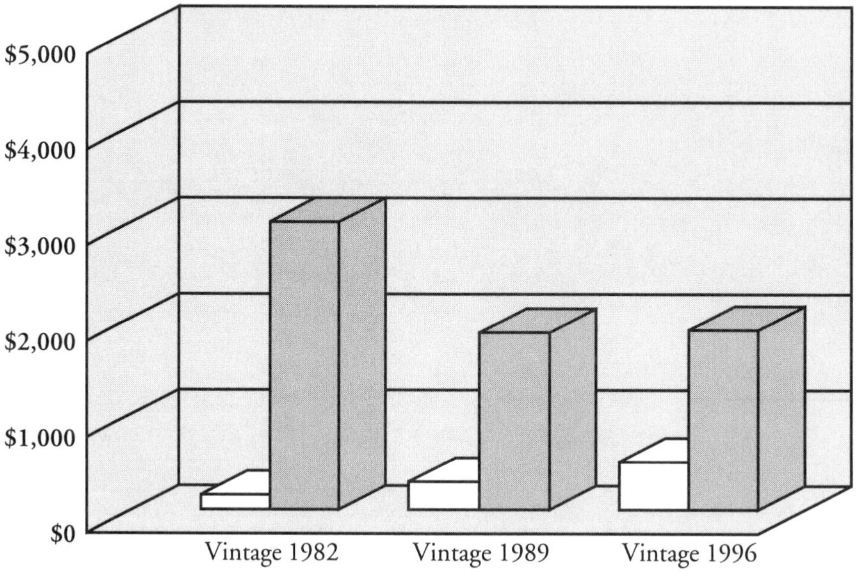

	Vintage 1982	Vintage 1989	Vintage 1996
☐ Opening Price/Case:	**$140**	**$300**	**$500**
▩ 1998 Price/Case:	**$3,000**	**$1,800**	**$1,800**

than taste the wine, in order to determine whether or not the château had successfully overcome its problem, he had simply consigned the wine to his "no buy" list. She waxed livid for a few moments, finally calming down when I told her that I had always enjoyed her wines, and that in any event I didn't have anything to do with Parker or his reviews.

Ultimately the situation was resolved. Parker reevaluated the wines, wrote that they had conquered the fermentation problem, and gave the 1982 Pichon his endorsement.

Today, Pichon-Lalande—the technically correct name is Pichon-Longueville, Comtesse de Lande—is a second growth. It is one of the top châteaux in Paulliac, producing some of the best wines in the Médoc, that aren't first growths, but may be equal to them.

Vintage years: 1982, 1983, 1985, 1989, and 1990.

Return on Investment—Léoville-Las-Cases

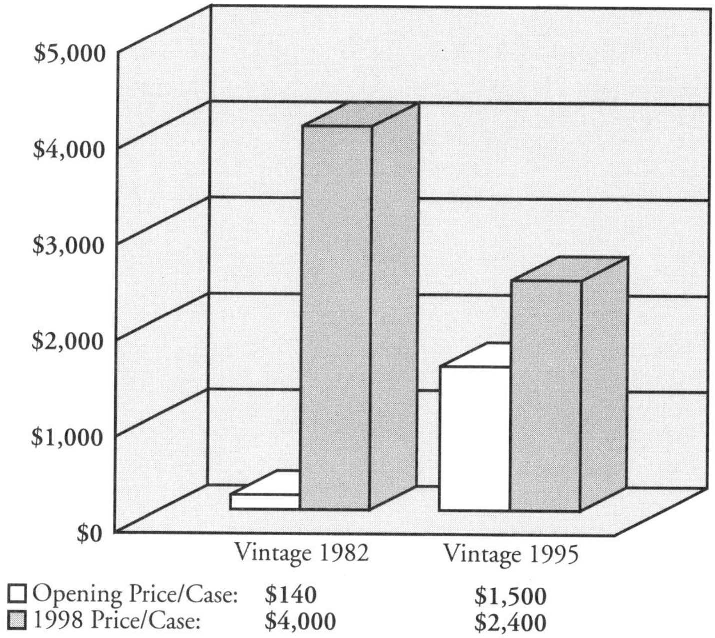

Château Léoville-Las-Cases Léoville-Las-Cases is adjacent to Latour, somewhat surrounded by Beychevelle, Talbot, and Pichon-Longueville. Overlooking the Gironde, its position calls to mind the Bordeaux saying that vineyards with a river view make the best wine. Many critics have given Las-Cases the title of the "poor man's Latour"—both wines are big and fleshy, becoming subtle after long aging. The wine is a "super second growth," and is very highly regarded. Many critics think it is the best second growth in Bordeaux. When my clients can't afford first growths, I suggest one of three wines: Pichon-Lalande, Ducru-Beaucaillou, and Léoville-Las-Cases. Despite its high production, there's never enough Las-Cases to go around.

How does a wine achieve such status? In his book *Grand Vins*, Clive Coates offers an interesting illustration of what makes a wine great. In addition, he says, to all the basics—such as soil and vinification techniques—it is the attention to detail that does it. He goes on to describe one late afternoon when he was at the château. It was raining, and the grapes had been loaded into a truck. Another vineyard owner, he said, might have just thrown a tarpaulin over the grapes and brought them to the cellar. But not at Las-Cases. Instead, they carefully tipped the truck with the tailgate in place, and an amazing amount of light pink fluid drained off the fruit. That pink liquid was water colored by the grapes, dozens of gallons of water that otherwise would have diluted the wine had it not been drained off.

Vintage years: 1982, 1985, 1986, 1989, and 1990.

Château Cheval Blanc Cheval Blanc is one of the few first growths to have remained in the hands of the same family since its inception. That sort of continuity is invaluable when it comes to establishing a wine's reputation. In 1980, I read several writers' comments about the 1947 Cheval Blanc, which they described as the "wine of the century." My curiosity was piqued, so I bought a bottle and tasted it. Frankly, the taste was less than overwhelming. To me the wine seemed faded, suggestive perhaps of a former complexity, but definitely past its prime. About a year later, in Paris, I encountered an old collector who wanted to sell 25 cases of the 1947. The bottles were in an unacceptable disarray: Some of the labels were faded; they needed new corks and cases. After my recent experience tasting the "wine of the century," I only agreed to the sale on the condition that the collector first send the bottles back to the château for recorking, fresh labels, and new cases. The renewal process took almost a year.

We took delivery of the wine in New York in 1982, and over the course of the year sold each case for $3,200. The pres-

Return on Investment—Cheval Blanc

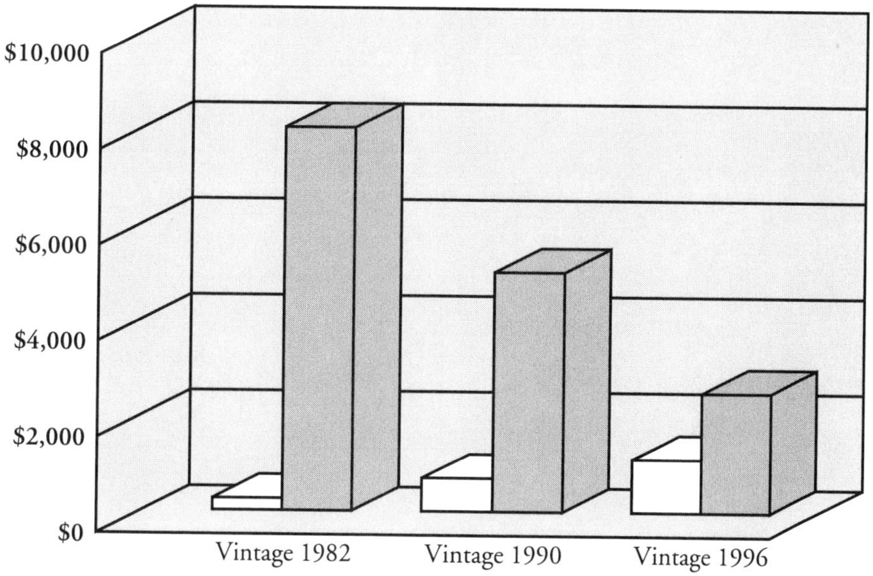

	Vintage 1982	Vintage 1990	Vintage 1996
□ Opening Price/Case:	$250	$700	$1,100
■ 1998 Price/Case:	$8,000	$5,000	$2,400

ent value of a case of 1947 is around $50,000—if you can find any. Collectors who've sampled their purchases tell me the wine is delicious, an argument perhaps for the preservative power of Parisian cellars over their American counterparts.

In the right vintage, Cheval Blanc can be the most outstanding wine in Bordeaux—round, supple, harmonious, with an unbelievably long finish. The 1964, a poor vintage in Bordeaux generally, produced a wonderful wine at Cheval Blanc. As a wine merchant, I have an obligation to taste many wines in the course of my business—too many—and I've always denied myself the pleasure of buying expensive wine for my own home. Cheval Blanc has been my one exception to the rule.

Vintage years: 1947, 1964, 1982, 1985, and 1990.

Château Palmer The name of this château comes from John Palmer, whose family came from the Bath area of England. John was a wealthy man and highly successful politician. One of his main accomplishments was initiating a mail-coach service between Bath and London.

It was his son, Charles, who bought the estate in Bordeaux that bears the Palmer name. The story goes that Palmer, who had fought in the Napoleonic Wars and had achieved the rank of Major General in the British Army, was in France, on a coach, when he met an attractive lady named Marie Brunet de Ferriere, who was on her way to sell the property owned by her recently deceased husband. The woman was distraught because legal necessities were forcing her to sell the property quickly, which meant she would only get about one-quarter of its value. But by the time the journey—which took three days at that time—ended, Palmer had nobly bought the property for a handsome 100,000 francs. The château had been called de-Gascq, but he renamed it Palmer.

For years now, Château Palmer has combined great wine with great marketing. An easy name, a distinctive black label lettered in gold, and a superb wine with a history of superior vintages in the '60s and '70s have all made Palmer a good investment value. The last owner, Peter Sichel (now deceased), was a lean, soft-spoken, scholarly man who typifies for me the refined Bordeaux winemaker. Under the Sichel family's management, the prices of Palmer have risen to first-growth levels, despite the estate's official third-growth classification.

I recall one spectacular evening at the château, the food overshadowed by the wines. Sichel had arranged a blind tasting of wine, which he asked the guests to identify. The wines were later revealed to be 1952, 1953, and 1955 Lafite. Sichel's confidence in his own wine may be measured by the fact that he later served us the 1962 Palmer, a rich, supple wine that compared very favorably with the Lafites.

My attitude toward investing in Palmer is very optimistic. There's plenty of it around and it has a high price, suggesting that its present popularity has a more solid basis than simply fashion. It appreciates quite rapidly.

Vintage years: 1970, 1983, and 1990.

Château Lynch-Bages What's a Lynch doing in Bordeaux? As one might guess, an Irishman married a Frenchwoman.

At the time, in 1749, the property Domain de Bages, named after the hamlet of Bages, was owned by Pierre Drouillard. When he died, the property passed to his brother, Jacques Gregoire, who died a year after Pierre. The property then passed to their sister, Elizabeth, who was married to Thomas Lynch.

André Cazes, the owner of Lynch-Bages, and I once sat next to each other at a lunch given by Lafite. Before the lunch, a group of people in the wine trade, proprietors, *négociants*, and merchants, had sampled a selection of recently bottled 1981s. The samples were numbered, their identities concealed, so we had to make our selections exclusively on taste. My two choices were both wines I recognized and loved, Latour and Peyrabon, both from opposite ends of the price spectrum.

I no longer recall the choices of Monsieur Cazes, but upon hearing my selections he immediately agreed that the 1981 Peyrabon was a very good wine, especially in its price range. He also informed me that his own goal was to produce great wine that people could afford to drink. Great wine that people can afford to drink pretty much sums up Lynch-Bages. Problems with history prevent Lynch from equaling the big three (Pichon, Ducru, and Las-Cases) that wine lovers inevitably buy when they don't want to pay the price of the first growths. Still, it's a very good wine that deserves elevation to second-growth status.

> Burgundy is a province of eastern France known there as Bourgogne. It is also known for its fabulous red and white wines, the former produced mostly from Pinot Noir grapes and the latter from Chardonnay.

Vintage years: 1982, 1985, 1989, and 1990.

Château Clinet In his 1985 book, *Bordeaux: The Definitive Guide for the Wines Produced Since 1961*, wine critic Robert M. Parker, Jr., characterized Clinet as "very poor value for the money."

Parker couldn't say that today, however. Now the wine is worthy of IGW #1 first-growth status. It all goes back to a belief I have that the most important element in the vinification process is the winemaker.

For much of its existence, Clinet produced wines that suffered from a case of the blahs. In four years—1947, 1950, 1955, and 1959—some respectable, more-than-ordinary wine had been produced, but observers felt that was due more to luck than design.

Then, by way of marriage, Jean-Michel Arcaute got involved in the vineyard. In 1985, he made a number of important changes at the winery with the help of his friend, the renowned enologist Michel Rolland.

One of the changes made was in the harvesting. Around the time Arcaute took over, 25 percent of the blend was Cabernet Sauvignon. Arcaute noticed something very wrong: The Cabernet Sauvignon was being picked before it was fully ripe, which occurred a full 10 days after the other grapes.

Tactfully, Arcaute had to persuade others that one must have more patience with this grape and not worry so much about rain—apparently the reason for the early harvest. It took him, and Rolland, some time to make an impact, but gradually they succeded. The amount of Cabernet Sauvignon was reduced—today it is closer to 15 percent, with 10 percent Cabernet Franc, and 75 percent Merlot.

There had been a picking machine in use, which was discarded in favor of hand picking. In addition, Arcaute made other changes, including switching to shallow plastic trays to carry the grapes during picking, instead of big wicker baskets in which many grapes were crushed. He also extended the time for storing the wine in vats, and bottled the wine after 24 months instead of 13 months.

Arcaute is a devotee of the process the French call *effeuillage*, or leaf stripping. This allows more sun to reach the grapes, and increased air movement militates against rot.

The wine started to improve, and by 1989 and 1990, the vintages were outstanding. Ordinary had turned into extraordinary.

Château Clinet—the château is a *maison bourgeoise* from the latter part of the 1800s. Its vineyard consists of 17.3 acres of very gravelly soil and produces 3,000 cases a year.

Vintage years: 1989 and 1990.

Le Pin If a château—though this one is not yet called a château—deserves the description of miniature, it is Le Pin, which up until 1985 amounted to 2.6 acres. That year, the Thienpoint family, who bought the vineyard in March 1979, was able to buy another 2.47 acres from the local blacksmith. Still, annual production is only about 1,500 cases.

The Thienpoints made a much more profound change in the vineyard than merely increasing its size. When they took it over, it was suffering from neglect, and they vowed to make a wine on a level with Pétrus. If it hasn't achieved that as yet, it is on its way, and well deserves being regarded as an IGW #1.

The vineyard is in the middle of Pomerol, and the soil can be described as poor—the previous owner neglected to fertilize it. It consists of clay that is about 2.5 meters deep, gravel, and a little sand. As a result, the production of wine is a low yield, normally no more than 3,000 liters per 2.47 acres. But the low yield, as often happens, results in great wine. The grapes are virtually 100 percent Merlot (there is some Cabernet Franc), just like Pétrus.

One can consider Le Pin to be a new wine that has been in development since the Thienpoints took over the vineyard. Some Le Pin was first sold in 1979 and 1980, but 1981 should really be considered the first vintage. Much needed cleanup and upgrades had to be done in order to get the winery in shape for producing fine wine.

Le Pin is high-priced but still a bargain if you can find it. It's not that easy, since most of the small production, perhaps two-thirds, is sold in England.

Vintage years: 1982, 1983, 1985, 1989, and 1990.

Troplong-Mondot In 1980, the château of Troplong-Mondot, perched on a bluff 100 meters above sea level, was languishing in mediocrity. While it produced a lot of wine from its flinty, limestone 74.1 acres—much more than surrounding châteaux, none of which was larger than 24.7 acres—it wasn't very good.

Then, in 1980, the old winemaker died and Christine Valette, daughter of owner Claude Valette told her father that she believed the château could produce great wine. The proof was that it already had, because Christine had done tastings on aging bottles in the cellars and saw the potential for greatness.

She could, she told her father, put the greatness back into those bottles.

Her father gave her a free hand, and she started to make some changes. She contracted with Michel Rolland to help her, and one of the things they determined was that the picking had been done too early, which Rolland had also discovered in other vineyards. Today, the harvesting is done one week later than surrounding châteaux because of its microclimate.

The yield of grapes was also reduced to less than 5,000 liters a year. The grape blend was made 70 percent Merlot, 15 percent Cabernet Franc, and 15 percent Cabernet Sauvignon.

Today, Christine Valette has realized her vision. The wine that she puts into the new bottles is every bit as good as the wine that she first tasted almost two decades ago. As the saying goes, "It takes time to bring you good wine," and that's exactly what she and her colleagues have done.

Vintage years: 1989 and 1990.

Château L'Angelus I remember reading somewhere that the name L'Angelus was not its given name. As it happens the château is located near Saint-Emilion, within earshot of three churches and the bells playing the Angelus. The château was renamed in honor of this.

L'Angelus has always sold its wine well, but then in 1981 the famed winemaker/consultant Pascal Riberau-Gayon did a tasting. His sensitive palate tasted something beneath the wine that could be developed, and at his behest the château set out to do exactly that.

For a long time the wine had been aged in concrete vats, but these were replaced with oak and stainless steel casks. The effect on the wine was dramatic, and it started its rise toward becoming the world-class wine that it is in today.

Vintage years: 1989 and 1990.

Le Tertre-Rotoboeuf In two decades this vineyard has risen from of the pack with a superb wine that is as much a product of the winemaker as the soil.

Francois Mitjavile has always been a rugged individualist, and in 1977, he and his wife Miloute took over the 13.8 acres of Le Tertre vineyard. She had inherited the property from her father in the '60s, but had rented it out to some cousins who, until that time, had produced a passable, but by no means extraordinary, wine.

Francois had prepared himself for the job. Starting in 1975, he apprenticed at Château Figeac, learned the wine trade, and than returned to Le Tertre, which they renamed Le Tertre-Rotoboeuf because there were a number of other Le Tertres in the area already.

Francois was determined to make a superior wine, and though he didn't have a lot of money, he did have elbow grease to spare, and he and his wife worked in the vineyards, getting them into shape.

It was difficult in the beginning, because the couple was starting virtually from scratch, and there wasn't any winemaking equipment available.

They struggled for eight years, taking chances by harvesting late, keeping production small, meticulously observing and monitoring all processes, and finally produced the quality wine they wanted.

But it wasn't doing them any good. No one was noticing, and they started to spiral downward, almost surely headed for oblivion despite having produced what they thought was a great wine. Then, in 1985, the French magazine *Que Choisir?* held some blind tastings of the 1982 vintage, and Le Tertre-Rotoboeuf came in first. They never looked back.

Today, their production is about 2,000 cases year, 80 percent Merlot and 20 percent Cabernet Franc.

Vintage years: 1982, 1985, and 1990.

Château Rausan-Segla Like other châteaux, Rausan-Segla has had more than its share of ups and downs, but by the 1920s it appeared to have the same chances of success as Hemingway's fisherman in *The Old Man and the Sea:* ". . . his sail when unfurled looked like the flag of permanent defeat."

Everything was run-down and in disrepair. The area that produced grapes had been reduced to 49.4 acres, the vines were old, and the equipment was antiquated and broken. The equipment was so primitive, in fact, that the grapes were being crushed by the old reliable method—with the soles of one's feet. This method was also extremely uneconomical. Rausan-Segla was the last major Bordeaux estate to use it.

It wasn't until 1956 that the château started on the road back to what had once been vinous glory. A. M. de Melon purchased it and instituted changes that included replanting Merlot grapes. While he did not appear to be a dedicated winemaker—although he was dedicated to getting a good return on his investment—his changes were a step in the right direction.

In 1960, de Melon sold the estate to John Holt and Co., a Liverpool firm that brought in the Bordeaux *négociants* Eschenhauer to manage the property. They made many improvements.

Some of the Merlot vines were eliminated and replaced with Cabernet Sauvignon, and the dilapidated wooden fermentation vats were replaced with epoxy-lined steel ones.

A new storage cellar and cuverie were built where once wild weeds grew. They brought in other equipment and got advice from enologist Emile Peynaud.

Today the château is a super second growth, vying with Palmer for the top spot. The wine is a blend—65 percent Cabernet Sauvignon, 30 percent Merlot, and 5 percent Cabernet Franc.

Vintage years: 1983, 1985, 1986, 1988, 1989, and 1990.

Château Lafleur This Pomerol château is only 200 meters north of Château Pétrus. It has always been known for high quality. Indeed, Clive Coates writes that "If you were to ask Jean-Pierre Mouiex or his son, Christian, whether there was any property in the area that could rival Pétrus they would tell you Château Lafleur. Which means that these experts believe that Lafleur might equal their legendary First Growth."

The only criticism of Lafleur is that it uses old winemaking methods, as well as old fermentation vats, which can lead to uncleanliness. The château is reportedly clean, but there are doubters.

Clive Coates, who has been involved in vertical tastings of Lafleur, says he has not encountered any dirty bottles, just wine that was a little "stewed," something that can be cured by letting the wine breathe for a half-hour or so before drinking.

Vintage years: 1982, 1985, 1989, 1990, 1995, and 1996.

Château Cos d'Estournel In the early '70s I hosted a weekly radio show called *Wine and Other Things* on WNCN. Robert Mondavi and Alexis Lichine were two of my early guests, as was a young, aristocratic man who was just starting to make wine at Cos d'Estournel. His name was Bruno Prats.

From 1919 to 1971, Cos was the property of the famous Ginestet family, and was most recently administered by

Bernard Ginestet. When financial difficulties caused the Ginestets to break up many of their holdings, Cos went to Bernard's aunt, Madame Prats. Her son Bruno now runs the estate. I recall Bruno Prats as an elegant, highly informed young man who defended Cos as an example of the older style of Bordeaux wines. On the face of it, however, his wines indicate a change of heart. The Cos of the '80s drinks much sooner than vintages two decades earlier.

Prats does an admirable job as representative and publicist for the new style of Bordeaux wines. In an interview with the *Wine Spectator*, he took pains to point out the role of Emile Peynaud in defining and changing the way wine has been made, not only at Cos, but all over Bordeaux. Says Prats: "Traditionalists say that in the old days, the wines were hard, but they kept well; today, they are so supple they will never hold up. I'll take that bet, if only because I don't believe that one must have a detestable character in childhood to have a likable one as an adult."

Vintage years: 1982, 1985, 1988, 1989, and 1990.

First Growths (Premier Crus)

Château	Region
Lafite	Pauillac
Latour	Pauillac
Margaux	Margaux
Mouton-Rothschild	Pauillac
Haut-Brion	Pessac

(continues)

Second Growths (Deuxièmes Crus)

Château	Region
Rausan-Ségla	Margaux
Rausan-Gassies	Margaux
Léoville-Las-Cases	Saint-Julien
Léoville-Poyferré	Saint-Julien
Léoville-Barton	Saint-Julien
Durfort-Vivens	Margaux
Lascombes	Margaux
Gruaud-Larose	Saint-Julien
Brane-Cantenac	Margaux
Pichon-Longueville Baron	Pauillac
Pichon-Longueville Comtesse de Lalande	Pauillac
Ducru-Beaucaillou	Saint-Julien
Cos d'Estournel	Saint-Estéphe
Montrose	Saint-Estéphe

Third Growths (Troisièmes Crus)

Château	Region
Giscours	Margaux
Kirwan	Margaux
d'Issan	Margaux
Lagrange	Saint-Julien

Château	Region
Langoa-Barton	Saint-Julien
Malescot Saint-Exupéry	Margaux
Cantenac-Brown	Margaux
Palmer	Margaux
La Lagune	Haut-Médoc
Desmirail	Margaux
Calon-Ségur	Saint-Estéphe
Ferriére	Margaux
Marquis d'Alesme-Becker	Margaux
Boyd-Cantenac	Margaux

Fourth Growths (Quatièmes Crus)

Château	Region
Saint-Pierre	Saint-Julien
Branaire-Ducru	Saint-Julien
Talbot	Saint-Julien
Duhart-Milon	Pauillac
Pouget	Margaux
La Tour-Carnet	Haut-Médoc
Lafon-Rochet	Saint-Estéphe
Beychevelle	Saint-Julien
Prieuré-Lichine	Margaux
Marquis-de Terme	Margaux

(continues)

Fifth Growths (Cinquièmes Crus)

Château	Region
Pontet-Canet	Pauillac
Batailley	Pauillac
Grand-Puy-Lacoste	Pauillac
Grand-Puy-Ducasse	Pauillac
Haut-Batailley	Pauillac
Lynch-Bages	Pauillac
Lynch-Moussas	Pauillac
Dauzac	Margaux
d'Armailhac	Pauillac
du Tertre	Margaux
Haut-Bages-Libéral	Pauillac
Pedesclaux	Pauillac
Belgrave	Haut-Médoc
de Camensac	Haut-Médoc
Cos Labory	Saint-Estéphe
Clerc-Milon-Rothschild	Pauillac
Croizet-Bages	Pauillac
Cantemerle	Haut-Médoc

Burgundy

BURGUNDY IS A province in eastern France, known by the French as Bourgogne. It is also known for its fabulous red and white wines, the former produced mostly from Pinot Noir grapes and the latter from Chardonnay.

Burgundians have been making wine for at least 2,000 years, but it really flowered in medieval times when the monks were the winemakers. There was peace, and the political stability made it easier to concentrate on such worldly pursuits.

The monks had several advantages in making wine. They had the cool, dark cellars and store rooms to safely store and age the wines that they made. They were also able to keep scrupulous records of the various wines, including tastings, notes that would serve them well in improving the wines as the years went by.

Around the year 925 A.D., the Benedictine monks of Burgundy became the first group of monks to acquire vineyards, but the practice soon became commonplace. As time went by, the Benedictines acquired more and more vineyards and fine-tuned their viticultural skills. They were to leave a lasting influence on the area.

The Cistercians, another group of monks, also had an impact on the area. One of the things they learned, and acted upon, was the effect different soils had on the same grape variety. It was an insight that was to serve winemakers for centuries to come.

The Cistercians purchased a number of vineyards, including those of the Benedictines, and also produced the first Chablis. Indeed, in the 12th and 13th centuries, drinking water was less than pure and clean, and clear white wine was preferred over water, and over red wine.

For years, Burgundian wines did not have wide distribution because transporting them by horse over bumpy roads was

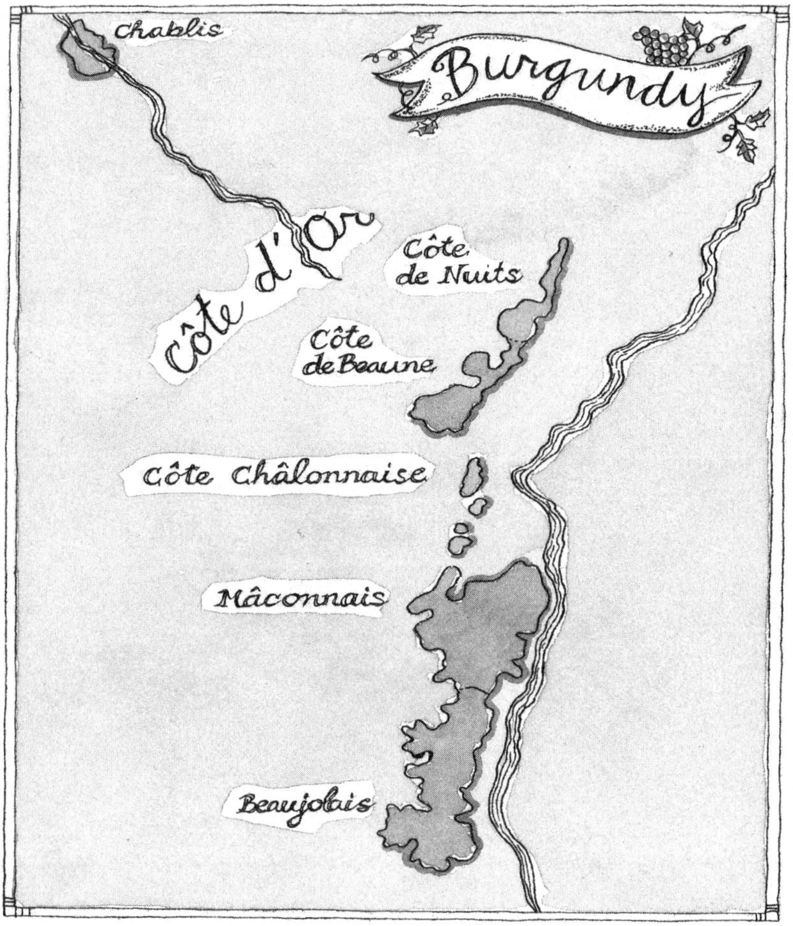

unsettling to the wine, and its potential worth was not widely known. But then Pope Clement V moved the Papal Court to Avignon. Clement V's court reveled in excess, and located close to Burgundy (then known as Beaune), barrels and barrels of wine from Burgundy were shipped to Avignon.

Dukes governed Burgundy until the mid-15th century, and Burgundian wine became a symbol of their importance. The church was still in control of most of the vineyards, but as time went by the monarchy slowly became more powerful, and the church sold off most of the vineyards in the 17th century.

In the 18th century, transportation improved, and it was possible to ship more and more wine made in Burgundy to other regions. As Burgundy wine was distributed, its fame spread even further.

Aside from making wonderful wines, the thing that Burgundy succeeds at best is confusing people! There are so many winemakers in the relatively small region of Burgundy, each producing wines of certain qualities, that it's a grim harvest of hundreds of names. As wine writer Paul de Cassagnac, author of *French Wines*, said in 1930, "But in every corner where the earth is deep enough and mellow enough, the vine has been planted. It has been done in strips and bits and pieces. . . . That is why Burgundy, whose riches and glory are known in the whole world, looks as though it were clothed in a secondhand garment; patched, darned, and borrowed; a beggar's coat on a millionaire's shoulders."

The wine lover/investor need not delve into such complexities, but just be aware of some basics, at least to start.

Burgundy may not be regarded as highly for its wines as Bordeaux, but it does produce some superior wines.

There are five different regions in Burgundy. Many of the subregions are preceded with the word *côte*, which means slope, and describes the topography of the named area. The five areas are: Chablis, Côte Challonais, Maconais, Beaujolais, and Côte d'Or, which is divided into Côte de Beaune and Côte de Nuits.

There is also some confusion in the way people refer to the region. Sometimes when people talk about Burgundy they mean the entire region, but oftentimes they're just referring to the center of the area, Côte d'Or. Also, both Beaujolais and Chablis are often spoken of separately.

The area produces both white and red wine, and is famed for both. As mentioned, the white wines are made from Chardonnay grapes while the red Burgundies are made from the Pinot Noir variety. In the southern part of Burgundy, known as Beaujolais, the red grape used is the Gamay, a grape that is not as highly regarded as some other types. Burgundy also uses some Pinot Blanc for white wines.

IGW #1: Burgundy

Burgundy now has three blue-chip wines that I consider IGW #1, but a number of #2 wines should be watched.

Domaine de la Romanee Conti At the top of any list of Burgundian wines has to be Romanee Conti. It is one of the usually superb red wines produced by the Domaine de la Romanee Conti, which includes Romanee Conti among its other fine wines. A world-renowned red wine, it always commands top dollar when it is released. The only problem with Romanee Conti is that it is difficult to get. But if you can, and you store it in your cellar, it's like storing gold bullion. And if you drink it, you will be drinking one of the greatest wines ever made.

According to Matt Kramer, in his 1990 book *Making Sense of Burgundy*, the reason Romanee Conti's wine is so great (though, of course, not all vintages are equal) is because of the moral commitment of the family who owns it. "The domaine," he said, "goes to great lengths to point out to visitors, and, especially, journalists, its expensive risk-taking in harvesting grapes later than just about any other grower. You will see photographs of grapes being harvested in the snow."

Vintage years: 1978, 1985, 1990, and 1996.

Musigny Comte de Voguë Musigny is a 26-acre vineyard that has had a number of owners.

In the California Napa Valley, roses are planted along the edges of vineyards to detect early signs of disease that may attack the vines.

Autumnal vineyards in the Napa Valley, California.

Two-thirds of it is owned by Monsieur Georges de Voguë, who makes both red and white wine. The red is the IGW.

Vintage years: 1978, 1985, 1990, and 1996.

Domaine Leroy By the late '80s, this vineyard had become a good example of what a vineyard should not look like, but then came new owners. Lalou Bize-Leroy took over (changing the name to Domaine Leroy), and today it is a model vineyard, encompassing the latest high-tech winemaking machinery and vast experience. Lalou Bize-Leroy is a driving force behind another vineyard—Domaine de la Romanee Conti.

Domaine Leroy consists of 35 acres, and produces both red and white wines. The reds are typical of Leroy, designed for the long haul, and perfect IGW.

Vintage years: 1978, 1985, 1990, and 1996.

IGW #2: Burgundy

There are a number of IGW #2 in Burgundy, both red and white. Here is my capsule guide.

Domaine Atone Sauzet This 26-acre estate makes a number of white burgundies. Check out their top white wine.

Vintage years: 1985, 1990, 1995, and 1996.

Domaine Ramonet There are fewer than 2,500 acres of Chardonnay planted in the Côte d'Or, of which Domaine Ramonet is a part, the smallest part, being only 9 acres. Its Montrachet is the IGW.

Vintage years: 1985, 1990, 1995, and 1996.

Domaine Lafon This estate has slightly more than 32 acres and from its vines come some of the finest whites anywhere. It is considered the leader in Meursault-style wines.

The domaine boasts one of the coldest natural cellars, which allows it to keep wine for two years on its lees (the sediment found at the bottom of the cask). This seems to handle the potential problem of bacteria forming quite well.

Lafon's winemakers are also chance-takers, preferring to pick the grapes as late as possible, which has resulted in some wines that were not up to the domaine's standard. However, when everything goes right, the wine is spectacularly good.

Vintage years: 1985, 1990, 1995, and 1996.

Domaine Coche-Dury This vineyard produces a small amount of wine, which is said to be the key to its success.

The winery is run by Jean-Francois Coche-Dury, who took it over for his father. The wines are high priced, but are still much in demand. Check out the red wine.

Vintage years: 1985, 1990, 1995, and 1996.

Domaine Leo Camuzet This domaine was founded in 1983 when the Leo and Camuzet families went into partnership. Their vineyards are on 25 acres. The 1985 vintage was superb, but other vintages were spotty. Now, in the '90s, there have been a number of excellent red wine vintages.

Vintage years: 1985, 1990, 1995, and 1996.

Domaine Laguiche Its white wine is the IGW.

Vintage years: 1985, 1990, 1995, and 1996.

Domaine Rousseau This domaine was the first in Burgundy to bottle its wine. There are 35 acres of vineyards that produce excellent red wine using traditional methods. The only problem is that it only produces a few hundred cases per year.

Vintage years: 1985, 1990, 1995, and 1996.

Domaine Laurent Its red wine is the IGW.

Vintage years: 1985, 1990, 1995, and 1996.

Rhône Valley

THIS WINE-PRODUCING AREA is in the southern part of France. Because of the weather, wines of the northern part of the district are different from those in the southern part.

The district produces both red and white wines. In the north, one of the most startling geographical characteristics is the steepness of slopes that comprise the vineyards—some are at 50-degree angles. A number of the slopes have flags designating ownership. It is quite a sight!

The main grape used to make red wine is the Syrah, which loves the granite soil, warm summer climate, and those steep slopes. A number of white wines are produced, but reds are more common.

The southern Rhône Valley also produces reds and whites. The reds tend to be softer than other reds; the Syrah is not used exclusively but is blended with other grapes that do not have Syrah's intense taste.

IGW #1: Rhône Valley

La Mouline Guigal Etienne Guigal is one of most accomplished producers in the Rhône Valley. He manages Côte Brune and Côte Blonde and produces both reds and whites.

Vintage years: 1985 and 1990 (red wine).

Rayas Châteauneuf-du-Pape In his 1990 wine buyer's guide, Robert M. Parker, Jr., described an interesting trip he made to Château Rayas, which is north of the village Châteauneuf-du-Pape in the Rhône Valley. Parker described coming onto a scene filled with screaming workers, "undisciplined" dogs, and chaos in general, and recalled that the owner, Jacques Reynaud, put off seeing Parker three times and once didn't show up to a scheduled meeting with the most influential wine critic in the world.

Even so, Parker writes: "Rayas is a unique wine in every respect. For those who say Grenache cannot produce majestic wines on a level with the Mouton-Rothschild and Cheval Blancs of the world—taste Rayas (Châteauneuf-du-Pape)."

Enough said.

Vintage years: 1985 and 1990.

Perrin Beaucastel Beaucastel has a reputation for producing the longest-lived red wine in the southern Rhône area, a minimum of 20 years. The producers believe, as the late Jacques Perrin did, in using natural products to work the 272-acre vineyard. No chemicals are used. Indeed, it's a choice with implications. It now takes about 500 tons of manure to fertilize the vineyards.

Vintage years: 1985 and 1990.

Sauternes

ALTHOUGH FRANCE MAKES dozens of sweet wines, and while it is a good idea for the wine investor to know all about these, there's just one I'd recommend now for investment purposes. Labor-intensive production makes sweet wines a good value, but it also makes them very expensive. The best of them command fabulously high prices.

The word *Sauternes* often leads to confusion. True Sauternes is a sweet wine that is named after the place it is made, Sauternes, France. In fact, Sauternes is but one of five communes—Sauternes, Barsac, Bommes, Preignac, and Fargues—in the district of Sauternes. In other words, there are two Sauternes. It is as if all of the five boroughs in New York City were referred to as Manhattan, and one of the boroughs was also named Manhattan. Adding to the confusion, one also sees wine that is not from Sauternes but is labeled as such—or mislabeled by dropping the last "s."

Making Sauternes: A Tense Experience

The making of Sauternes is every bit as tense an experience for the winemaker as it was for Wallenda in walking the high wire. And it is filled with surprises.

Sauternes is made from a blend of grapes, mostly Semillon with about 20 percent Sauvignon. But they must first be allowed to be attacked by what is known in English as "noble rot," or "porriture noble" in French, which makes the grapes overripe. In fact, by the time they are picked, the grapes hardly look as if they could produce great wine. As Alexis Lichine says in his *Encyclopedia of Wines and Spirits:* "The bunch of grapes, ready for . . . picking, is dried and folded and (while it is not a pleasant comparison) has a marked resemblance to the wizened, leathery, folded-in appearance of a hanging bat. Covered over with porriture noble, it hardly gives promise of the golden nectar it is to produce."

If this process fails, then the wine will lack the extra sugar—as much as 16 to 17 percent—that is necessary for making an entirely natural sweet wine, that is one to which no sugar is added. But if the winemaker goes too far, the necessary bouquet will be lost in the richness of the wine. Ideally, what happens is that grape skins shrivel, and the grape loses water but not sugar. The ratio of sugar to other elements in the grape increases.

Another reality that may have the nervous winemaker drinking Alka-Seltzer instead of wine is that the forced overripening must happen late in the growing season, making the grapes vulnerable to an attack of frost. Daily, you will see a concerned winemaker treading through the vineyard a number of times, evaluating which grapes are overripe enough, giving the order to pick, or not pick, the grapes as the case may be. In other words, the grapes are picked gradually, as ripeness dictates, perhaps 10 or 12 times before the process is completed successfully . . . the winemaker hopes. The mold, or mushroom as it is also called, increases the grape's elements—pectins and glycerin—which increase the wine's smoothness.

Classification of Sweet Wines

In Sauternes, the wines are classified, and controlled by the government, in the same way wines in Bordeaux and Burgundy are. There are three classifications.

The best Sauternes you can get is classified "Grand Premier Cru," and there is only one wine in this classification. It towers above all, and it is the only one I see as an IGW: Château D'Yquem. It is the world's number one sweet wine, and in good years an incredibly concentrated nectar redolent of honey, with prices to match.

I first brought D'Yquem into my shop in 1965; we were selling the 1962, a great vintage. The price for a case was a heart-stopping $150, yet even then lovers of sweet wine gobbled it up in no time. I remember in the '80s I came across a chance to buy 50 cases of the 1975 for the bargain price of $600 per case. Within one afternoon all 50 cases disappeared from my shop—at $750 each. Six months later the price was over $1,000.

D'Yquem is one of the few wines I've ever personally coveted. On first visiting the Florentine restaurant Enoteca Pinocchiora I was flabbergasted to discover a carpeted corridor with floor-to-ceiling racks containing magnums and double magnums of this wine. I made the owner an offer on the spot, which, of course, he cheerfully refused.

A friend of mine told me a story about Château D'Yquem that is one of the saddest wine stories I ever heard. It seems that back in the '60s, before Château D'Yquem was as famous as it is today, this friend went to a wine merchant and said that he wanted to buy a bottle of the best wine he had in the shop. He was giving it to a good friend as a gift.

The wine merchant wrapped up a bottle of Château D'Yquem for him and he left the store. His trip to his friend's house was particularly long, but he was almost there, going down the steps of a subway when someone bumped into him. The wine bottle tumbled out of his hand and crashed on the street. The only consolation was that he didn't realize that a truly great wine had just bitten the dust.

The other two classifications are premier cru and deuxième cru.

There are 11 excellent Sauternes that go in the premier cru classification, some of them quite excellent.

The deuxième cru wines are delicious, though not as valuable as those in the premier cru classification.

Vintage: 1975, 1976, 1983, 1988, 1989, and 1990.

Champagne

Champagne is the name of a drink, but first and foremost it is the name of a district in France, a parcel of land about 100 miles east and slightly north of Paris. It is an area whose weather challenges grapes to achieve perfect ripeness, and when they don't, which is more frequent than not, the champagne made and shipped is a blend of several vintages, some better than others. When grapes do ripen perfectly all at once, a single vintage is declared, something that only occurs three or four times every 10 years.

Champagne is a lovely area, 60,000 acres of it carpeted with neat, green vineyards that are crimson–gold in the fall. The climate is cool, the soil chalky, and the vines yield a wine of great delicacy.

Some of the best vineyards lie between the co-capitals of Champagne, Reims and Epernay. According to law, only three types of grapes may be grown: Chardonnay, Pinot Noir, and Pinot Meunier. Since champagne appears clear, people are usually surprised to hear that three-quarters of the grapes grown in Champagne are red, but this relates to the way the wine is made.

The natural color of champagne would be red or pink, except that when the grapes are crushed, they're pressed in wide, shallow presses for a short period of time. The juice that emerges is clear, however, because the color is not in the meat of the grape but in the skin. If the winemaker wants pink champagne—rosé—he adjusts the contribution of the skin to the wine.

Many people wonder why champagne is bubbly. It wasn't until the 17th century that people understood where the bubbles came from. A blind priest named Dom Pierre Perignon was in charge of the wine collection at an abbey in Hautvillers, a town a little north of Epernay. Perignon noticed that some still wines developed bubbles every spring, and he correctly deduced that this was related to fermentation. The cold cellars of Hautvillers slowed the wine's fermentation, leaving behind a little unfermented sugar that dissolved into the wine as the weather got warmer. This, he theorized, somehow produced the bubbles. In fact, the process produces carbon dioxide as a by-product. When the bottle is opened the carbon dioxide is released, creating effervescence.

Knowing this allowed Dom Perignon to control the effervescence by controlling sugar levels. He also used bottles of thick glass that wouldn't explode, topping them with tight corks so the bubbles couldn't escape.

Today, champagne goes through fermentation twice. The first fermentation occurs while it is stored in casks; the second time occurs while it is stored in bottles, and a little extra sugar is added.

Different houses—they call them châteaux in Champagne—make champagnes of different taste and style, some of them with blends made up of many different vintages. Top-quality champagne may be aged for five years before it is released, but it is capable of aging many more years.

Curiously, most of the grapes come from small vineyard owners, some of whom may own the equivalent of a vegetable garden. There are a huge variety of brand names, many produced by 19,000 small-vineyard owners. But the major houses, such as Moet et Chandon, Krug, and Roederer Cristal produce most of the champagne.

Moet et Chandon Dom Perignon

Moet et Chandon makes the blue-chip of champagne, Dom Perignon.

Return on Investment—Dom Perignon

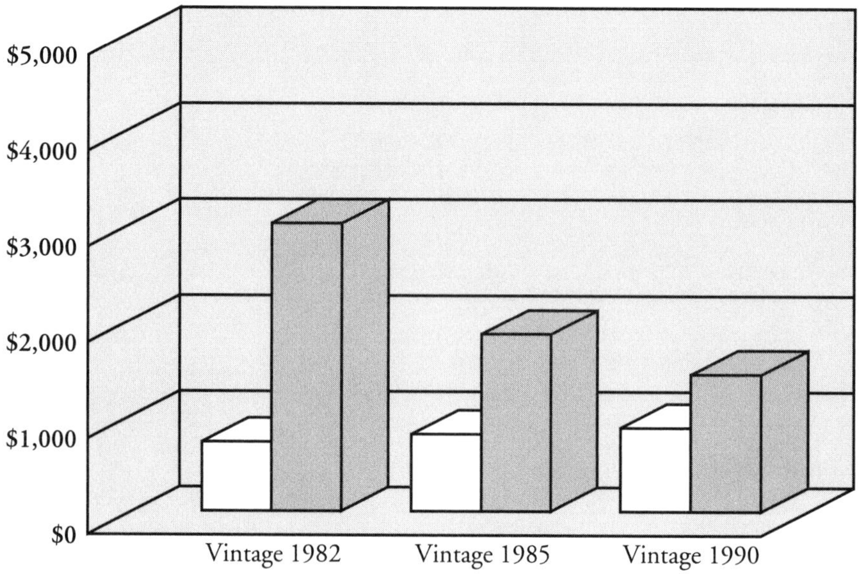

	Vintage 1982	Vintage 1985	Vintage 1990
□ Opening Price/Case:	$720	$780	$840
■ 1998 Price/Case:	$3,000	$1,800	$1,440

The champagne is light and crisp with a hint of almonds; it is very long-lived. A number of years ago, I went to visit the Moet et Chandon at Château Seran, which entertains guests in high style at its palatial country house. The night I happened to be there, the French race-car team was also invited. I left with the feeling of having been feted in the most indulgent manner possible—an appropriate image for Dom Perignon.

This is as sure a thing as you'll find in wine investing.

Vintage: 1990.

KRUG

In 1983, I visited the house of Krug and was treated to one of the most reverential disquisitions of an estate's history that I'd

Return on Investment—
Roederer Cristal

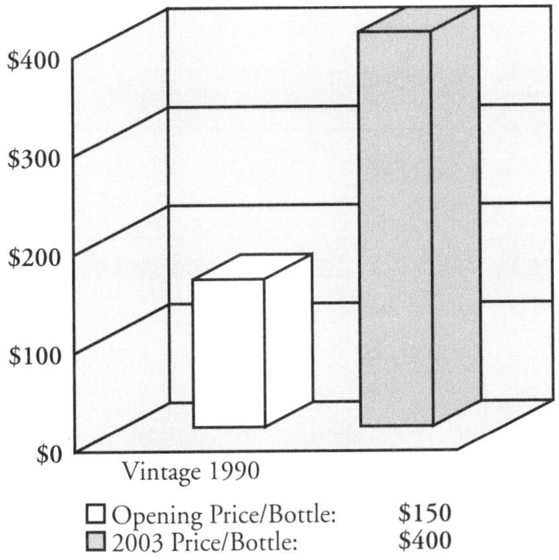

ever heard. Despite the fact that I liked the champagne, I only allotted myself 30 minutes for the visit.

At the time, Krug was a relative newcomer to the United States; its vintage champagne had only been marketed there for three years—and I thought it would probably take another three or four for it to catch on. It did. In England, where Krug is known and popular, old vintages command large sums. Like many other wineries, Krug ferments its wine in wood. The champagne has a sturdiness that's lacking in other wines. I thought it was built to last back then—and it is.

Vintage years: 1982, 1985, and 1990.

Roederer Cristal

This is a very expensive, delicious champagne, and in the United States, it's a favorite both of Hollywood wine mavens and members of East Coast's upper-class society. About 30,000 cases are produced each year.

Vintage years: 1982, 1985, and 1990.

Important Points

- Even great wine-producing areas, like Bordeaux, have had bad wine-producing years.
- IGW #1 are blue-chip wines; IGW #2 are wines to watch.
- Before investing in any wine, do your homework.
- The most important element in the winemaking process is the winemaker.

Chapter Eight

California Investment Grade Wine

California can make great wines, as the French discovered in 1976, when some California wines (Château Montelena and Stag's Leap) beat the powerhouse Bordeaux wines in blind taste tests.

For the wine lover/investor, this state is an exciting place to watch. It currently produces 90 percent of the wine consumed in the United States, and some of this wine is as good as you can get, period.

There are many indications that the wine is on the move. In June of 1988, Christie's of Los Angeles conducted its first all-California wine auction. A month before that Sotheby's in New York said that California wines were leaving the place like frightened pigeons, and in this year's Napa Valley auction, a

15-litre bottle of "Maya," a blend of Cabernet Franc and Cabernet Sauvignon from the Dalla Valle winery sold for $160,000. It all points to a very rosy future for California wines—and investors.

If you live in California or even just visit, it now seems that there is a danger, if you stand still long enough, that somebody will turn you into a vineyard. Grapes for wine are grown in 45 of the 58 counties and blanket 378, 603 acres. There are 680 commercial wineries in the state. The largest 25 of these, incidentally, sell 90 percent of the wine, and though the Napa and Sonoma counties are best known for wine, there are vineyards as far south as Santa Barbara.

In the Beginning

WINE GOT STARTED late in California. In 1769, Father Junipero Sierra planted a single vine—more than 225 years later, millions of vines are flourishing.

Franciscan monks made the first wine, a sweet wine, in 1782 at the celebrated Mission of San Juan Capistrano.

Wine took a good step forward in 1833, when an émigré from Bordeaux, Jean Louis Vignes, planted cuttings he had brought from his native Bordeaux in what is now downtown Los Angeles. This started the hub of California wine activity. Surprisingly, the Napa Valley, which is today quintessential California wine country, did not see vineyards until 1838.

The arrival of a Hungarian immigrant named Agoston Haraszthy gave the California wine scene a giant boost. While in California, he had planted cuttings of *Vitis vinifera* around the Sonoma area, but when he returned from Europe in the 1850s he brought with him an astonishing 100,000 cuttings from hundreds of European vineyards and started to plant them. When they bore fruit it allowed winemakers to make better wine simply because they started with better grapes.

As immigrants and gold prospectors flooded into California, the population grew from 1.5 million in 1856 to 4 million in 1858. Many of the transplants were Dutch, English, French, and Italian immigrants—people used to drinking wine in their homelands.

> And what do French winemakers think of California? Enough to invest in producing their own wines in the state. For example, Moet et Chandon, Christian Moueix, and Mouton-Rothschild have all invested in California vineyards (as well as those in Oregon and Washington).

In the beginning, most of the wine made in California was sweet, but dry wine gradually took over. (It took until 1967, however, before the dry white wines beat sweet wines in total gallons produced.)

California is an ideal place to grow grapes and make wine, even though it is not immune to attacks by vine-destroying lice and other problems. The industry survived such attacks in the early 1900s, and winemakers continued to plant vines. In the 1920s, the Gallo brothers began growing and selling grapes, and over the course of time, they got into making wine. Their enterprise grew so big that eventually they were selling more wine than a number of countries.

By 1946, the state wine output totaled 1 million gallons; by 1996 it had catapulted to 407 million gallons.

The truth is, however, that California wine's reputation in the 1960s did not cause Bordeaux vineyard owners to lose any sleep. Then along came Robert Mondavi.

Mondavi started out working for Charles Krug at his family's winery in California, which he left to start his own vineyards. Now in his 80s—though he looks much younger—Mondavi is a brilliant winemaker and publicist. He was and is a person who stands above all for quality wines—California quality wines—and that's the message he has spent his life beaming across the United States and the world.

Other winemakers got the message, too, and in the '70s the image of California wine started to move from the "Hearty Burgundy" jug wines to wines called varietals—that is those described by the chief grape from which they were made, such as Cabernet Sauvignon or Chardonnay. (Since 1983, the law states that to be classified as a varietal, a wine must contain 75 percent of the grape that it is named after.)

California Varietals

TODAY, WINES MADE from Chardonnay grapes set the pace in California. In 1986, some 29,000 acres were devoted to producing it. By 1996, that had vaulted to more than 82,000 acres. Cabernet Sauvignon is a winner, too, having grown from almost 19,000 acres to 40,500. Some examples of producers of Cabernet Sauvignon are Caymus, Heitz, Stag's Leap, Opus One, and Robert Mondavi. Chardonnay-wise, respected names include Mondavi, Kistler, Château Montelena, Grgich Hills, and Peter Michael.

The big red wine in the state is made from the Zinfandel grape. Ridge, Ravenswood, and Turley are a few of the leading producers.

And what do French winemakers think of California? Enough to invest in producing their own wines in the state. For example, Moet et Chandon, Christian Moueix, and Mouton-Rothschild have all invested in California vineyards (as well as those in Oregon and Washington).

Investment Grade Wines

A NUMBER OF wines in California are, in my view, #1 IGW. Following is a profile of each of the relatively few vineyards that have accomplished this feat, and the years of their best vintages. All the California IGW is red, Cabernet Sauvignon, or a blend.

Joseph Phelps, St. Helena

Joseph Phelps was a builder in Denver who had a clearly identifiable adventurous streak. In the early '70s he left Denver, arriving in the Napa Valley. He purchased a ranch in Spring Valley and then proceeded—without previous experience—to create his own winery, which, not unsurprisingly, is known for its architectural panache.

Today, Phelps is big. He owns 300 acres of vineyards in the Napa, Yountville, and Stag's Leap areas. Some 98 acres are devoted to Chardonnay; 82 acres to Cabernet Sauvignon. There are also 12 acres devoted to Syrah, some of the earliest vines planted in California. There are other varieties of grapes as well. Phelps fulfills 70 percent from his own vineyards; the rest he buys from other vineyards.

Phelps established his reputation with white wines made from Riesling grapes, but today his reds are attracting the attention of wine lovers and collectors. He puts out a variety of labels, such as Backus Cabernet and Eisele, which are rich with concentrated fruit, as well as Insignia, blended from Cabernet, Merlot, and Cabernet Franc. A number of critics mark this as his best wine.

Address: P.O. Box 322, St. Helena, CA 94574.

Vintage years: 1987, 1990, and 1994.

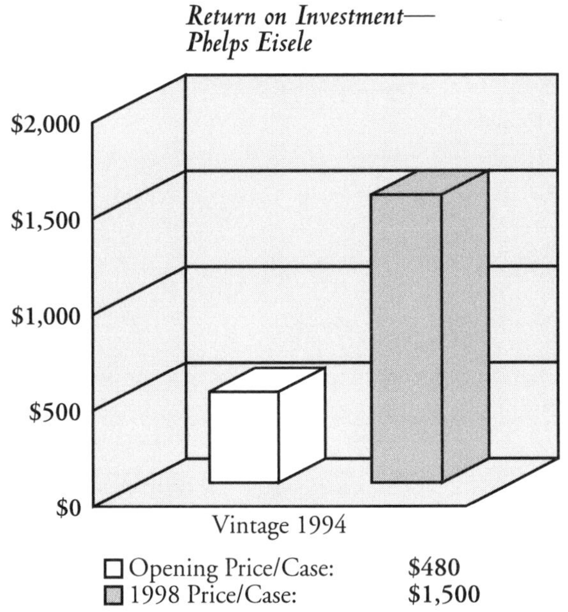

Dominus Estate, Yountville

This vineyard involves an international collaboration, between Christian Mouiex, producer of Château Pétrus in France, and Americans Robin Lail and Marcia Smith, daughters of John Daniel, who created the Dominus Estate.

Like the other international linkups, the symbolic value was clear: When a world-class winemaker gets involved with a vineyard, it most certainly indicates that he expects to produce high-quality wine.

The estate produces full-bodied reds that could hold their own in a Bordeaux blind tasting. The 125-acre vineyard is currently producing about 6,500 cases of wine annually under the Dominus Estate label—which shows a picture of Christian Mouiex on it. The vineyards are 69 percent Cabernet Sauvignon, 15 percent Cabernet Franc, 14 percent Merlot, and 2 percent Petit Verdot.

Return on Investment—
Dominus Estate

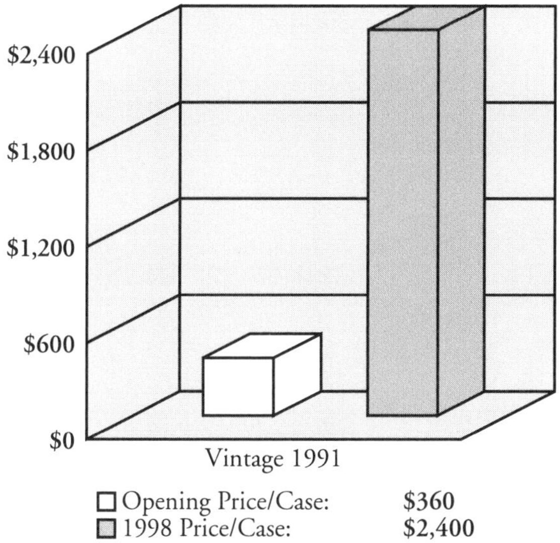

The wines are not cheap: They'll run you about $50 a bottle. But Americans are not complaining. Many people think Dominus makes the best reds produced in America. The reds are not expected to mature for years, which is typical for IGW.

Address: P.O. Box 3275, Yountville, CA 94599.

Vintage years: 1987, 1990, 1991, and 1994.

Opus One, Oakville

As a joint venture between the legendary—and deservedly so—Robert Mondavi in Napa Valley and the equally legendary Rothschild family in France, this vineyard certainly has a lot going for it. Opus One is expensive, and it is bound to become even pricier in the future.

The winery has not been without problems. About 10 years ago, it was subject to a bad case of phylloxera, requiring that many acres of vineyards be torn up. Mondavi has since moved the winery to Oakville, where the vineyards comprise 110 acres.

The varietals produced are consistently among the top wines, however, proving that the move to Oakville did not slow the winery's momentum in the slightest.

Address: 1144 Oakville Cross, Oakville, CA 94562.

Vintage Years: 1987, 1980, 1991, and 1994.

Far Niente, Oakville

This meticulously run vineyard, whose name means "without a care" in Italian, was a stone winery that had been abandoned during Prohibition. Its owner, Gil Nickel, started to restore it in 1978. He rebuilt it from top to bottom, even revamping the 15,000 square feet of stone underground caves that had been used for storage.

Far Niente has 150 acres of vineyards with two-thirds planted in Chardonnay and the rest in Cabernet Sauvignon. Annual production is an impressive 35,000 cases. Definitely a winery to watch.

Address: P.O. Box 327, Oakville, CA 94562.

Vintage years: 1985, 1987, 1990, 1991, and 1994.

Grgich Hills Cellar, Rutherford

The owner of Grgich (pronounced GUR-gitch) Hills Cellar, Miljenko "Mike" Grgich, arrived in Canada in 1956, traveling from his native Croatia, then went onto the Napa Valley. He worked at a variety of vineyards, honing his winemaking skills. Then, he electrified his colleagues when his 1973 Château Montelena Chardonnay placed first in the 1976 tasting contest in Paris, where American white wines competed with those of Burgundy.

Obviously, this feat did not go unnoticed, and in 1977 Grgich teamed up with coffee giant Austin Hills to form his own vineyard. During a recent trip to California, my wife, Gloria, and I reacquainted ouselves with the 75-year-old Grgich, and he's still going strong.

Grgich wines are always among the best, and they now produce more than 65,000 cases of wine a year, 65 percent Chardonnay, 20 percent Cabernet Sauvignon, 10 percent Fume Blanc, and 5 percent Zinfandel. He uses both his own grapes and grapes from select vineyards in the area.

Address: 1829 St. Helena Highway, P.O. Box 450, Rutherford, CA 94573.

Vintage years: 1985, 1987, 1990, 1991, and 1994.

Grace Family Vineyards, St. Helena

This Napa Valley vineyard produces rich 100 percent Cabernet Sauvignon wines that only have one problem—they're difficult to find. At last count, Grace was only producing 300 cases a year, a minuscule amount. But if you can find it, it makes a fine wine for drinking or investment.

Dick Grace, an ex-stockbroker who got into winemaking full-time in 1978, built the winery in 1987. His winemaking philosophy dictates that the closer together the vines are, the better, so his vines are planted that way to achieve flavor intensity.

He surely is doing something right. His wine sells for $125 to $150 per bottle. At the 1990 Napa Valley wine auction, a bottle of the 1987 vintage was sold for $20,000, one of the highest prices ever paid for a wine in the United States.

Address: 1210 Rockland Road, St. Helena, CA 94574.

Vintage years: 1985, 1987, 1990, 1991, and 1994.

Dunn Vineyards, Angwin

The Gault-Millau *Guide to the Best Wineries of North America* says that the saga of Dunn Vineyards "is one of the biggest American wine success stories of the 1980's, the tale of a great winemaker and one of the generation's superstar wines."

Randy Dunn and his wife Lori were working for another winery when they decided to try to rehabilitate an ancient Cabernet Sauvignon vineyard surrounding their home on Howell Mountain.

They set about the task and in 1979 produced about 600 cases of outstanding wine, not only showing that they had resuscitated the vineyard, but that they had brought it to vibrant life.

In 1982, Randy took a chance and started his own winery, and since then has been producing wine that has a virtual cult following. He produced some 4,000 cases a year, but there was more demand than Dunn could meet, so he purchased 47

Return on Investment—
Dunn Vineyards

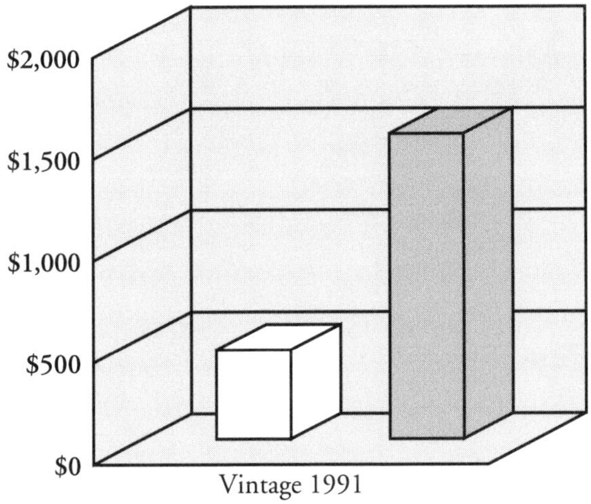

Opening Price/Case: $420
1998 Price/Case: $1,500

acres from the nearby Park-Muscatine Vineyard and planted it entirely with Cabernet Sauvignon.

Address: 805 White Cottage Road, Angwin, CA 94508.

Vintage years: 1985, 1987, 1990, 1991, and 1994.

Spottswoode Winery, St. Helena

This winery, like so many in California, looks like a living postcard. It hugs the side of the Mayacamas Mountain range in St. Helena. And from its picturesque vineyards come some of the best Cabernets in the state.

The winery was given its name by the Spotts family, who purchased it in 1910. Over the years the postcard had become a little frayed at the edges, but when it was purchased in 1972 the new owners, named Novak, restored it to former glories. They also refurbished the lovely Victorian home on the property.

It is a 40-acre vineyard, with 37 acres devoted to Cabernet Sauvignon and 3 acres to Cabernet Franc. Sauvignon Blanc is purchased from other vineyards. All told, the vineyard turns out about 7,000 cases of wine a year.

Address: 1401 Hudson Ave., St. Helena, CA 94574.

Vintage years: 1985, 1987, 1990, 1991, and 1994.

Harlan Estate, St. Helena

The great Bordeaux winemaker Michel Rolland gets around—and this is one of the places he goes. He has been consulting with the Harlan Estate since the early '90s, and it's no small wonder that Cabernet Sauvignon is the predominant grape grown. First release of its wine was in 1990, only 100 cases, but that has steadily risen since then.

Vintage years: 1985, 1987, 1990, 1991, and 1994.

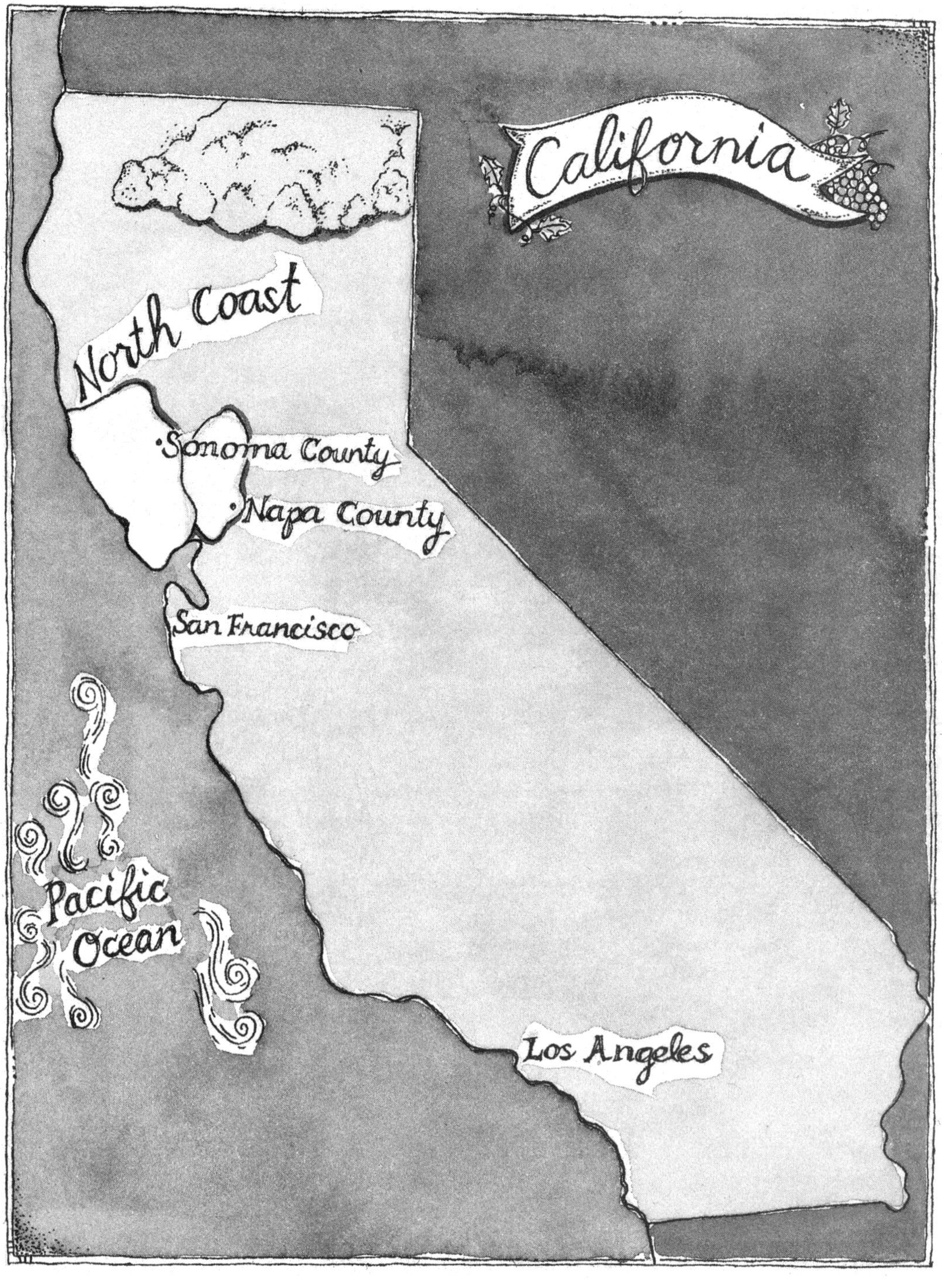
California
North Coast
Sonoma County
Napa County
San Francisco
Pacific Ocean
Los Angeles

Bryant Family, Napa Valley

World-famous winemaker, Helen Turley (who is highly regarded by Robert M. Parker, Jr.) has practiced her craft at these vineyards. The vineyards are exclusively Cabernet Sauvignon, and the yield is low, 2 tons of grapes per acre, or 1,000 cases a year. The red wine is dense and concentrated.

Vintage years: 1985, 1987, 1990, 1991, and 1994.

Araujo Estates, Napa Valley

In 1989, Milt and Barbara Eisele sold this estate to William Farley. The vineyards needed replanting and Farley, in turn, sold the estate to Bart and Daphne Araujo. Bart Araujo, a very successful homebuilder replanted the vineyards and overhauled the winery while he was at it. The vineyards produce great Cabernet wines.

Vintage years: 1985, 1987, 1990, 1991, and 1994.

Colgin, Napa Valley

Helen Turley has shared her expertise with this estate too. It produces Cabernet Sauvignon wine and offered its first release in 1992. Colgin Cellars now has a waiting list of 3,000 people who want to purchase their wine.

Vintage year: 1994.

Dalla Valle Winery, Oakville

Naoko Dalla Valle has been presiding over the winery for the last few years. The 1994 Maya was released at $80 a bottle and has doubled in value.

Return on Investment—Colgin

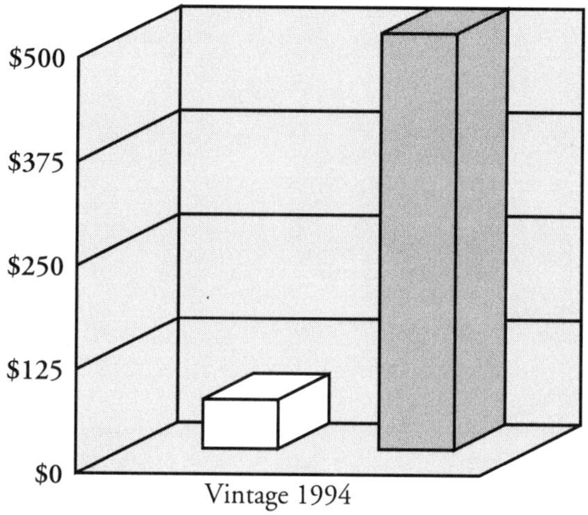

□ Opening Price/Bottle: **$60**
■ 1998 Price/Bottle: **$500**

Important Points

- All California IGWs are red—Cabernet Sauvignon or a blend.
- French winemakers think enough of California to have invested in vineyards there.

Chapter Nine

Port and Miscellaneous Investment Grade Wine

In the last decade or so other winemaking regions have deservedly worked their way into the IGW spotlight. They are Italy, the North Fork of Long Island, Australia, Spain, Lebanon, South Africa, and New Zealand. As with other wines, there are both IGW #1 and IGW #2; the first are IGW now, the second are the wines to watch.

Another wine, vintage port, is always IGW #1.

Port

For years, Port was enjoyed mostly by the British. It perpetuated the image of an elegant-looking Englishman raising his pinkie as he sipped the drink. (The reason you see so many English names on Port is that when France and England went to war in the 1600s the British stopped getting wine from France, shipping it in instead from Portugal. Eventually many English people moved to Portugal and opened up wine establishments with English names.) But in the last few years that image has changed. Today people in many countries drink Port, including Americans. Port can be at the heart of any IGW portfolio for a simple reason: It lasts longer than any other wine. In fact, Port is not considered drinkable until 10 years after it is bottled. It is expected to age much longer before it's at its peak. There are ports older than 100 years that are sensational.

Today people in many countries drink Port, including Americans. Port can be at the heart of any IGW portfolio for a simple reason: It lasts longer than any other wine.

Because the best Port is made in Portugal, one might logically assume that its name comes from this country. In fact, it is so named because all the makers of Port, or "shippers" as they're known in the country, are located in Oporto, a city in the north of Portugal at the mouth of the Duoro River, where the wine is known as *porto*, and the estates are called *quintas*.

As it is made, brandy is added to Port, which is why it is considered "fortified" wine. It is allowed to age for six months or so at the quinta before it is shipped down the river to the port lodges, which are clustered across the river from Oporto. It is allowed to age, usually in wood casks, for another half a year.

The addition of spirits to the mix makes all the difference in Port's taste. Originally, it was not fortified and the taste was raw, harsh, and tannic. But then someone had the bright idea of adding brandy to stop the fermentation process, causing it to change to sugar earlier. The result was a much sweeter drink. Today Port is fortified to up to 20 percent; in other words, it consists of 80 percent wine and 20 percent brandy.

Of all the regions in which wines are made, the vineyards from which Port comes have the harshest soil. Most of the soils in which Port grapes are grown are granite; they also contain schist, a soft, crystalline rock that easily splits and crumbles.

The vines grow on terraced hillsides that allow the torrential rain between May and October to run off harmlessly. Vines that produce a variety of grapes are used, but they are all grafted into American vines from phylloxera-resistant rootstock.

There are a variety of Ports, but whenever the vintage is great, the winemaker will earmark these grapes for making True Vintage Port. Here's how Port is categorized:

Ruby Port: This is the inexpensive, simple Port. After being poured into bottles it is allowed to age for a couple of years, then sold. Like other Ports it is thick and sweet, but it has a higher alcohol content—18 percent—than other Ports.

Vintage Port: This is investment grade Port. When the vintage is exceptional—and there are usually only three or four every ten years—the Port shippers "declare" a vintage, meaning the Port of that year is of exceptional quality.

Tawny Port: The are two types of Tawny Port. The inexpensive version merely refers to the color. The more expensive version has much more going for it (see "Tawny Port," later in this chapter).

Making True Vintage Port

To make True Vintage Port, the makers blend various grapes, let the wine age two or three years in wood casks, then bottle it. It is neither filtered nor refined, so as it ages a sediment builds up. In the trade, they describe this as "to throw a deposit."

Port should be stored with the label up, so the deposit builds up on the other side. Also, before it is drunk it must be decanted, unless you like to chew on sediment.

True Vintage Port is an outstanding drink, a dark purple, with concentrated fruit and spice flavors.

Tawny Port

Tawny Port is also made from a blend of grapes and then aged in wood for at least six years. Tawny Ports age quite a long

Return on Investment—Port

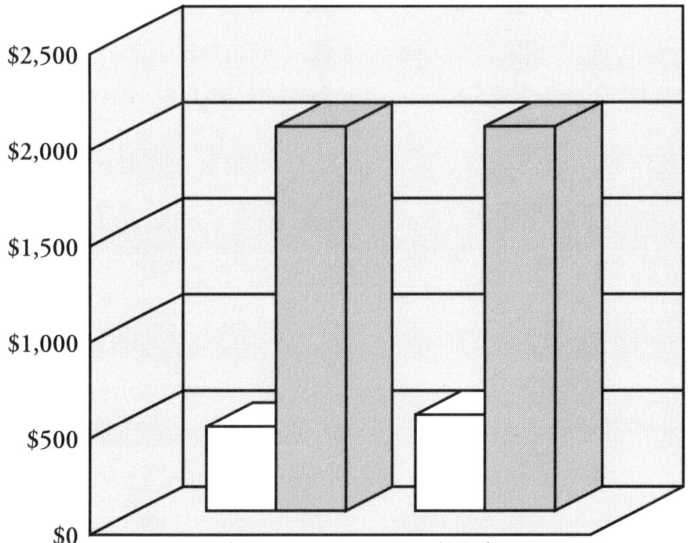

	1994 Fonseca Port	1994 Taylor Port
☐Opening Price/Case:	**$450**	**$500**
■1998 Price/Case:	**$2,000**	**$2,000**

time. Stores commonly carry tawny Port that is 10, 20, 39, and 40 years old.

Tawny Port is brown rather than purple and tastes of caramel, vanilla, hazelnuts, and the like. Mature Tawny Port is even smoother than True Vintage Port, but TVP is the superior drink, mainly because it starts with only the best grapes.

The three best investment grade Ports are made by Taylor, Fonseca, and Graham. These are the only Ports you should consider.

Vintage years: 1948, 1955, 1963, 1977, 1985, and 1994.

Italy: Biondi-Santi Brunello

WINE LOVERS ACCUSTOMED to the taste of the Sangiovese grape in Chianti are often astonished upon tasting its incarnation in Brunello di Montalcino. Italian law requires that Brunello age four years in oak casks, a treatment that contributes to the raw, leathery quality of the wine in its youth. A *riserva* must age for one additional year, although the final year need not be in barrels. Such wines, obviously designed for the long haul, may take a decade before the first chinks appear in their tannic armor.

The Biondi-Santi family first developed Brunello in Tuscany in the 1840s. Although there are now many producers of Brunello, none has acquired the legendary status of the Biondi-Santis, or the prices, which equal those of Bordeaux first growths.

While there have been some mixed results from the Biondi-Santis' winery of late, there have still been some superb vintages.

Biondi-Santi Brunellos are all made in the same manner. Grapes are handpicked and crushed, destemmed, then macerated and fermented in concrete vats. Then the wine is transferred to large oak casks. It is released five years later.

According to the owner of Biondi-Santi, Franco Biondi-Santi, Brunellos can age 100 years, like port. If the wines need to be recorked, the wine producer will do it. They don't charge for the service, just the wine used (of the same vintage, of course). The youngest vintage that I've heard of being recorked was 1975.

Vintage years: 1968, 1971, 1985, and 1990.

Sassicaia

Producer of leading Tuscan wine, made from a blend of Cabernet Sauvignon and Cabernet Franc.

Vintage years: 1990 and 1995.

Tignanello

The proprietary name of the first super-Tuscan wine to be successful using a blend of Sangiovanese and Cabernet grapes.

Vintage year: 1990.

Australia: Grange Hermitage

Wine has been around in Australia since the 1700s, but Australian winemakers only got busy trying to make better wine around the 1970s. The world started to notice Australian wine in the 1980s.

Australia is a huge country, and it is hardly covered with vineyards. Vineyards are clustered in the southeast and southwest, like the population. Australian wineries make both red and white wines. The most famous and most valuable IGW #1 is Grange Hermitage, a red wine made by the Penfolds Estate. It is made from Shiraz grapes and is aged in small, American oak barrels à la some Bordeaux wines. Originally the wine was made from 100 percent Shiraz, but now Cabernet Sauvignon grapes are also used.

When mature, the wine is full-bodied and very much like Bordeaux wines.

Vintage years: 1985 and 1990.

Spain

SPAIN'S WINES, EXCEPT in rare cases, have not been known for being particularly wonderful. This was partly due to the naturally arid conditions, including very little water for irrigation, as well as antiquated viticultural methods. Although the country had an appellation system that purportedly rated the wines, it was said to be lax, allowing wines that were not high quality to nevertheless be rated highly.

Spain is trying to change its image now, and it seems to be succeeding. Everything has been upgraded in many different areas, and a new appellation system has been established, along with strict enforcement.

The most prestigious estate in all of Spain is Vega Sicilia, which was established in 1864. The French varieties of Cabernet Sauvignon, Merlot, and Malbec are planted, as well as other more native grapes.

Spain's red wines are particularly good, and Unico (IGW #2), a red wine that is barrel-aged for 10 years, is known as its premier wine.

Vintage year: 1985.

Lebanon: Château Musar

IT SEEMS AN odd location for a winery, but just 18 miles from the place that is synonymous with bloodshed and heartache, Beirut, there is a world-class winery called Château Musar (IGW #2). It produces stunning wines from blends of Cabernet Sauvignon, Syrah, and Cinsault.

Harvesting grapes has sometimes been a bizarre, yet understandable, problem for owner and winemaker Serge Hochar: People were unwilling to go there and risk their lives!

Hochar learned to make wine from his father, and also spent some time in Bordeaux learning his profession.

The war is gone from Lebanon now, but the great wine remains.

Vintage years: 1966 and 1970.

South Africa: Plasir Di Merle

IT MAY COME as a surprise, but South Africa has been producing wine since the 1600s. Most vineyards are planted in the southwestern part of the country.

Like most wine-producing countries, South Africa has had its ups and downs, particularly in the early 1900s when overproduction brought big problems. Happily, this led to a government induced control system called "Wines of Origin."

Currently South Africa is producing a wide array of red and white table wines as well as semisweet wines.

South Africa bears careful watching. A few years ago, Paul Pontellier, the winemaker at Château Margaux in Bordeaux, took up residence in South Africa and started to make wine there. The result is 1995 Plasir Di Merle (IGW #2), and it is every bit as delicious and valuable as anything coming out of Bordeaux.

Vintage year: 1995.

New Zealand

FOR A LONG time no one was interested in wine in New Zealand. It was a beer-drinking country. In 1960 there were fewer than 1,000 acres of land devoted to vineyards. Most of the wines made were usually hybrids, and the wine was fortified.

Then, in the 1960s, New Zealand winemakers started to experiment with European grapes, such as Cabernet Sauvignon. The experiments were successful, but the winemakers determined that they had more luck with white wines than with reds, perhaps because the climate is cool (New Zealand is between the 35th and 45th parallels).

By the 1990s, there were 15,000 acres under vine. Mulderbosch and Providence are the country's best wines.

Vintage years: 1993 and 1994.

New York's Long Island: The New Bordeaux

THERE WAS ONCE a young winemaker named Eric Frye. He liked the challenge of new vineyards and spent eight years at Mondavi, five years at Jordan (Sonoma–Alexander Valley), and two years in Bordeaux. One day, he asked the legendary winemaker André Tschelistcheff where he should go next.

"Go," Tschelistcheff said, "to the next great wine region of the world."

A Day with a Winemaker

ONE OF THE best times I've had in recent years was spent with Sean Capiaux, the winemaker at Jamesport in the North Fork wine country area of Long Island, where I live.

Capiaux is one of a number of world travelers and world-class winemakers who have come to the North Fork; Eric Frye at Lenz and Ric Hearn at Pelligrini.

Sean and I talked for about four hours, although it seemed more like four seconds, and I was very interested in the man and his observations.

Early in our meeting we went into a local vineyard and Sean observed that there was rot on the leaves. Not good he said, but then, in a manner typical of the winemaker's invincible spirit, he made some comments on how to fix it. Winemakers do not give up and walk away, but they stay to fight!

According to Sean, there is little chance of the phylloxera louse invading the North Fork. The soil is mainly sand-based and the little creature cannot endure this.

"Where's that?"

"The North Fork of Long Island."

Tschelistcheff was not having a mental breakdown. In fact, many experts predict that the North Fork will be the new Bordeaux. And the region is already proving it. There are cur-

Sean thought that promotion-wise, Palmer and Pindar have done a good job, and he likes them. I do, too.

Sean loves Paumonok 1995 Cabernet. There were only 40 to 50 cases produced that year, and it is a bit pricey—about $50 a bottle. (Of course that's cheap when you think of California's Screaming Eagle at $1,500 per bottle!)

Sean also likes Bedell Merlot, which has been around for about 20 years. He also admires Schneider—as they have no facilities, Bedell makes the wine for them.

Sean feels that the North Fork vineyards should specialize, go the same route as some California wineries, such Mondavi Fume Blanc, Phelps Eisele, Le Pin, and other world-class châteaux where one wine has made the entire winery famous. The same thing can happen on the North Fork, Sean says.

Sean feels that the opinions found in *Wine Spectator* magazine are more accurate than those of Robert M. Parker, Jr. I agree. It all swirls down, as it were, to the fact that *Wine Spectator* has a lot of different tasters, rather than just one.

rently 20 vineyards on the narrow strip of land that is adjacent to the Hamptons on the south shore and boasts land bathed in trade winds that would allow one to grow flowers in December. There is room for 30 more vineyards, and the wine emerging from the region is absolutely superb.

Lenz Barrel Fermented Chardonnay has proven it. While a bottle still costs only $25, there's no reason the price shouldn't climb like other great wines. Over the next decade I see it going to over $1,000 a bottle.

Port is not considered drinkable until 10 years after it is bottled. It is expected to age much longer before it's at its peak. There are ports older than 100 years that are sensational.

Why the interest in Long Island? For the same reasons that wineries have succeeded everywhere else: good soil and good weather. Though people might think of Long Island as ice-bound in the winter, lashed by rain, and subject to freezing weather—and it can be—the climate on the North Fork is generally moderate, protected from bad weather.

The North Fork has the same growing season as Bordeaux, and the weather and well-drained soil are not dissimilar. The grapes start growing in the spring, and by October they are ready to be harvested. Both red and white wines are produced, and as the years have gone by, they have gotten better and better. Though I would not yet put any in the first tier of IGW, the wines from a number of vineyards qualify for #2 status.

And another important ingredient has been added to the mix: Bordeaux winemakers. There are at least four I know of who have brought their expertise to the North Fork. To me, their convergence on the scene in such numbers is of great significance. Bordeaux winemakers are not into wasting their time.

Following are wineries and some of the wines to watch. (I get a chance to watch them closely, because I have a home and shop in Southampton. Not too shabby for a wine fanatic such as myself!) I see them all as IGW #2.

Paumanok Vineyards, Aquebogue

When Paumanok owners Charles and Ursula Massoud were researching how to plant in the 1980s, they did something clever. Ursula had her uncle Werner come from Germany to advise them. As a result, they planted *Vitis vinifera*, classical European wine grapes, and used European methods. Such techniques include growing smaller vines so, as Charles Massoud says, "the fruit would have more intense flavor and no vegetative character. The solution there was dense planting. The method spread and is now used extensively in California."

At a tasting in 1996, critic Robert M. Parker, Jr., complimented Massoud on his barrel-fermented 1993 and 1994 Chardonnay. And the *Wine Spectator* waxed enthusiastic about the 1993 red wines, the Grand Vintage Merlot, Grand Vintage Cabernet Sauvignon, and Assemblage, the new Bordeaux blend.

There doesn't seem to be anything that will keep this winery from going on to greatness.

Corey Creek, Southold

In 1993, when Joel and Peggy Lauber first tasted the Chardonnay grapes they had grown on their then 18-acre vineyards, they were all set to sell the grapes. But the magnificent taste of the fruit turned them around, and they decided to make some wine. They commissioned a graphic artist to design a label, had the wine made at a neighboring vineyard, and bottled it.

Everything clicked, and the first wine, a 1993 Chardonnay, was a big hit. Indeed, wine critic Howard Goldberg, wrote in the *New York Times* that if there was a Rookie of the Year award it would go to Corey Creek. To add to the new winery's luster, in 1994 the *Wine Spectator* gave Corey Creek's 1994 Merlot a "top pick" status and the Chardonnay a "best value."

An additional 7 acres were added to the vineyard in 1994, mostly planted with Merlot and Cabernet Franc. Planting Pinot Noir is also in the future, but they do not plan to plant Cabernet Sauvignon. "We have limited space," says Joel, "and it doesn't make sense for us—we're better off with the earlier-ripening varietals."

Bedell Cellars, Cutchogue

One of the specialties of this winery is Eiswein, a sweet white wine, made with German Gewürztraminer and Riesling grapes and has the scent of pineapple and honey. It is said to have intoxicated (not literally!) the judges of the 1997 International Eastern Wine Competition, who awarded it a gold medal.

Lenz

Lenz is one of the oldest wineries on the North Fork of Long Island. A pair of Westhampton restaurateurs named Peter and Patricia Lenz founded it in 1979 and then sold it in 1988 to Peter Carroll and his wife, Debbie, who were growing grapes on the nearby Dorset Farm.

Peter Carroll's first order of business was to call in experts. He hired winemaker Eric Frye, who had worked with two American winemaker superstars, André Tschelistcheff and Dr. Konstantin Frank, the pioneer of *Vitis vinifera* in New York state. *Vitis vinifera* (originally from Europe and Asia) is a type of vine from which 99 percent of all grapes in the world are grown. Frye replanted the vineyards—about 60 acres—a task eased by vineyardist and consultant Sam McCullogh.

The goal has always been to produce a wine that was both delicious and complex. Frye and company share a belief that a wine's greatness is both in the fruit and in harvesting it at just the right moment. Rather than following a schedule, "I pick on taste," Frye says. "I'm looking for the true expression of the grape."

> True Vintage Port is an outstanding drink, a dark purple, with concentrated fruit and spice flavors.

The results have been dramatic. In blind tastings, the 1995 Cabernet Sauvignon and Merlot wines scored as well or better than such superstars as Château Pétrus, Château Latour, and California's Opus One and Duckhorn.

Palmer Vineyards, Aquebogue

In 1997, Palmer broke new ground for Long Island vineyards by going national, with sales distribution to 39 states. Palmer opened the market in California to Long Island wines in a big way. Today it also sells wine in China, having been chosen by a Chinese delegation in a series of closed blind tastings.

The vineyard has won many awards. Its 1995 Merlot won a double gold medal at the 1997 New York Wine and Food Classic. Its 1992 Brut sparkling wine was the only wine to win two gold medals at the 1992 San Francisco Wine Competition, winning over such great sparkling wines as Moet et Chandon and Domaine Chandon.

Pellegrini, Cutchogue

Pellegrini Vineyards is making a name for itself. James Ottenritter had enough respect to come from ZD Winery in

California's Napa Valley to manage the vineyards at Pellegrini in 1997.

Pellegrini's 1993 vintage put it on the map, when Howard Goldberg of the *New York Times* characterized the production of Pellegrini's winemaker, Russell Hearn, thusly: "He made—with ease, it seems—what may well be the finest Merlot, the finest Cabernet Sauvignon, and the finest Bordeaux-style blend of the vintage."

Like other North Fork wineries on the rise, Pellegrini understands the fundamental importance of fruit. Its wine has just gotten better and better.

Important Points

- Vintage Port is always IGW #1. It can last over 100 years.
- A variety of wineries are IGW #2, but may go to #1 status. Keep a close eye on North Fork, Long Island producers.

Chapter Ten

Hot Investment Grade Wine

A DECADE AGO, WHEN I predicted the investment potential of a number of wines, it might have appeared as if I had lost my marbles a second time, the first being when I decided to put my liquor business more or less aside and get heavily into wine.

But time proved me right. And investors who had plunked down their money based on my predictions as contained in my book *Liquid Assets* are very happy now indeed. The wines I'd recommended have increased in value many times over.

That being said, I have a specific new set of predictions to serve up, and I can only hope that I am as successful as on the first go-round. These wines represent the "hottest of the hot," the most promising IGW I see now.

A word about the list. After each wine in the following list, you will see a per case price. My recommendation is to not buy the wine above the prices given. As you delve into the wine market you will see that prices can vary considerably.

In terms of what to spend, I would suggest the following based on individual income.

If you net $50,000 per year and are a wine nut, you can spend up to 5 percent of your income. A $150,000 net per year can go 5 percent to 10 percent. $500,000 per year? Try 10 percent. A million? 10 percent to 15 percent. $5,000,000? 20 percent if you're a wine nut. $10,000,000 and up—whatever you want!

Wine	Price per Case
Bordeaux	
Mouton-Rothschild 1982	$5,000
Mouton-Rothschild 1988	2,000
Palmer 1990	1,500
Pichon Lalande 1985	1,200
Cheval Blanc 1982	5,000
Latour 1982	4,500
Rausan Segla 1990	1,200
Margaux 1995	3,000
Margaux 1996	3,300
Latour 1996	3,000
Latour 1961	12,500

Wine	Price per Case
Clinet 1989	$ 3,000
Haut-Brion 1989	4,500
Margaux 1983	3,300
La Mission Haut-Brion 1975	4,800
Montrose 1990	2,000
D'Yquem 1975	4,800
Latour 1990	4,200
Margaux 1990	4,000
La Mission Haut-Brion 1989	2,500
La Tache 1993	4,800
L'Eglise Clinet 1996	1,500
Burgundy	
Romanee Conti 1990	36,000
Dom Perignon 1985	1,800
Dom Perignon 1990	1,020
Dom Perignon Rose 1982	3,000
California	
Dunn Vineyards 1986	1,200
Caymus Regular 1994	750
Maya Dalla Valle 1992	3,000
Berringer Reserve 1991	1,000

(continues)

Wine	Price per Case
Port	
Fonseca 1994	$1,600
Taylor 1994	1,600
Italy	
Tignannello 1990	1,500
Sassicaia 1994	1,200
Sassicaia 1995	1,200
Africa	
Plasir Di Merle 1995	250
North Fork	
Pindar Merlot Reserve 1995	240
Lenz 1995	300

CHAPTER ELEVEN

Protecting Your Investment

A FEW YEARS BACK, an animated woman came into my wine shop and showed me a bottle of Château D'Yquem, the finest Sauternes wine in the world, and wanted to know how much it was worth.

"I have a lot of it," she said.

I examined the bottle and tried to show nothing in my face, but I felt a sickening sensation in my gut. The wine was brown, as opposed to its natural color of amber.

"Where do you have it stored," I asked.

"In my garage."

Later, inspection confirmed my suspicions. All the wine was ruined. Wine that might have been worth $200 to

$400 a bottle was worth $1 a bottle. The cause? Poor storage conditions.

Good Storage Is Crucial

WINE LOVERS CAN extol the virtues of a vineyard's soil, tally up the days of sunshine or rain, and judge an enologist's skill by the number of great wines he's coaxed from his vineyards. But once a wine is in the bottle, one factor becomes preeminent in determining its future: storage. Hiccups in the market, the influence of fad and fashion, bad weather, and poor vintages—each presents a danger to the investment value of wine. But bad storage kills investment grade wine.

Throughout my time in the industry, I have seen horror stories of ruined wine that would make Steven King lick his lips in anticipation of writing about it. This is why provenance—a bottle's history—is so important at auction: You have to know as much as you possibly can about just who owned the wine, how it was treated, and how it was stored.

Storage is just one aspect of protecting your investment, but it is the most important one. There are a variety of ways to store your wine depending on your particular physical and fiscal situation.

The well-known definition of the best storage conditions for wine is that the temperature should be 55 degrees Fahrenheit, the wine not subject to light or movement, and humidity level about 60 degrees. In fact, that is a cliché, and does not apply in every situation.

If you store wine at 55 degrees, says Robert M. Parker, Jr., it will age so slowly that your grandchildren will be toasting you or your headstone with it. If you want it to age faster, the temperature should be higher.

Carrying grapes off the hill in traditional baskets at Ferreira's Quinta do Seixo near Pinhao in the Douro Valley, Portugal.

Harvest time at Soutelo do Douro in the hills of the Douro Valley near S. Joao da Pesqueira, Portugal.

Heat: Wine's Worst Enemy

You should not store wine in temperatures higher than 75 degrees. Heat and wine do not mix, and if the temperature rises too much in your wine storage area, bad things happen. James Laube, a columnist for the *Wine Spectator* described what could happen in his August 31, 1995, column. On a trip to Bordeaux he and his colleagues shared some wine at a local restaurant. "After a round of Champagne and a pair of pleasant Loire Valley Reds, we opened the Bordeaux we'd just bought (at the restaurant), all less than ten years old, from very good vintages and well-known châteaux within a few miles of the place. Each of the wines was tired, with that cooked, dried-fruit edge to the flavor that points to poor storage." Laube was referring to storage conditions that were too warm.

On the other hand, wine should not be frozen either. If you let it sit in the freezer too long, the wine will expand and possibly push the cork upward, loosening it and creating a gap for oxygen and microbes to hustle inside.

Temperature fluctuation is another no-no. According to Michael Davis, president of Michael Davis & Co., "a cellar which has stable temperatures has less impact on a wine's condition than one that is subject to severe fluctuations." Davis says that collections that are temperature-and-humidity controlled usually bring higher prices than those stored in cool underground cellars. He adds that cellars in the south, below the Mason–Dixon line, can offer unreliable storage conditions.

Light

Excessive light is another thing to avoid. Most people know that direct sunlight is bad, but many people also feel that fluorescent light can have harmful effects on wine. This is not proven, but it is a prudent idea to keep your wine out of such light except for brief periods when you are in the storage area to inspect it. Light, of course, is the reason dark-colored, light-resisting bottles are used.

Don't Feel the Vibes

Vibration represents another peril to fine wine. It plays havoc with the wine's sediment, which is an important component in the aging process. Tags with the name of each wine will also diminish the need to examine (and move) each bottle.

> . . . once a wine is in the bottle, one factor becomes preeminent in determining its future: storage.

Vibration is less a problem with storage (unless you live over a subway line) than transportation. Roger Livdahl, who was one of the premier wine appraisers in the United States, used to subtract value automatically for wine that hadn't been bottled at the château or winery. Part of the discount relates to the shade of doubt regarding authenticity, which is always present when a wine is not estate-bottled. But the greater rationale pertains to the additional rough handling the wine may have received in passing through so many hands—estate to salesperson *(négociant)* to shipper to importer to bottler—before bottling, treatment that may shorten the life span of the wine. Move your wines from place to place or cellar to cellar as little as possible. If, perchance, you find yourself investing in wines in the English market, try to store your purchases in England. Facilities are inexpensive and often easily arranged through an auction house or broker. Your wine will be more valuable in the long run if it isn't shuttled back and forth across the Atlantic.

Humidity

Excessive humidity encourages the growth of fungus, that is, mold. The fungus eats at the label and cork. Allowed to continue unchecked, the fungal aroma that gets into the cork will penetrate the wine, giving it an "off" flavor (hence the term "corked" wine). The resale value of wine is also partially a function of the bottle condition. If the labels are falling off (indicating excessively dry storage) or rotting away (too much humidity), the wine will be worth less than the same bottles whose labels are impeccable, indicating good provenance.

High humidity also makes it easier for other odors to affect the wine. For example, I once tainted a valued case of Romanee Conti by leaving it in a humid closet in my apartment during the summertime. My apartment was air-conditioned, so I wasn't concerned about the temperature, but my wife stored some winter coats lined with mothballs in the same closet. The wine carried an unmistakable aroma of mothballs for several months after I moved it out of the closet into a storage vault. The taint faded as the wine rested in a cellar with proper ventilation, but for almost a year I waited on pins and needles to see if I had inadvertently destroyed my wine. I hadn't, fortunately, but it still had a slightly "off" aroma.

Even though you don't want too much humidity, some humidity is necessary, however, because it means there is moisture in the air. Without some moisture, the cork could dry up and shrink, which causes leakage. Humidistats, sold at hardware stores, can be used to monitor the amount of humidity in the air.

It's also important to store wine on its side so the liquid is in constant contact with the cork. A wet cork won't shrink.

Another downside is that some people are allergic to the molds that grow under humid conditions. If you see mold

Occasional Tasting

TASTE YOUR IGW once in a while. You should hold a few bottles for this purpose. Don't become so obsessed with the appreciation of your wine that you deny yourself the pleasure of marking its progress toward maturity. Over the years, some wines have appreciated so quickly that many of my clients can't bring themselves to open a bottle. "It's too expensive for me to drink!" they cry. Nonsense. Taste it now and then or you'll never know why people are willing to pay so much money for wine.

Tastings are also important to ensure that the wine doesn't turn bad before it is drunk or sold. It is also important to understand, in

forming anywhere in your storage area—it can be black, gray, and a variety of other colors—you can wash it away with a solution of bleach and water (1 cup bleach to 1 gallon of water). In fact, bleach is the only chemical that will kill mold. You should wear gloves and ventilate the area while you clean so bleach fumes don't build up.

The important thing to remember here is not to become cowed by the facts of storage. If you stay around the 55-degree temperature mark, don't use the wine bottles as maracas, and don't store them in the sun, you should be fine. And you can—and should—check their taste from time to time. (See sidebar: "Occasional Tasting.")

general, which wines should be drunk first. In the 1995 edition of *Parker's Wine Buying Guide*, Robert M. Parker, Jr., tells of visiting a "prominent businessman" at his home and touring his "impressive cellar," which was "enormous, immaculately kept, with state-of-the art humidity-and-temperature controls." The wine investor was storing about 10,000 bottles in his cellar, but among his collection, to Parker's amazement, "there were also hundreds of cases of 10- and 15-year-old Beaujolais, Pouilly-Fuisse, Dolcetto, and California Chardonnays—all wines that should have been drunk during their first 4 or 5 years of life." Parker politely suggested that the man inventory his cellar for wines that should be drunk now, already knowing that he was looking at expensive vinegar.

Storage Options

JUST WHERE THE wine will be stored will depend on what you can afford and the size of your collection. Fortunately, there are a variety of ways to do it. In some instances, you may decide to build your own storage facility in the basement or elsewhere. If you build it yourself, you can find simple plans for building one in various do-it-yourself magazines, such as *Today's Homeowner*, *Popular Mechanics*, and *Family Handyman*.

There are also a variety of readymade or ready-to-assemble wine racks you can buy. They are advertised in magazines such as the *Wine Spectator*. Insulated, climate-controlled wine vaults may be purchased in various sizes too, at fairly modest prices. Your wine merchant can recommend a manufacturer or dealer, or you can investigate the various cellar makers yourself. Most of these also advertise in wine magazines or in newspapers. If you have limited resources, reserve your storage area for IGW. And sometimes it pays to be creative. I had one client who perused the "For Sale" sections of restaurant trade publications until he found exactly what he wanted at a liquidation sale: a used walk-in refrigerator. He put it in his garage and now has a superior cellar.

> Vibration represents another peril to fine wine. It plays havoc with the wine's sediment, which is an important component in the aging process.

People will go far, and spend a lot of money, to store their wine properly and safely. One wine lover I know bought an abandoned speakeasy located beneath Dag Hammarskjöld Plaza in New York City; columns arch into groined vaults overhead and on one wall a mosaic dating from the days of Prohibition depicts cavorting revelers. A Southern physician with an insatiable appetite for wine converted a hillside behind his house into a facility that would make many a wholesaler envious, as well it should, for the doctor has almost $10 million invested in vintage wines. A few years ago, the *Wine Spectator* carried a coast-to-coast roundup of wine cellars, some of which cost hundreds of thousands of dollars to build.

For most people, storing wine at home need not be an extravagant venture to be effective, as long as you pay attention to the basic requirements. If you're doubtful about temperature or humidity, take a few readings in your intended storage space over the course of several days using a thermometer and humidistat.

Any storage unit you buy should be able to accommodate the present and future collection. If you are going to be liquidating part of your collection for cash sometime down the road, remember that investors pay a premium for wine in its original case. To make sure you're storing it in conditions conducive to preservation, an inexpensive thermometer and humidistat will do the trick nicely.

Custom Built: Two Cautionary Tales

About a year ago, a Milwaukee homeowner contracted with a home improvement contractor to build a custom wine cellar in his suburban home. The contractor assured the homeowner that he was experienced and knew all about wine cellars. After all, he drank a lot of it himself.

Part of the job involved excavating a portion of the cellar. To make a sad story short, it resulted in the house having its foundation removed on one side so that it sagged to the tune of tens of thousands of dollars in repairs. During subsequent legal action (from which it is unlikely the homeowner will get complete satisfaction, a not uncommon occurrence) it was discovered that the contractor was unlicensed, uninsured, and had no experience building wine cellars. It was true, however, that he drank wine.

In another instance, a San Francisco resident contracted with a wine-cellar builder who in fact did have experience and had some good ideas, so the homeowner gave him a $5,000 advance toward "materials" and never saw the contractor—or the $5,000—again. It turned out that the contractor was in dire financial straits and had taken money from several customers without performing any work.

Stories like these—and just plain common sense—illustrate the importance of proceeding with caution if you decide to have a custom wine cellar built in your home or elsewhere. Approach it like you would any home improvement project, and take pains to make sure you get someone specifically experienced at building wine cellars. There can be a number of issues involved, from obvious ones like structural considerations to more specific ones like ventilation. With regard to ventilation, remember that while some mold may be inevitable with high humidity, you don't want to build a mold manufacturing plant.

Protect Yourself

If you want to hire someone to build a wine cellar, follow a procedure that will keep you safe and ensure that you get a good job. It is suggested that you adhere to the following system of checks and balances:

1. Check the contractor out at your local Consumer Affairs office. The vast majority of towns and cities have local offices, and they can be invaluable. (If there isn't one in your town, you can check with your state attorney general's office).

Check to see if the contractors you're considering have licenses to do home improvements. If they don't, don't even think about hiring them. For one thing, if they're not licensed, it means that if a dispute arises between you and the contractor, you can't rely on public agencies (like Consumer Affairs) to intercede for you.

If a dispute occurs over the job, the agency will send an investigator experienced in home improvements to see if your complaint has merit. Only 20 percent of consumer complaints about home improvements are valid: the other 20 percent of the time the contractor is right, and 60 percent of the time they're debatable.

Checking for a license (some communities call it being registered) is also particularly important in some areas that have what is known as a contractor refund program. This states that if there is a dispute between the customer and contractor and Consumer Affairs determines that the contractor is at fault, Consumer Affairs will pay if the contractor doesn't make amends. There are only seven or eight areas in the United States that have this program. Depending on the area, refunds range from $5,000 to $20,000. As of this writing, New York City had a refund program of $20,000; residents in Suffolk and Nassau Counties on Long Island can get back up to $5,000; Hawaii pays up to $12,500; Virginia pays up to $10,000; and Maryland pays up to $10,000.

> For most people, storing wine at home need not be an extravagant venture to be effective, as long as you pay attention to the basic requirements.

But here's the kicker: Unless the contractor was licensed on the day you hired him, you are not eligible for the refund.

Ask Consumer Affairs if there are any complaints lodged against the contractor. There may be complaints, but the key information is if they were resolved. And remember: Just because someone filed a complaint against a contractor doesn't necessarily mean he was at fault.

2. Check references and jobs. The contractor should be able to give you the names of 5 to 10 people for whom he has built cellars. Call one or two and see how they liked his work.

You may also want to visit the site of one of his jobs, not only to see how the cellar looks and functions but how the customer got along with the contractor.

3. Before starting the job, you should have a visual plan in hand, just as you would for any home improvement plan.

> Wine theft is a serious and often unreported problem.

Here are some other key points to observe:

1. Have a written agreement. The main purpose of this is to avoid misunderstandings, and make sure that both parties understand what is to be done and with what products and materials. The agreement should also contain the dates when the contractor will start the job as well as when it will be completed.

2. Don't give any money up front directly to the contractor. If he wants money for materials, make arrangements to pay the supplier directly, or give the contractor a double-endorse check, made out to him and his supplier. The reasoning here is that if for any reason the contractor doesn't pay the supplier, then under the lien laws in many states the supplier can come at you to collect; and he *can* collect. In other words, you can end up paying twice. If you don't pay, the penalty ranges from a black mark on your credit to having your home foreclosed. It depends on the state. In some states, such as Utah, foreclosure is possible; in New York, you can fight the action, but this will entail hiring a lawyer.

3. Pay as you go, making the final payment on the last day after you are satisfied with the work. It's smart to remember that the key to controlling the job is to control the money.

Professional Storage Space

Because of space limitations in your own home, you may want to consider renting professional space. One reason is security. One of my clients spent $120,000 in my shop in the course of an afternoon. He didn't take delivery until the next week, insisting that I personally drive the truck to his Long Island home under the cover of darkness. I thought my truck-unloading days were long behind me, but when I arrived it was just the two of us. We spent the better part of three hours hustling the wine into his house. He is, to put it mildly, concerned about security. And while insurance is not a panacea, it is far better than no protection. (For more on insurance, see section later in this chapter.)

Wine theft is a serious and often unreported problem. Unless the victim is directly involved in the wine trade—a merchant, a wholesaler, or a restaurateur—he or she rarely notifies the authorities and especially avoids the press. The last thing a wealthy collector wants to do is draw attention to his rare bottles. The wealthy or well-known personalities who have been robbed almost always try to avoid any publicity. I know of a number of cases. One fellow New York retailer lost $60,000 worth of wine when his home cellar was looted; a California entertainer was robbed of $120,000 worth of wine from his home; and a Long Island attorney had 830 select bottles, worth $372,000, removed from his cellar while other nearby bottles were untouched. In each of these cases, the thieves knew precisely what to take and what leave; they were wine experts themselves. (Life does sometimes provide amusing anecdotes. When a London restaurant was robbed of its wines a few years ago, the thieves concentrated exclusively on what were inexpensive red Bordeaux wines, pushing aside the far more valuable collection of rare California Cabernets.) Since wine crimes often go unreported, it makes it difficult for authorities to track down the criminals or the wine.

Another major reason to opt for professional storage is space: You may simply not have the room in your home.

Whatever your situation, professional storage space is available, but it is not all created equal. Some warehouses cater to wine—most do not. As a rule, you pay more for space that guarantees ideal cellar conditions.

Whatever your situation, professional storage space is available, but it is not all created equal. Some warehouses cater to wine—most do not. As a rule, you pay more for space that guarantees ideal cellar conditions.

There are many storage facilities throughout the country for this express purpose. In general, at this writing, they are charging a dollar a case a month, some more, some less. The lineup at the end of this chapter contains the names of some of these (check your local Yellow Pages for others). I heartily suggest that you confirm rates and other details noted—and also personally visit a facility to ensure that it enforces good storage practices—before renting space there. One Boston consumer was glad he did. When he inspected the "high-tech" facility advertised in the glossy ad in a wine magazine, he found a lot of wine sitting around stored in cardboard boxes in obvious disarray. Though he was only in the building for 15 minutes or so, and it was cool, his forehead was glistening with sweat when he left, perhaps in part because he had had such a close call!

Whatever facility you choose, you should ask them the following questions:

1. How long have you been in business? It's best to choose someone who's been around for a number of years. While longevity doesn't confer sainthood, it does indicate that the facility is likely to stay in business. If it goes out of business, or the owners can't pay their electric bill, your collection will be at risk. And it happens. Years ago, a New York outfit overextended itself on wine futures, which brought the entire business down, including the storage division.

2. Will you furnish an affidavit for my collection? This a legal document that gives all the particulars on how much wine you will be storing there and for how long. Without a written record, you have nothing.

3. Do you have a backup power system? You want to be sure that in case there is a power failure, the facility has a backup power system that will kick in to ensure that your collection stays at the optimum temperature.

4. Do you carry cellar liability? Is the facility covered in case of loss or damage to your wine? How much is it insured for?

5. What kind of security system does your facility have? You don't want to be prey to professional thieves, or even a bunch of kids sneaking in one night and getting high on your 1947 Château Lafite magnums and then attacking the rest of it with lump hammers.

Also, make sure that the facility's arrangements are convenient to you. Some facilities will allow weekend access, some won't; some will allow more or less unfettered access while others require that you supply code numbers that correspond to numbers on boxes. Also, in some cases, you have to give advance warning before you can get access to your wine; in other cases there is no delay. Find out if you can get to your collection immediately, something that might be handy if you want to convert to cash right away. Of course if you use your own cellar the only inconvenience will be walking down the cellar stairs.

Recorking

THE SAYING GOES that the best wines live only as well as their corks, so IGW older than 40 years should be recorked as a matter of course; if the wine's level is down, then refilling and recorking will make it more valuable. So, too, if the cork gives signs of failing—seepage or a sinking level are the main signs—then recorking is also called for.

Recorking is not a wondrous event. Opening up a bottle can expose the wine to bacteria or oxidation, and unless scrupulously handled, it can raise the specter of fraud or misrepresentation, something that can make the value of the wine plummet.

There is debate on whether recorking affects the wine. Some experts feel you should not recork, because once bottles are opened the wine starts to deteriorate slowly. Denis Foley, a consultant to auctioneer Butterfield and Butterfield, said that he believes this is so after tasting wine older than 25 years. Another expert Michael Davis says he's been tasting recorked wines for many years, some that go as far back as the 19th century, and there hasn't been a problem.

So far, there does not seem to a definitive ruling on the subject. However, there are some new recorking methods.

As mentioned in Chapter 4, the usual method of recorking and refilling Bordeaux wines is to have it done at the château in France. Château Lafite recorks its own wine at the château and during regular trips to the United States. At this writing, Lafite is the most respected château for recorking Bordeaux wines.

Insurance

TAKING THE TROUBLE to store fine wine properly and then not insuring it is like buying an expensive horse and then not locking the barn door. The standard homeowner's policy makes no special provisions for wine. In the event of disaster, your coverage may not even indemnify you for the original purchase price on particularly expensive bottles. This situation is remedied in two ways: You can either request a rider to your homeowner's policy that will extend your coverage to include your bottles of fine wine; or you can purchase a policy designed exclusively for the protection of wine cellars.

Whether you wish to insure your wine with its own policy or as an addition to your homeowner's coverage, you should look for protection against fire, theft, flood, excessive vibration, and accidental breakage. If climate-control equipment is used in the storage facility, your coverage should also protect you against any loss as a result of equipment or power failure.

If you store your wine in a professional facility you will almost certainly need an individual policy. Facilities should gladly explain the limits of their own liability before renting you space. Their policy will most likely not cover you for the following contingencies:

- An act of war
- Ullage
- Temperature changes (except in climate-controlled settings)

- Radiation
- Mold or rot
- Insects, vermin, or rodents
- Spoilage

This type of coverage is just about the same as that sought by wine merchants. The factor to keep uppermost in your mind is the extent of liability. A typical insurance company will want to have the following information about your collection: the number of bottles you keep, their size, a description that includes château and type (that is, Bordeaux, Port, Sauternes, Burgundy, etc.), the vintage, and the current market value of each. This may mean having an appraisal of your collection done by a creditable appraiser or wine merchant, or reaching some other type of agreement with the insurer about what it will accept as fair market value. Prices fetched at public auctions are sometimes accepted as fair market value, or prices listed by certain wine merchants might be acceptable.

> Taking the trouble to store fine wine properly and then not insuring it is like buying an expensive horse and then not locking the barn door.

Insurers will also want to know if your cellar or storage area is equipped with security and smoke alarms or fire detection systems, the location and construction of the area, whether the area is climate controlled, type of climate-control equipment used, and type of backup for this system.

This information, including the estimated fair market value of the wine, should be updated at least every two years, and in the case of rapidly appreciating wine, every year. In the event of a loss, the insurance company will generally have the option of either reimbursing you or replacing your wine.

In 1998, a typical premium was $7 a case, per year for all wine valued at less than $30 per bottle or less than $3,600 per case. Above those values, premiums need to be individually factored. Clearly, if you store costly wine haphazardly, your insurance rates will be exorbitant.

Again, I recommend that you keep a cellar book or record. It comes in handy when purchasing insurance. Cellar records should include these entries: the name and year of the wine in each bottle, the total amount of each type purchased and from whom and on what date, the name of the shipper, and the price paid. If you drink the wine rather than sell it (or drink one bottle), you should also enter your own comments on taste and the date adjacent to the other technical information.

Appraisals

HOW DO YOU assess the value of your wine? By having it appraised. The two primary times to conduct an appraisal are when purchasing insurance and when liquidating. And you should have it done by a professional! Most amateur estimates vary wildly—20 percent or so, in my experience. Private collectors just don't have the time, expertise, and information to make accurate appraisals. You would be wise to have your wine appraised about every two years, just in the interest of keeping yourself informed.

Wine merchants sometimes do appraisals, or can recommend a creditable appraiser. Don't hesitate to ask for the credentials of whomever you're considering for the job. At the very minimum, the appraiser should have a working knowledge of the current retail and auction prices and some sense of market trends. Most merchants won't do it. They simply do not have the time to maintain up-to-the-minute files on the thousands of vintages and names about which collectors inquire.

When selecting an appraiser, one insider also offers this advice: "Beware of anyone who bases his or her fee on a percentage of the cellar's appraised value. There's always the temptation to inflate the wine's worth."

Transporting Wine

A FEW YEARS ago, a lawyer named Anthony Root was transferred by his company from the United States to Hong Kong. Root had a little problem: He had a 1,600-bottle wine collection and wanted to take the lion's share with him. "The moving company," he told *Wine Spectator* magazine, "tried to get me to ship it by boat," but he demurred. He was well aware that to get it to Hong Kong the ship would have to pass through the Panama Canal, which at the time would've raised the temperature inside the ship to that of a sauna.

Happily, Root came up with an out that allowed him to drink his wine and ship it safely too. His company allowed him 1,000 pounds for shipping airfreight and he used 900 pounds of it for shipping slightly less than half his collection, wrapping each bottle in bubble wrap. The wine left at home was stored in a climatized storage unit and the wine that arrived in Hong Kong was stored in a climatized warehouse until his storage unit arrived.

Shipping Dangers

Shipping overseas or anywhere else is something to be very cautious about. While there is some debate on how well wine can take jostling (which can move the sediment in unfiltered wine) and heat or cold (which can pop the cork because wine expands when heated, leading to oxidation), it is best to err on the side of caution. Though Root's collection was undamaged, for example, he said that his Beaujolais lost taste. Also, his Burgundies have matured more rapidly, a sure sign that they were affected by heat.

If you want to ship wine across country by air, there are a number of commercial outfits available. Your best bet is to shop around. Prices can vary from $4 to over $30 a case.

But carefully check the conditions under which your wine will be shipped. Trucks and the like that carry wine commonly do not have cooled storage areas. As Robert M. Parker, Jr., points out, most importers claim to ship in "reefers" (the trade jargon for temperature-controlled containers), but only a handful actually do. Parker also says that American shippers of Bordeaux say that reefers are not needed in shipping wine across the ocean, but he says they should have witnessed a shipment of Rausan-Segla, Châteaux Margaux, and other fine wines that arrived in Washington after a 1986 ocean voyage. The labels were stained and the corks pushed up, the wine obviously ruined, and perhaps bought for high prices by unsuspecting consumers.

Many of the filtered, fined, and otherwise processed wines can go through virtual hell and not get damaged. But the untampered-with Bordeaux and similar fine wines are particularly susceptible to heat damage, something to be acutely aware of when having wine shipped.

Cellar records should include these entries: the name and year of the wine in each bottle, the total amount of each type purchased and from whom and on what date, the name of the shipper, and the price paid.

Important Points

- Ideal wine temperature for storage is 55 degrees. The lower the temperature, the slower the wine ages.
- Wine should be stored with the following in mind:

  Fluctuating temperatures can harm wine.

  Excessive light is an enemy.

  Vibration is not good for wine because it agitates the sediment.

  Humidity should range between 60 and 75 percent.

  Wine should be stored on its side so the cork is always wet.

- If having a custom wine rack built, observe the following:

  Make sure the contractor is licensed and that he doesn't have unresolved complaints lodged against him with your local Consumer Affairs office.

  Have a plan in hand.

  Check the contractor's references and visit some active job sites.

  Never let the contractor get ahead of you on the payments: Pay as work is completed, and be sure to review the job before making the final payment.

  Make sure the supplier is getting paid for materials.

  If subcontractors are used, make sure they're getting their money, too, because they also have lien rights.

- Recork wines when they are over 40 years old or as necessary.

- Make sure your collection is insured, whether you store it at home or in a professional facility.
- Take great care when shipping wine and when having it shipped to you.

Storage Warehouses

Chicago

Sam's Wine and Spirits
1720 N. Marcey St.
Telephone: (312) 664-4394
Fax: (312) 664-7037
Rates: $3 per case.

Wine East Bank Storage
429 W. Ohio St.
Telephone: (312) 644-2000
Fax: (312) 644-7878
Rates: $95 per year for a 12-case locker; $145 per year for 18 cases; $190 per year for 24 cases; $280 per year for 36 cases; $690 per year for 90 cases.

Houston

Houston Wine Cellar
4645 SW Freeway, Suite 130
Telephone: (713) 840-1243
Rates: $23 per month for a 9-case locker; $25 per month for 12 cases; $28 per month for 15 cases; $32 per month for 18 cases.

Los Angeles

Bel-Air 2020 Wine Merchants
2020 Cotner Ave.
Telephone: (310) 447-2020
Fax: (310) 475-2836
Rates: $175 per year for 25 cases; $450 per year for 50 cases; $675 per year for 75 cases; $750 per year for 100 cases; $1,500 per year for 250 cases; $4,000 per year for 2,500 cases.

L.A. Fine Arts & Wine Storage
2290 Centinela Ave.
Telephone: (310) 447-7700
Fax: (310) 447-7070
Rates: $275 per year for 24 Bordeaux cases; $125–$199 per year for 15–20 cases; $125 per month for 90–100 cases in a walk-in room; $170 per month for 150–160 cases in a walk-in room.

The Wine House
2311 Coo Ave.
Telephone: (310) 479-3731, (800) 626-WINE
Fax: (310) 478-5609
Rates: $650–$725 per year for a 72-case locker.

Miami

International Wine Storage
601 SW Eighth St.
Telephone: (305) 856-1208
Fax: (305) 758-6124
Rates: $25 per month for 18 cases.

New York City

Morgan Manhattan
2100 Hunters Point Ave., Long Island City, New York
Telephone: (718) 786-3304
Fax: (718) 786-2969
Rates: $20 per month for 1–14 cases; $1.40 per case per month for 15–25 cases; $1.30 per case per month for 26–50 cases.

Vintage Warehouse
665 11th Ave.
Telephone: (212) 245-4889
Fax: (212) 245-4839
Rates: $1.20 per case per month ($12 minimum).

Philadelphia

My Cellar
4560 Route 130 North, Pennsauken, New Jersey
Telephone: (215) 625-3928
Fax: (215) 592-4744
Rates: $1 per case per month (3-case minimum).

San Francisco

Extra Space Storage
4050 19th Ave.
Telephone: (415) 333-3191
Fax: (415) 333-1256
Rates: $16 per month for a 9-case locker; $19 per month for 12 cases; $26 per month for 18 cases; $185 per month for 225 cases.

John Walker & Co.
175 Sutter St.
Telephone: (415) 986-2707
Fax: (415) 421-5820
Rates: $15 per case per year for 1–9 cases purchased from them; $12.50 per case per year for 10 cases or more purchased from them; $17.50 per case per year for 1–9 cases purchased elsewhere; $15 per case per year for 10 cases or more purchased elsewhere.

K&L Wine Merchants
3005 El Camino Real, Redwood City
Telephone: (650) 364-8544
Fax: (650) 364-4687
Rates: $1 per case per month.

Subterranean Private Wine Storage
2227 San Pablo Ave., Oakland
Telephone: (510) 451-3939, (800) 357-1188
Fax: (510) 451 5753
Rates: $14 per month for a 16-case locker; $32 per month for 40 cases.

Seattle

Seattle Wine Storage
122 Terry Ave. North
Telephone/Fax: (206) 628-4802
Rates: $1–$10 per case per month.

CHAPTER TWELVE

Liquidating Your Investment

THERE MAY COME a time when you want to liquidate some of your IGW portfolio. If so, there are three basic ways it's done:

1. Sell or trade between private individuals.
2. Sell it at auction.
3. Sell it to a wine merchant.

Private Sales

UNFORTUNATELY, THE FIRST way is illegal. Since wine is an alcoholic beverage, it is under state control and cannot be sold legally without a license. And if one is caught, the consequences can be nasty. I remember reading about one New Jersey collector who advertised the sale of his $30,000 cellar in a local newspaper. He got some inquiries and invited one of the buyers to view his cellar. Unfortunately, the buyer was an undercover operative from the New Jersey Alcohol and Beverage Commission and the resulting legal wrangles included the collector's arrest and the state selling off his cellar—a total loss to the owner.

Margaux for medical research? Pétrus for PBS? It's not as far-fetched as you might think.

Effective stings like that are rare, however, and a run-through of the advertisements of many wine newsletters indicates that despite the chance of getting caught, many wine lovers do indeed sell their wine directly to private buyers. Collectors tell me they resent the state telling them what they can and cannot do with their wines. Also, private sales between individuals are quite common in Europe and those nations do not seem to have suffered from them.

Until now, the IGW "gray market" communicates via print media and word of mouth. But at this writing I understand that someone is about to go online with a sort of clearinghouse for wine to be sold between private individuals.

Why do the vast majority of people get away with it? Because law enforcement doesn't care enough to pursue malefactors, nor does it have the manpower to enforce laws.

"The last thing I wanted when I was a district attorney," said one ex-DA, "was for an undercover detective to come to me and say that he knew a liquor store was selling an occasional six-pack to an under-aged individual. It's not the kind of case I want. I have too many murders, rapes, and other serious offenses to cope with."

Wendell Lee, a lawyer with the Sacramento-based Wine Institute, believes that the major factor in whether law enforcement gets involved is the "amount of wine that is sold (or traded). The DA isn't going to go after pocket change."

Not only is gray market selling done, it's done by experts. It's been rumored—and I believe the rumors—that a number of prominent wine consultants have served as middlemen for some important sales. Small wonder. One of the hazards of buying from a private collector is that you have no legal recourse if you get scorched. You can't appeal to any governmental agency, nor can you take your case to court. So consultants are employed to appraise the seller's collection to make sure that the buyer doesn't buy the vinous equivalent of a pig in a poke.

As for why the government does not allow private individuals to sell wine, the heart of the matter appears to be taxation: When private collections change hands, the state loses a pound of flesh. Like the Romans said, to understand a situation ask yourself, "Que bono?" Who benefits?

Auction

A LEGAL WAY to liquidate your collection is to sell it to an auction house (see Chapter 4, "Auctions"). There are two types of auctions: commercial and charitable.

Margaux for medical research? Pétrus for PBS? It's not as far-fetched as you might think. The fastest way to exploit your IGW's appreciation is to give it away: Donate your wine to charity. Wine lovers from all over the country annually contribute to their favorite charity wine auctions—a particularly Californian approach (learned from auctions in Europe)—to raise money for hospitals, public radio and television stations, and other nonprofit enterprises. While it stands to reason that Golden State fund-raisers would focus on wine, gifts of appreciable property such as real estate, art, and antiques are welcome too. A friend of mine donates rare wine to a yearly dinner for a research hospital—and deducts it. Uncle Sam's loss is science's gain. Note that giving your wine away won't bring you the same return as selling it. But if you were planning a cash donation to your favorite cause, a gift of the same amount—in wine—can provide double benefits: You reduce what you would have paid in taxes had you sold the wine and at the same time you boost the value of your donation. Generous bidders pushing a given wine to twice its fair market value are so commonplace that appraisers completely disregard charity prices in their calculations.

> When the wine sells, it will be months before you actually receive your money. If you are in a hurry for cash, selling it at auction is not the way to go.

A Note About Taxes

Since 1985, donors of appreciated property have had to take a little extra care when filling out their tax returns. Filers must now notify the IRS about non-cash gifts totaling over $500; if the total exceeds $5,000, they must also have the property appraised and provide a brief description of the appraiser's qualifications. Certain people are excluded from appraising your gift (if the gift is wine, for example, the merchant who sold it to you cannot act as your appraiser).

Your accountant or tax attorney should determine the size of your deduction. Your other income, the type of organization you wish to benefit, whether you qualify for the alternative minimum tax, and exactly how the beneficiary decides to use your gift will all have a bearing on your final deduction. In the meantime, you can sit back and enjoy the satisfaction of knowing that good taste can serve a good cause.

Commercial Auctions

You make an arrangement with the auction house to sell your wine, the auction house puts your wine up for bid, and you get the proceeds, minus the auction house's fees. (For more details, see Chapter 4.)

Today, auction houses won't take collections that are worth less than a certain amount in value. Since there are auction houses only in New York, Chicago, and San Francisco, how do you sell your wine? You call the auction house and someone comes to you to examine your collection. That person tells you how much the auction house will bid it out for: This is the minimum amount they will accept for your wine. If no one makes the minimum bid, the wine will be returned to you.

Added to the fees that you pay, you will have to figure the cost of shipping the wine. There are various ways to do this (as detailed in Chapter 11).

You do not have to be present at the auction.

When the wine sells, it will be months before you actually receive your money. If you are in a hurry for cash, selling it at auction is not the way to go.

Different auction houses charge different rates for their services. For example, at a recent auction in New York run by Acker Merrill, there was no charge. This may change, but that is certainly an attraction. Christie's, Sotheby's, Butterfield and Butterfield, and Chicago Auction House currently charge 15 percent service rates.

Selling to Wine Shops

Certain states allow you to sell your wine to someone who is licensed, such as a wine shop. For example, New York State allows it. There are some pros and cons to doing it this way. One pro is fast cash. Once the merchant receives the wine, he or she writes you a check for the agreed-upon amount—and that's it. The problem may come with how much the wine merchant is willing to pay. He may just want to pay you the wholesale price for your collection, which may be well below what you can make at an auction. On the other hand, you may be able to immediately deduct the fees that the auction house would collect.

Shop Around

Whether you sell your wine to an auction house or a wine shop, shopping around for the best price is an excellent idea. Prices are bound to differ, and there's no question that you can make extra hundreds, even thousands, of dollars by being choosy. And all it will cost you is your time and telephone calls.

Important Points

- Selling or trading wine between individuals is illegal.
- The amount of wine sold between individuals seems to correspond to how forcefully the authorities respond.
- The most common legal way to sell wine is through auction houses.

- Wine given to charities may be used as a tax deduction.
- In some states, wine may be legally sold back to wine merchants.
- Shop around for the best prices when selling your wine.

Chapter Thirteen

Enjoying Wine

World class financier Ron Perelman once said to me: "Bill, I want to learn all about wine in five minutes."

"Fine," I said, "you can teach me all about making money in the same amount of time."

The fact is, no one can learn all about wine in five minutes, or even five weeks, however, should you decide to literally liquidate your investment, you can learn quickly enough to make the experience more enjoyable. The plain fact is that drinking wine is not the same as drinking beer, soda, milk, or any other beverage. It encompasses everything from getting the wine to the proper drinking temperature to using the right glass.

Following are some things you'll want to know.

Temperature

Some folks get crazy about what temperature wine should be at before imbibing, but they needn't.

All that's necessary to know is that white wine is served cool, but not cold, and storing it in the refrigerator for an hour before serving should do the trick.

Red wine should be served a few degrees cooler than room temperature, because room temperature in the United States is warmer than abroad.

Champagne and sparkling wines should be served quite cold. However the same idea mentioned before applies: cold mutes taste so it should not be overly chilled. Between 45 and 50 degrees should be about right.

It's not a good idea to refrigerate sparkling wines and champagne for longer than two hours prior to it being served. Rather, speed-chill the wine by submerging the bottle in a container containing both cold water and ice, which does a quicker job of chilling than ice alone (because there's more cold contacting the glass).

Removing the Capsule

The kinds of wines we're talking about in this book are sealed with a cork, so the first job is removing the cork without accidentally getting fragments of it in the wine.

Before doing that, however, it is first necessary to remove the capsule, the metal or plastic casing that covers the cork and lip of the bottle. To do this, you can use a specialized foil cutting tool or, simply, the tip of a knife. Cut about ¼-inch below the top of the capsule, then pull it off and use a damp cloth or towel to remove any capsule residue.

Up and Out

REMOVING THE CORK comes next, and for this you use either a corkscrew or a corkpuller. These devices are designed so you don't have to be Arnold Schwarzenegger to use them. (Curiously, it is estimated that 30 percent of the people in America do not own any sort of device for removing a cork.).

To use a corkscrew, center the screw over the cork, then turn it clockwise so it bites into the cork and penetrates downward deep enough to grab it securely, but not so far that it punches through the bottom (this could push bits of cork into the wine).

Once the corkscrew is solidly in place, pull it out gently. If the cork breaks during the process, back the corkscrew out and reinsert it.

Your other option is to use a corkpuller (also called an *ah-so*). Corkpullers have two long prongs, which you push down between the sides of the cork and the inside of the bottle neck. Then, pull and turn the device until the cork comes up and out.

With the cork out, use a damp cloth to wipe the top of the bottle to remove any bits of cork. To remove any pieces in the wine, you can pour it through a fine sieve, such as cheesecloth, into a wide-mouth bottle or decanter.

Decanting

RED WINE THAT is 8 or 9 years old usually has a sediment or buildup of a sandy residue. If you hold the wine bottle against the light you'll be able to see it. As mentioned elsewhere in the book, though harmless, it should be removed before drinking.

The removal process is known as decanting. To do this, gently pour the wine into a decanter, taking care not to disturb the sediment. As you pour, you may shine a flashlight through the wine so you can see the sediment. Once you spot it, stop pouring. Show-offs light a candle under the bottle for this purpose.

Opening Champagne

HOW MANY TIMES has this scene played in a movie: someone opens a bottle of Champagne and the cork goes flying while the top of the bottle suddenly resembles Old Faithful at Yellowstone National Park? (And if it's a comedy, somebody takes the cork directly in an eye!)

In actuality, those scenes indicate poor technique! Opened properly, the cork will not pop, nor will the Champagne gush out.

First, remove the capsule from the bottle, then untwist the wire holding the cork in place. Do this with your hand over the cork and, of course, never have the bottle pointing at anyone.

Keeping your hand in place over the cork, rotate the bottle. When the cork starts to push up, use your thumb to control it until it releases gently. You should hear a sort of "poof" rather than a gunshot!

Tasting Wine

BEFORE SERVING WINE, you should taste it to ensure that it's drinkable. Sometimes wine can change for the worse, but will not give any clues until it's on your palate.

When tasting wine, disregard the usual rules about wine temperature. When a wine is tasted it should be just a few degrees above room temperature. Why? When it's warmer, it's full of flavor, and any flaws are easier to detect than when it's cold. As mentioned before, cold mutes taste.

With the wine at the proper temperature, fill a glass about halfway. Swirl it around a bit in the glass; this helps release the aroma.

Color

Take a look at the color. With red wine, the deeper the color the better the wine will usually taste. There are various colors. Following is a lineup of what they usually indicate in terms of taste.

Brownish amber This usually indicates that the wine has deteriorated because of oxidation.

Tawny Only desirable when the wine is a Tawny Port.

Purple Indicates a very young wine.

Ruby or crimson Wine that has not been aged long; also the color of very young Vintage Ports.

Red Wine that has been aged for awhile, such as Pinot Noir that has aged 1 to 3 years or a Cabernet Sauvignon that has aged 3 to 5 years.

Brick red Here, the red color has a hint of brown. The color usually indicates very good taste. Also indicates that the wine is well aged.

Reddish brown This color is lighter and browner than brick red. Usually indicates wine that has matured fully.

Following are white wine colors and what they usually indicate.

Pale greenish yellow Indicates very young wine.

Straw Also very young.

Yellow gold Wine aged 3 to 4 years old.

Gold Wine aged at least 6 years.

Brown tingeing Indicates that the wine is excessively aged. Exception: sherry. This can have a brownish tinge and still be good.

> The plain fact is that drinking wine is not the same as drinking beer, soda, milk, or any other beverage. It encompasses everything from getting the wine to the proper drinking temperature to using the right glass.

Clarity

Examine the wine for clarity. Wine should be clear, though as mentioned earlier, it is natural for wine to have some sediment in it.

Smell

Second, hold the glass under your nose and sniff. How does the wine smell? Usually, if the wine has a light smell it will have a light taste. One that has a more intense or aromatic "nose," as they say, has a more intense taste.

Do you smell a variety of aromas in the wine? Complexity of smell is a sign of good taste.

Wine and Food

As Harvey Steiman, editor at large of the *Wine Spectator* magazine says, "The first thing to remember about matching food and wine is to forget the rules. Forget about 'should' and 'shouldn't.' Forget about complicated systems for selecting the right wine to enhance the food on the table. This is not rocket science. It's common sense. Follow your instincts."

I couldn't have said it better myself!

Of course you may wonder about the age-old rule of drinking white wine with fish and red wine with meat. As Steiman points out, such rules made "perfect sense in the days when white wines were light and fruity and red wines were tannic." But wines these days don't always fit these descriptions, so the "color coding does not always work."

Taste

Professional wine tasters, such as Robert M. Parker, Jr., know that you don't need to swallow wine to taste it. Fortunately, they don't—they just swirl it around in their mouths for awhile—otherwise, we'd be running out of wine critics!

Happily, as a non-professional taster, you can swallow.

There's no great mystery to performing this phase of the operation. Just take a small sip and taste. You'll either like it—or you won't!

Wineglasses

A VARIETY OF stemware is available for drinking wine, but most share one characteristic: The rims are turned in to capture the bouquet and flavor. For most wines all you need is a few Bordeaux glasses. You can use a sixteen-ounce glass, but only fill it halfway (six to eight ounces). This leaves room for the wine to breathe.

The exception to the rule is Champagne. For drinking this you should use a Champagne flute.

Incidentally, my idol Thomas Jefferson said he limited his drinking to two glasses of wine a day. I wonder what size they were?

Important Points

- Don't go crazy trying to figure out the temperature at which wine should be served. It shouldn't be confusing. Cool for white, slightly below room temperature for red, and cold for Champagne.
- To detect sediment in wine, shine a light through it as it's pouring. Decant as necessary.
- Taste the wine before serving it.
- Remember, when selecting a wine to go with your meal, there are no hard and fast rules, just follow your instincts.

APPENDIX A

How Wine Is Made

The winemaker is a warrior. He has to fight the vagaries of nature, storms, disease, rot, hail, and bad luck. This is why every bottle is worthy of respect and every glass must be drunk with the honor it deserves. That soil, that man, that fight, are embodied in your glass.

—*Anonymous*

BEFORE DESCRIBING HOW the two main kinds of wine, red and white, are made, it would be smart to talk about the raw material wine is made from—grapes.

GRAPES

There are an estimated 1,000 varieties of grapes, some of which are used to make the world's great wines and others, at the other end of the scale, are used for jams and jug wine.

Also, wines with the same name may have differences, making even more "varieties," depending on where they're grown.

Still, when it comes to IGW or fine wine the plain fact is that only a small number of grape varieties are used. Here's a look.

Cabernet Franc: This grape is blended with Merlot and Cabernet Sauvignon to make classic red Bordeaux wine. Since it is light and has less tannin than other grapes, it is used to make several light-style reds.

Cabernet Sauvignon: When it comes to the magisterial red wines of the Médoc district of Bordeaux, arguably the best in the world, the name of the game is Cabernet Sauvignon grapes. They make some of the best reds in the world, such as in Bordeaux where winemakers combine them with other grapes like Merlot, and where the Cabernet grape's thick skin provides plenty of tannins, which act as preservatives and provide longevity.

Chardonnay: Someone once said that if Chardonnay wine didn't exist, it would be necessary to invent it. Its fame spans the globe. Indeed, no other grape is more famous. It is used in making upscale white wine and is considered the "house white" in a wide variety of countries including the United States, New Zealand, and Australia. It is also grown in southern France—the only areas in which Chardonnay is not grown are Bordeaux and the Rhône Valley.

Grenache: This is the second most commonly planted red grape in the world. It is key to making world-class wines in the southern Rhône Valley such as Chateauneuf-du-Pape and Côtes du Rhône.

Malbec: Mostly used in Chile and Argentina to make varietals.

Merlot: This is a thick-skinned blue–black grape that gives softness and roundness to the red wines of the Médoc district in Bordeaux. It is often used with Cabernet Sauvignon to make the classic Bordeaux blend. In California the two are combined in a blend called Meritage. Years ago, Merlot grapes were planted in Bordeaux as insurance against the failure of other grapes. Merlot is tougher than most varieties. Today there are a number of Bordeaux reds that are made with 100 percent or close to 100 percent Merlot, primarily those from the Pomerol and Saint-Emilion districts. Merlot grapes are also used in winemaking in Chile, Washington State, Argentina, New York, and elsewhere. Americans seem to like wines made with Merlot grapes because they are less tannic than some other types and therefore offer a smoother drinking experience. Classically, Merlot grapes give off mint, black pepper, cherry, olive, vanilla, and other aromas. However, Merlot grapes do not impart the same complex taste sensations to wine as other varieties.

Pinot Noir: This is one of the great winemaking grapes of the world. It needs the right soil and the right vine and is only moderately prolific, but if conditions are perfect, it makes the sensational red wines of Burgundy, such as Nuits-Saint George, Chambertin, Pommard, Volnay, and the like. It is the base ingredient in making champagne and slightly pink sparkling wine. The winemakers of Burgundy believe in letting the grape find its own *terroir*; that is, they plant different grapes in different areas until they get the best match.

The Pinot Noir grapes grown in California are generally fruitier tasting (with cherry, raspberry, and strawberry flavors) than those of Burgundy, which have a more subtle taste. The thin-skinned Pinot Noir grapes are also less tannic than wines made with Cabernet grapes, and lighter in color. In general, wines made with Pinot Noir grapes are drunk relatively young—two to six years—but there are also a number of *grand cru* wines made with Pinot Noir grapes that can age for decades and still be highly drinkable.

Sangiovese: This grape is used in making Italian Chianti, as well as the world-class Brunello di Montalcino. It is also starting to be used in California.

Sauvignon Blanc: This grape is used frequently in the production of white wines. In the United States, New Zealand, and Australia, wines from the grape are called Sauvignon Blanc. These wines are also known in the United States as Fumé Blanc. Chile also uses the grape in production of white wine. It's the grape of choice in a number of whites from France, such as Pouilly-Fume, Sancerre, and whites from the Loire Valley. It is also an ingredient in dry white wines from Bordeaux, such as Graves and Entre-Deux-Mers and sweet wines from Sauternes and Barsac.

Its taste has one very surprising aspect, which authors Leslie Breener and Lettie Teague reveal in their book *Fear of Wine:* "Sauvignon blancs are crisp, refreshing, aromatic wines, known for their distinctive nose (smell), which is often described as freshly cut grass, bell peppers, asparagus or even, believe it or not, cat pee. When a Sauvignon blanc has a cat-pee nose, it's considered a positive thing, because this smell is a good example of the wine's variety."

Sauvignon Blanc makes for delicious wine, despite its unusual nose, but perhaps part of the reason it's not as popular as Chardonnay is that it hasn't been promoted as much. Years ago, Robert Mondavi was going to use it in his famed California winery, but decided against it. The word was that he felt that Americans might have trouble pronouncing "Sauvignon." Eventually, he did bottle it, but rechristened the wine "Fumé Blanc," which he thought people would have less trouble pronouncing.

Sémillon: This grape is usually blended with other grapes, though it is unblended in California and Washington State. Sémillon is a yellow grape with low acid levels, but it ages well. It is also susceptible to the botrytis mold, which ultimately leads to Sauternes (sweet wine). It is blended with 80 percent Sauvignon Blanc and a little Muscadelle, about 20 percent, another grape variety and making up the chief white wine from the Graves region of France. This white wine and Sauternes are much better after aging, and they will drink well after decades in proper storage.

Syrah: This grape makes dark red wines such as those made in the northern Rhône Valley like Hermitage and Côte-Rotie. In Australia and South Africa, the grape is known as Shiraz, which may be its original name. Experts suspect that the grape came from Persia.

Zinfandel: This red grape's claim to fame is that it was born in America. It is quite popular for making wines in California, including rosés and sparkling wines. When drunk young it has plenty of "fruit."

Making Wine

Winemaking starts in the vineyards. The growing season starts in the spring; the grapes are harvested in the fall. Ideally, what the winemaker hopes for is a long summer so the grapes can get good and ripe, and no rain before harvest. Rain can waterlog grapes and dilute their taste. Quite obviously it is the weather that is key in how grapes, and ultimately the wine, turn out.

The winemaking process is similar for white and red wines.

Making White Wine

As grapes grow and the sugar content increases, they get sweeter. This is key. The winemaker wants the grapes to get as sweet as possible, so as harvest time approaches you'll see him or her out there tasting the grapes, or measuring sugar content with a refractometer.

At some point, the winemaker will give the go-ahead to pick, and the experienced harvesters will pick, in bunches, only the good grapes, trying not to get any leaves in the big baskets they use. It all can impact the wine's flavor.

The harvested grapes head for the winery where they are destemmed and crushed. The juice that results is called "free-run juice." The skins—which give the wine its color—and stems are pressed to produce more juice, then they are discarded.

Next comes the fermentation process. The wine is placed into stainless steel or epoxy-lined vats or oak barrels and yeast is added. The yeast eats the sugar in the wine, and in the process produces carbon dioxide in the form of bubbles and alcohol. The bubbles dissipate in the air (unless one is making champagne) and the alcohol is left behind.

The resulting product is called "must" and is fermented days or weeks until most of the alcohol is gone.

The yeast becomes inactive; the leavings are called "lees." These are either left in the wine—they settle on the bottom of the container—or the clear juice is racked (transferred into a fresh, clean vat, leaving the lees behind). It's all a matter of what kind of flavor the winemaker is trying to achieve.

The wine is then aged, either in oak barrels or stainless or concrete vats. Chardonnay grapes are frequently aged in oak, because the winemaker wants the flavors in the wood to seep into the wine.

After aging, it is racked (if it hasn't been already), and then it is "fined"—a chemical is added to attract extra particles floating around—and filtered.

Making Red Wine

In making red wine, the winemaker follows essentially the same steps as in making white wine. However, when the grapes are crushed, the skin is left on to impart color and tannins (the harsh-flavored chemicals that give wine a solid structure and enable it to age properly). The skins are left in during fermentation too. The skins naturally rise to the surface, but they are continuously pushed down into the liquid. This process is known as maceration.

Red wine may be filtered and fined, but this is not done with finer wines because it strips the wine of the solids, which impart flavor and longevity.

After being bottled, the wine—red or white—starts to age gradually, losing the tannins and other harshness until it's ready to drink.

Fine Wine Is Complicated

Wine writer Hugh Johnson describes freshly made wine as a "complex of unresolved principles: of acids and sugars, minerals and pigments, esters and aldehydes and tannins." He goes on to explain that the finer the wine, the more it contains of all of these elements, and the longer it takes for them to chemically harmonize. Fruity, simple wines intended for immediate consumption contain relatively small amounts of these brash, competitive elements. Year-old Beaujolais makes good picnic wine because it provides a mouthful of uncomplicated fruity flavor, the taste equivalent of a bright yellow balloon. A Margaux, or meaty Cabernet, if tasted at the same age, is a cacophonous Spike Jones band of strident impressions, each vying for attention.

Winemaking Decisions

A number of different choices by the winemaker determine the intensity of these rival elements, as well as how long the wine lives. First, for example, comes the variety of grapes used, the quality of the particular vintage, and the type of fermentation used in making the wine. Some grapes are higher in tannins than others, a vital ingredient for long-lived wines. Cabernet

Sauvignon grapes contain more than Merlot grapes, for example. A winery may blend its wine from Merlot and Cabernet Sauvignon in traditional proportions, but an exceptional vintage in one or the other of these grapes may cause the winemaker to rethink his or her traditional strategy. That ratio will affect the life of the wine. How much "press wine" should he or she blend with the "free-run wine?" After fermentation, about 80 percent of the wine runs out of the fermenting vat without requiring any pressing of the grapes at all; this free-run wine tends to be light and fruity. Press wine, as its name suggests, follows afterward, when the fermented grapes are pressed. Highly tannic and dark-colored, press wine is added in varying percentages to wines intended for aging.

The Aging Process

Until as recently as the last century, the chemistry of how wine ages was barely understood at all. Our taste for aged wine has itself only developed in the last several hundred years. Before the 1700s, most wines were vinified to be drunk fairly soon. The odd barrel of wine that now and then escaped everyone's notice and was allowed to sit undisturbed for several years spoiled more often than it aged. Older wines that managed to avoid bacterial contamination were treated as medicines or curative tonics, more valued for their miraculous powers of preservation (as witnessed by their proven ability to resist turning into vinegar) than for their complexity of tastes. According to Hugh Johnson, the aging of wine didn't come into its own until the technology of the cork and the corkscrew came along in the 17th century. Even so, the general public still preferred coarse concoctions of young wines or raw wine fortified with brandy.

The first real scientific inquiry into the aging of wine began with Louis Pasteur. In 1863, Napoleon III and several prominent winemakers, distressed at the deterioration of their wines during travel to faraway markets, invited Pasteur to research the question of how winemakers might control the effects of aging. Pasteur himself had been born in a winemaking region, the Jura in eastern France, and he eagerly took up the challenge. After a series of experiments that involved sealing wine in glass tubes with precisely measured amounts of air he discovered that oxygen is integral to the aging process. Wine in half-filled test tubes aged faster than wine in full tubes, proving that too much air, too soon, will age wine to vinegar. Too much oxygen causes wine to age rapidly and turn brown; too little, and the wine doesn't age at all.

Oaken casks have the advantage over cement or stainless steel vats because wood is porous: It permits the passage of air into the wine. On the negative side, wood also allows wine to evaporate. If the level of the wine in the casks isn't topped off, too much air collects in the top of the barrel, bacteria begin to grow, and the wine turns to vinegar.

Pasteur developed a process of heating and then cooling wine rapidly to kill microorganisms present in the wine, a technique similar to the pasteurization of milk. As an antidote to spoilage, the process is very effective. For fine wines, however, a reliance on sterile bottling practices and an emphasis on keeping the cuverie (fermenting room) sanitary at all times is preferable to pasteurization. Some bacteria are actually necessary for aging; without them, the chemical interaction of the wine's various elements takes place fitfully or not at all. Killing all the bacteria destroys a wine's ability to age properly and thus become valuable.

In fact, discoveries that one vineyard was pasteurizing its wines caused scandals in the wine trade. In 1930, a group of

British aristocrats who had purchased 1929 Lafite sued the château when it became known that a portion of the vintage had been pasteurized. We can only imagine the horror with which the old wine–collecting community regarded this practice. In the end, Lafite had to recall the wine and pay damages to the British buyers. Incidentally, the fears of the British wine buyers were unfounded; I've been fortunate enough to sample the 1929 Lafite and, though faded, it is still good.

Sometimes pasteurization can be profitable. A wealthy and well-known client of mine came into my shop one day and purchased a bottle of the pasteurized 1929 Lafite. We talked for a few moments and he began telling me about his father's wine cellar. The old man had started collecting wines in the early 1900s, passing on the unconsumed fruits of his labor, some of which were quite rare, to his offspring.

The client told me about one of his father's most precious acquisitions—a magnum of 1858 Lafite that had once belonged to Louis Pasteur! Pasteur had received the bottle from Lafite in recognition of his service to the wine industry. My client, who had not heard of the 1930 lawsuit, was flabbergasted that quite by coincidence he had purchased one of Lafite's pasteurized wines. The magnum he owned, I informed him, was worth at least $25,000, and if the bottle's history and storage could be verified, perhaps as much as $100,000; a wealthy wine lover with an interest in Pasteur might have paid even more. Remember the discussion of mystique in Chapter 2? Here it was in action.

Pasteurized fine wine is usually something to beware of, however, if only because so many people in the fine- and rare-wine trade oppose the process.

Glossary of Wine Terms

à point [ah-PWAH(N)] The time when wine becomes drinkable.

abbocatto [ah-boh-KAH-toh] An Italian word used to describe a flavor that's not completely dry.

acetic A sweet, vinegary aroma and taste created by the vinegar bacteria's presence during production.

acid This helps give wine its ability to age "gracefully" at the same time giving it a fresh, tart, zesty taste.

aftertaste Taste left by the wine after it has left the palate; one can taste it mentally as well as physically.

agrafes [uh-GRAF] A metal clamp used to hold temporary corks in place on champagne bottles.

alios Sandstone rock rich in iron content, found in the subsoil of the Médoc and Graves.

amateur [ah-mah-TOOR] Describes a wine enthusiast who is "in it for the love."

Appellation Contrôlée [ah-pehl-lah-SYAWN kawn-traw-LAY] Refers to the highest quality French wines and the governmental controls that involve their production.

argile [ahr-JEEL] Clay, as in the clay-like quality of some of the Bordeaux region's soil, like the Pomerol.

aroma Also referred to as "nose"; the odor that is judged and enjoyed before tasting.

aromatic Assessment of all the qualities that go into the "nose."

arroba A Spanish wine measurement of 16⅔ liters.

arrope Spanish term that describes the concentrated wine used to give body and color to sherry.

astringent The slightly dry, bitter taste of a wine after the taste of fruit has diminished.

auction Activity where wine is consigned to professional sellers and then sold to the highest bidder.

austere Describes a more subtle or "coy" taste of certain wines when compared to others.

backbone Alludes to the body and grip of wine combined with its structure.

baked An overcooked or burned taste in wine.

balance An assessment of the harmony created between the alcohol, acidity, fruit, and body of a wine.

Balthazar Bottle containing 416 ounces, or 16 regular-size bottles.

Banvin or ***Ban de Vendage*** The ancient French custom of deciding the date of the first grape picking.

Bardolino [bar-doh-LEEN-oh] A red Italian wine.

Barolo [bah-ROH-loh] A red Italian wine.

battonage Stirring the lees (dead yeast cells) in a cask to build flavor.

Beaujolais [boh-zhoe-LAY] A Gamay-based red wine from Burgundy.

Belleyme, Pierre A French geographical engineer who made maps of Bordeaux. Also, the name of maps themselves.

binning The storage of wine in bins.

bitter The taste in a young red wine that in small degrees might be expected and not regarded as negative.

black currants The defining fruit in Cabernet Sauvignon grapes' taste.

blanc de blancs [BLAHN(K)-day-BLAHN(K)] French for "white from whites"; wine extracted from white grape juice exclusively.

blanco Spanish for "white."

Blaye [BLA-yuh] A town on the Gironde River in Bordeaux.

blowsy Describes a wine that is fat (rich) but lacking in zestiness or acidity.

body The core or substance of a wine.

boisé [bwah-ZAY] French for "woody;" describes the taste left behind in wine after using new oak for too long. The wood gives the wine an "oaky" taste.

Bordeaux [bor-DOH] The name of the capital city of the French département of Gironde and region in the southwest of France. Commonly, a place where great wines come from.

Botrytis cinerea [boh-TRI-this sihn-EER-ee-uh] Latin for the pourriture noble, or noble rot, a key element in the making of Sauternes (sweet) wine.

bouquet The nose (aroma) of mature wines.

Bourg [boor] Town in Bordeaux.

bourgeois [boor-JWAH] Wines of lesser status, often referring to Médoc and Haut-Médoc.

breed Distinction, finesse, or degree of superiority a particular wine achieves.

briery A quite spicy and aggressive taste in wine, most common in a California wine like Zinfandel.

Brunello di Montalcino [broo-NEHL-oh dee mohn-tahl-CHEE-noh] A red Italian wine.

Bureau of Alcohol, Tobacco and Firearms (ATF) A division of the United States Treasury Department that enforces national regulations concerning the items named in its title.

Burgundy (Bourgogne) [boor-GOH[N]-yah] France's second-leading wine-producing region. Though more modest in output, Burgundy was France's chief producer during the historically important years of the English occupation of Bordeaux.

Cabernet Sauvignon [ka-behr-NAY-soh-veehn-YOHN] Though not the most widely grown, one of the major grapes used in making fine red wine in Bordeaux. It grows best in a variety of soils like those in California and Australia.

Also known for providing red wines with the distinctive black currant taste.

caillou [kah-YOO] French for "pebble" or "stone." One of the gound conditions found in vineyards.

calcaire French for "limestone" or "chalky." One of the ground conditions found in vineyards.

capsule The object that protects wine corks, made from metal or plastic.

cask The large, usually oaken container for storing wine.

casse [KAHS-eh] Chemical "disease" that occurs when wine has too much iron in it.

cave, celler,* or *cellier [kahv or sehl-YEH] All French terms for underground storage areas for wine.

cépage [say-PAHZH] Vine variety, or the stock from which it comes.

Chablis [shah-BLEE] Dry, white wine from Chablis, France.

chai [sheh] Above-ground or below-ground–level structures (usually kept dark) used for wine production.

chambrer [shahm-BRAY] The slow, careful process of bringing a red wine to room temperature.

chapeau [shah-POH] The matter—grape skins, etc.—that rises to the top of the "must" during fermentation, leaving a thick "hat" on the wine.

chaptalization [shap-tuh-luh-zay-SHUHN] The process of adding sugar to "must" to increase the alcoholic content of the wine.

character Complexity and depth in a wine's taste.

château [shah-TOH] The house or villa on a Bordeaux wine estate, also used to denote the estate itself.

château-bottled Applies to wines that are produced and bottled at the château.

classified growths In French, *crus classé;* these were the wines classified according to their merit in 1855, 1955, and 1959.

climat [klee-MAH] French for *vineyard*, but also includes meteorological conditions.

closed A wine not yet demonstrating its potential because it is too young.

coarse A wine that is badly made, vulgar, and lacking finesse.

Cocks and Féret Authors of the book *Bordeaux et Ses Vins*, which is known as the "bible of Bordeaux" for having kept records of main characteristics and a variety of other things since 1850.

collage French for "fining a wine."

commune French for "parish" or "township."

complex A highly subjective term used to describe the numerous taste sensations embodied in a wine. Highly complex wines are interesting to the drinker every time the wine is tasted.

Confréries [kohn-frayr-EE] A French word for "brotherhood," in this case specifically describing gastronomic or wine fraternities. Many are of ancient origin. One is Confrérie des Chevaliers du Tastevin, or Gentlemen of the Tasting Cup, in Burgundy.

cork Material used to stopper wine bottles, among other things. It is actually the bark of certain trees. The best cork is grown in Portugal.

corky or **corked** Wine with a "dirty taste," the result of a bad or deteriorating cork.

coulure [koo-LURH] Bad, humid weather at flowering time for vines, which can result in grapes failing to appear.

coupé [koo-PAY] A wine blended or mixed with another.

courtier [koo-tee-AY] A wine broker who negotiates between the grower and the *négociant* (seller).

crémant [kray-MAHN] Wine that is slightly sparkling or crackling.

croupe [kroop] Gravel mound or ridge, characteristic of the Médoc, extremely good for vine growth.

cru [kroo] Describes the vineyard, the vines that grow there; literally means "growth."

crus classé [kroo klah-SAY] The classifiable growths of wines. The Official 1855 Classification names five classes: *premiers crus* (first growths), *deuxièmes crus* (second growths), *troisièmes crus* (third growths), *quatrièmes crus* (fourth growths), and *cinquièmes crus* (fifth growths).

crust Deposit thrown off by red wines, mostly Vintage Port that has been in the bottle for a long time.

cuit [kwuee] French for "cooked."

cuvaison [koo-veh-ZOHN] Applies to red wines and refers to the period during which grape juice is kept in contact with skins and seeds during both fermentation and maceration.

cuve [koov] Fermentation vat.

cuvée [koo-VAY] The contents of the cuve.

cuvier [koo-vee-AY] The part of the cellar or warehouse where vinification occurs.

decanter A vessel into which wine is poured from the original bottle for later use.

decanting Pouring wine from the bottle into another vessel to separate it from sediment or allow it to breathe.

dégorgement [day-gorj-MOH(N)] Removing sediment from champagne during the final stages of production.

délicat [day-lee-KAH] French for "delicate"; neither harsh nor coarse.

delimited area The area that is entitled by law to have its wine named after the region in which it is grown.

demi French prefix meaning "half."

demijohn A bottle that holds between 4 and 10 gallons, and which is enclosed in a wicker basket.

département [day-parh-tehr-MAHN] The French equivalent of a state, a subdivision of the federal government.

deposit The normal sediment that accumulates in a mature bottle of wine.

dépôt [dee-POH] The normal amount of sediment one might see in a red wine.

depth A description of wine's flavor. The more, the better.

dosage [doh-SAHJ] In champagne making, the usual amount of sugar used.

doux [doo] French for "sweetness." If on a champagne label, it means the wine is very sweet—over 5 percent sugar.

downy mildew Fungus that attacks grapes.

dry Describes a lack of sweetness in wine and sometimes indicates that the fruit used to make the wine was not ripe.

dull Wine lacking in character and complexity.

dumb Young wine with character that is still not mature.

eclairissage [eh-klauhr-ee-SAHJ] Thinning out of a grape crop to enhance the success of what remains.

ecoulage [eh-koo-LAJ] The process of separating the wine from what remains of the solid matter, such as skins. Takes place after cuvaision.

égrappage á la main [eh-gra-PAHJ ah lah MAYH(N)] Removing vine stalks by hand.

égrappoir [eh-gra-PWAHR] A device that mechanically removes stalks.

élégant [eh-leh-GAHN] Possessed of the qualities of finesse and style.

en fermage [eh(n)-fayr-MAHJ] Tenant farming.

en primeur [eh(n)-pree-MUHR] The first wine sold after harvest.

encépagement [ah(n)-say-pahj-MAH(N)] Proportions of different types grapes that are used in making a particular wine.

enologist One who studies wines and their creation.

enology [ee-nahl-oh-JEE] Of the scientific study of wines and their creation.

estate-bottled In Burgundy, wine grown, produced, and bottled by the same estate.

ethyl alcohol Type of alcohol created during the production of wine and other alcoholic beverages.

fat Wine that is rich, concentrated, and high in glycerin but low or average in acidity.

fermentation The changing of sugar into alcohol. The word derives from the Latin *fervere*, which means "to boil;" it also describes the "boiling" appearance as carbon dioxide escapes during the process.

feuillaison [foo-yeh-SOH(N)] When leaves grow on the vine. It is also used to describe the time when the vine is most vulnerable to damage from even a minor spring frost; young buds are not able to withstand temperatures even slightly below freezing.

filter Removing solids from wine by pouring it through a strainer.

fining Another method of straining solids out of wine; involves adding a substance to the wine to which the solids attach; the extra weight carries them to the bottom of the vat or other container.

finish The final taste impression one is left with after swallowing wine.

first growth Describes those wines deemed to be of the best merit in 1855 by the Official Classification rating. Included are Lafite, Latour, Margaux, Haut-Brion, and Mouton-Rothschild.

flat Devoid of zest or acidity; dull.

floraison [floor-ay-SOH(N)] The flowering of the vine.

foudre [FOO-druh] The large oaken vat or tub used for wine storage.

fouloir-égrappoir [foo-LWAHR ay-gra-PWAHR] A device that mechanically removes the stalks and opens the grape skin.

four-square Lacking finesse and probably acidity, this describes the undesireable quality of heaviness in wine.

Franck, Wilhelm Author of probably the first truly comprehensive texts to explore the Bordeaux wine region, entitled *Traité sur les Vins du Médoc*, published in its first edition in 1824.

full A quality describing the body of a wine, as in "full-bodied"; likely to be high in alcohol.

futures Buying wine while it is still in the barrel. It normally takes 18 months to two years for wine to be released (sold).

gôut de bouchon [goo duh boosh-ON] A taste of cork.

gôut de pique [goo duh PEEK] A taste of vinegar.

gôut de terroir [goo duh tehr-WAHR] A taste of the earth, which is not necessarily bad.

grand crus [gran KROO] Literally, "a great growth," but in a loose unofficial sense.

grand crus classé [gran KROO kla-SAY] In the official sense, "a great growth" and classified as such in the classifications of the Graves and Saint-Emilion.

grand vin [grah(n) VAH(N)] Can loosely mean a great wine, but also indicates the first wine to be bottled with the château's name on it.

graves [grahv] French for "gravelly" or "pebbly," the quality of the Médoc area's topsoil, which also has excellent drainage; ideal growing conditions for the Cabernet Sauvignon and other essential grapes.

green May be used to describe an immature vine, but more often, it describes the not-quite-ripe flavor of a wine.

green harvest Pruning of excess grapes to ensure the success of the crop.

grip Sufficient acidity, which provides an excellent finish. The direct opposite of flat, this is most often seen in a youthful wine.

hard Wine that's excessively tannic or acidic (not necessarily a negative characteristic).

harsh Describes the same qualities as the term "hard," but to more excess; this is usually a negative description.

heavy A very full-bodied wine—maybe too full.

hectare [hehk-TAHR] An international unit of measure for land, the equivalent of 2.271 acres.

hectoliter The metric measure of 100 liters, which amounts to 11 cases of wine.

hogshead Original term applied by the British to the size of a Bordeaux wine barrel, which has traditionally held 225 liters.

hot A wine high enough in alcohol to leave a burning sensation in the mouth and throat.

horizontal tasting Tasting wines that are from the same vintage.

indivision [ih(n)-dee-vee-see-YOH(N)] The French term for an inheritance shared between a number of heirs.

informing grape The predominant grape used in a wine; it defines the character of the wine.

inky A taste in wine suggestive of metal.

Institut National des Appellations d'Origine des Vins et Eaux-de-Vie [ihn-stay-TOO nah-see-yoh(n)-NAHL dayz ah-pel-ah-see-YOHN dohr-ee-JEEN day VEH(N)] **(INAO)** The French federal agency that regulates wine growing and production, setting the rules for what wine is permitted and what it is to be called.

Jeroboam Double magnum, holds the equivalent of four regular bottles, or 104 ounces.

lees Settling of matter, such as dead yeast cells, in the bottom of the cask.

lieu-dit French for "place."

long Describes the amount of time that a wine's taste lingers in the mouth.

maître de chai [MEH-truh duh SHAY] The master of the cellar.

Malbec [mahl-BEHK] A principal grape in Cahors, also used in the Loire and to a lesser extent in Bordeaux.

marc [mahr] The amount of grapes required to load a champagne press. This is also a term applied to the distillate remnants of the pressing.

marne The clay–limestone soil in Bordeaux.

meaty Possessed of a sturdy, tannic grip; a young, very full wine with a rich substance.

Médoc [may-DOHK] Perhaps the most important wine-making district in Bordeaux. It is a peninsula, nestled between the Gironde River and the Atlantic Ocean, about 50 miles long and 6 to 20 miles wide. Divided into two regions, Médoc to the north and Haut-Médoc to the south, closer to the city. Haut-Médoc is home to the communes of Pauillac, Saint-Julien, Margaux, and Saint-Estéphe.

mellow An aged wine with rounded, soft body and the subtleties of maturity.

Merlot [mehr-LOH] A premier grape, widely used in Bordeaux; the principal grape in Saint-Émilion and the Pomerol.

Methuselah About twice as large as a Jeroboam (a double magnum bottle); holds seven to eight regular bottles, or 179 to 208 ounces.

mildew Specifically refers to the "downy mildew," a fungus that attacks wine.

millérandage Small, hard, underdeveloped grapes, which result when the vine does not flower properly.

millésime [mee-lay-ZEEM] The vintage year.

mise en bouteille á la propriété [mee-ZOH(N) boo-TYE ah lah proh-pree-ay-TAY] Bottled by the shipper, in contrast to a château- or estate-bottled.

mise en bouteille au château [mee-ZOH(N) boo-TYE oh shah-TOW] French for château-bottled (Bordeaux); similar to estate-bottled (Burgundy).

mistelle [mees-TEHL] Adding brandy to must to halt the fermentation at a 15 percent alcohol level. The result is a naturally sweet wine that is then used for aperitifs and vermouths.

Muscadet [moos-kah-DAY] This is the local Loire River name for the Melon grape that produces an extremely dry yet gentle white wine.

must Fermenting grape juice on its way to becoming wine.

Mycodermae vini [my-koh-DER-muh] The Latin name of the yeast that turns grape juice into wine.

Nebuchadnezzar A champagne bottle, even greater still than a Methuselah, capable of holding the equivalent of 20 regular-size bottles, or 520 ounces.

nose The aromatic qualities of a particular wine.

négoce A term used to refer to a wine broker or more typically, the wine trade in general.

négociant [nay-goh-see-YOH(N)] A wine broker or seller.

négociant-éleveur [nay-goh-see-YOH(N) eh-leh-VURH] An individual or firm that obtains wine from the grower, blends, bottles, and markets it.

noble The finest quality, superior in breed and distinction; the finest description one can assign to a wine.

off-taste Describes an indiscernible taste or aroma.

oïdium "Powdery" mildew, another fungus of the vine, which can be controlled by applying sulfur.

oxidized The process of oxidization, or prolonged exposure to air at any point, which leaves wine flat.

palus [pah-LOO(S)] An area of land close to the Gironde that is not good for wine production.

Passe Tout Grains [pahs too GRAH(N)] A Burgundy mixture with a minimum of one-third Pinot Noir and the rest Gamay grapes.

pasteurization A process invented by Louis Pasteur used to make certain beverages safer to drink.

Petit Verdot [puh-TEE vehr-DOH] A late grape that is known for its good color and backbone, rarely seen outside the best Médoc lands.

phylloxera vastatrix [fihl-LOX-er-uh] A grape-plant louse that was inadvertently brought from America to Europe among a shipment of experimental vines. The resulting infestation affected all the European wine-growing regions for years until it was found that by grafting traditional European vines onto hardy, louse-resistant American grape roots, they could circumvent the problem.

piéce [pee-YESS] A 60-gallon cask used commonly for wine in various wine-producing regions of France.

Pijassou, René The premier modern historian of Bordeaux wine country, author of *Le Médoc*, published in 1980.

piqué [pee-KAY] Literally *sour*, a term for vinegar or wine that is becoming vinegar.

pourriture grise [poo-ree-TYUR GREE] This is the same mildew, or "gray rot," that causes the pourriture noble that gives Sauterne its distinction. Pourriture grise is less desirable in humid weather, a now preventable danger.

pourriture noble [poo-ree-TYUR noh-BL] The "noble rot," or *Botrytis cinerea*, which is the mold or yeast that leads to extra sweet grapes and the making of Sauternes.

premier crus [preh-MYAY KROO] French for "first growth."

provenance [prohv-NAH(N)S] The history of a wine bottle including owner, location, and handling.

puissance [pwee-SAH(N)S] The French word for "strength" or "power" specifically describing those qualities in young wine.

quarter-bottle One-quarter the size of a normal bottle, this miniature holds about 6 ounces.

quinta [KEEN-tah] The Portuguese equivalent of a Bordeaux château.

racking In winemaking, the transferring of clear liquid wine from one vat into a fresh, clean one, leaving the lees behind.

récolte [ray-KAWLT] The bringing in or harvesting of the grapes.

red wine Wine colored red; the color comes from the inside of the grape skin.

refresh Mixing young wine into an older wine to enliven and rejuvenate it.

régisseur [ray-jee-SOOR] A château's manager or chief.

rendement [rah(n)d-MAH(N)] In numerical terms, the amount of grapes harvested.

réserve du château [ray-ZEHRV doo sha-TOH] The very best wine produced at an individual château and reserved to wear the château's highest standard.

rich Possessed of a number of important qualities for a red wine, like a ripeness and fullness.

rootstock The lower portion of a root and its buds.

rosé [roh-ZAY] Slightly pinkish-colored wine.

round Mellow. Refers to a wine's taste.

ruby A color characteristic of Port when it is young. As the Port grows older, and with repeated finings, it pales to a tawny color.

saccharometer A device to measure sugar content of wine.

Salmanazar A large champagne bottle that can hold the equivalent of 10 to 12 regular bottles, or 270 to 312 ounces, of champagne.

Sauvignon [soh-vee(n)-YOH(N)] One of the principal varieties of grapes used to define the dry flavors of Bordeaux wines, particularly those from the Médoc and Graves.

sec The French word for "dry," it also denotes a champagne of middle sweetness.

sediment Natural deposits from tannins, pigments, and the like in wine.

Sémillon [say-mee-YOH(N)] The most common white base grape of Bordeaux and a premier grape of the Sauternes; as important for dry white wines as it is for sweet ones.

severe Found commonly in immature wines, this term describes an excessive austere, hard quality.

sharp A term that describes a young wine that has a sour quality or extreme acidity.

smoky An aroma possessed of a smoky quality.

smooth A quality almost like silk; round and mature, lacking roughness.

soft Even softer or more diffuse than smooth; round and mellow, more mature.

souche [soosh] Vine rootstock, another term for *cèpage*.

sous-sol [soo-SOHL] French for "under soil;" literally, "subsoil."

soutirage [soo-teer-AJ] French term for the racking process, the separation of the clear liquid wine from the lees.

spicy Describes a very rich aroma.

stage Slang for an apprenticeship with a wine broker or producer.

stalky A quality that occurs when vine stalks are left too long in the wine during the maceration phase of production.

style A combination of a wine's character, finesse, and breed.

superficial Lacking complexity and depth.

supple A well-rounded wine that also retains qualities of grip and vigor.

sur souche [suhr SOOSH] French term refering to the sale of wine prior to harvest.

sur-maturité [suhr-mah-toor-ee-TAY] On the brink of losing acidity; the most perfect and desired ripeness.

Syrah [see-RAH] No longer used around the Gironde, this is a premier grape traditionally used in the Rhône Valley.

tannin An acidic chemical contained in the skins of grapes and a natural component in young wine. As the wine matures, the liquid gives up the tannins and the wine becomes smoother to drink.

tartaric acid An acid naturally present in grapes; the substance by which the total acid content is measured.

tawny The pale color quality of Port after repeated finings and aging in wood.

Teinturier [tihn-toor-ee-OOR] Dark-skinned grapes used almost exclusively for color.

tendre [TAHN-druh] Tender, young, delicate wine.

terroir [tehr-WAHR] The soil and geographic factors that influence grape growth and, therefore, the quality of the finished wine.

tête de cuvée [teht duh koo-VAY] The "head" or chief of the blend, a term usually used in Burgundy for an outstanding growth.

thin Wine lacking in body.

tonneau [tohn-OH] A bulk trade measurement term used mostly in Bordeaux for a unit that is about 900 liters divided into four units, called "barriques" or "highheads." In the end, this is about 96 cases of finished wine.

tranche [trah(n)sh] The French word for "slice;" part of the harvest yield.

tri or ***triage*** [TREE-ahj] Going through grape bunches to eliminate the substandard.

ullage [uhl-AH] The degree to which a bottle is filled.

usé [oo-SAY] Having passed the prime points of drinkability; a vintage in decline.

vats The containers where the fermentation process takes place.

velvety Extremely smooth, rich, and well-textured.

vendange [vahn-dahn-ZH] The grape yield or harvest.

vendage tardive [vahn-dahn-ZH tahr-DEEV] Literally, "late picking," which results in a harvest that usually has more verve and strength and can be sweeter.

veraison [vehr-ray-SOH(N)] Moment when grapes start to take on their mature color, such as those that change from green to black on the way to becoming red wine grapes.

vertical tasting Tasting different wines from the same property.

vigneron [veen-ayr-OH(N)] One who grows vines, the grape horticulturist.

vignoble [vee-NYOHBL] The vineyard itself; the area where grapes are grown.

vigor Describing the quality of an exciting but balanced taste, young and acidic.

vin blanc [va(n) BLAH(N)K] White wine.

vin cuit [va(n) KWEE] Literally "cooked wine"; a specially prepared concentrate that thickens wines deemed too thin.

vin de goutte [va(n) duh GOOT] The last pressing, usually an inferior wine.

vin doux [va(n) DOO] Sweet wine.

vin ordinaire [va(n) or-dee-NAIR] An inexpensive wine made for immediate use.

vin presse [va(n) PRESS] After the juice has run off, the remnants—skins, pips, etc.—may be pressed to extract a highly acid and tannic juice, which when blended with the free juice, adds a considerable amount of backbone to the wine.

viniculture All the various steps involved in the making of wine.

vinification The process during which the grape juice ferments into wine.

vinothéque [vee-noh-TEK] A French term for a collection of bottles; a library of wine.

vintage The year of the harvest. Also means wine that is superior to other years. It is common in some areas, like Champagne and Oporto, that wine is only dated during exceptional years, as opposed to dating each year.

viticulture The science of caring for the vines on which wine grapes are grown.

Vitis vinifera Vine from which most of the world's grapes come.

volatile Referring to acidity, a quality of all wines, but suggesting a sweet and sour quality.

well-balanced An equality of the characteristics of a wine; harmony.

wine The fermented product of fruit juices, most commonly grapes.

wine broker One who acts between growers and wholesale buyers, in French a *négociant-éleveur*.

woody Too much of a woody flavor, an off-taste, not necessarily from a new oak cask, but a faulty stave.

Zinfandel [TZIN-fan-del] Red-wine grape brought to California by Agoston Harasthy (known as the "father of California wine"). Now grown almost exclusively in Calfornia.

Where to Get More Information

THE DEGREE TO which you succeed in investing in wine, as well as enjoying it as a beverage, is directly related to what you know. The more you know, the more likely you are to be a successful investor, as well as a successful imbiber.

When I wrote *Liquid Assets* more than a decade or so ago, I also supplied some sources, but there is a whole new vineyard, as it were, from which to harvest information this time around. To wit, the Internet.

There is still a great deal of valuable written material out there—books, magazines, and other publications. Here is a roundup.

PUBLICATIONS

Wine Spectator: This is the bible of the wine industry, a big glossy publication that is published monthly and contains information on events that impact the wine trade, reviews, and ratings for wines worldwide. It also features articles by a group of highly knowledgeable columnists. It can be a treasure trove for the investor and certainly is a must for the wine drinker to peruse. It is available by subscription; some libraries also carry it. The *Wine Spectator* is published in New York City.

Wine Enthusiast: This is published 14 times a year and looks very much like the *Wine Spectator*—big, colorful, and glossy.

Wine Advocate: This is the publication put out by Robert M. Parker, Jr., the most adored, respected, and loathed—not to mention the most influential—wine critic in the world. This is a bimonthly publication that rates wines worldwide. For information on subscribing, write to P.O. Box 311, Parkton, MD 21120 or fax (301) 357-4504.

Decanter: This is a British publication. Your wine merchant can show you sample copies.

Books

There are many books on wine, including encyclopedias, broad-based looks at the world of wine, books devoted to specific wines (for example, James Suckling of the *Wine Spectator* has written two books on Port), and books that evaluate wines.

Robert M. Parker, Jr., has written books on the wines of Bordeaux, the Rhône Valley, Burgundy—and the world.

James Laube, a columnist for the *Wine Spectator*, has written an excellent book on California wines, aptly titled *The Wines of California*.

Matt Kramer (another *Wine Spectator* columnist) has written one of the best books on Burgundy wines, *Making Sense of Burgundy*. Making sense of Burgundy vineyards is not an easy task, since their ownership is so fractionalized and complex that you need a calculator and a computer to keep up.

Clive Coates, another expert, has a number of books out, including *Grand Vins*, which rates the wines of Bordeaux and provides a lot of information about the châteaux that they come from. Coates has also authored a book on Burgundy. People who like to explore the high end of wine, the first growths, and their equivalents in other areas favor Coates's ratings and writings.

For a comprehensive look at American wines and wineries, check out Gault Millau's *Guide to the Best Wineries of North America*. This book covers every state in the union, providing information on wineries such as their addresses, hours of operation, and the like, as well as a critical consideration of the wines.

Another book of interest is *Oz Clarke's Wine Guide*, which comes out yearly.

If you'd like to get a comprehensive dictionary of wine terms look no further than *Wine Quest: The Wine Dictionary*. You can get this at liquor stores and wine shops as well by mail order from the author by writing to 869 Union Church Road, Churchville, VA 24421. The author, Ted Grudzinski, tells us that the book retails for $28, but "discounts are available." This contains some 7,600 terms, it is very thorough, and its author is an obvious wine and language lover.

I recommend two wine encyclopedias: *The Encyclopedia of Wine* by Jancis Robinson and *Wine Lover's Companion* by Ron Herbst and Sharon Tyller Herbst.

You don't need to buy all these books, either. Most of them are available at your local public library. If your local branch does not have a copy of the book you're looking for, have your reference librarian check with neighboring—or even far away—libraries; it's likely that you can have the title sent over from a nearby branch. Reference librarians by definition—part nurse and part detective—will go a long way to help you find the book you're looking for. I remember a friend of mine who wanted to find *Peyton Place* by Grace Metalious. His local library didn't have it, and neither did any other library in Long Island, nor did any library in New York State. But about a month later it showed up at his library, loaned by a college library in Columbus, Georgia, thanks to the efforts of the reference librarian.

Electronic Information

Since I wrote *Liquid Assets* a whole world of wine information has been made available on the Internet. I don't pretend to be a computer expert, but I will say that I have been able to access some very valuable information online, and so will you.

The Internet is just that: a network of information containing vast numbers of "Web sites," which are places where the information is stored. Someone has compared the Internet to a library, and each particular Web site to one book in the library. I've also heard it referred to as a mall, where the stores are the Web sites.

There are various ways to reach this information. To do this, you don't need a library card but an online service or Internet service provider. Examples are America Online, Prodigy, or CompuServe. You pay a certain amount each month for access to these online services, say around $22 for AOL, which allows you unlimited access to the Internet—and all those "library books."

One of the advantages of using the Internet is that you don't need to leave your home. Reams of wine info are at your fingertips. And it's not difficult to use. For example I recently typed in the word *wine* on my computer, and the machine came back with what it characterized as the top 10 of 300,000 entries on wine. Now the vast majority won't be relevant, but many, many will.

Another advantage is that it's fast. Clickety-click a bit and within seconds you'll be deep in the area you want to explore.

I have a few basic suggestions for making the most of your Internet wine search:

- Once you've found a Web site you like, write the address down. It's very easy to get distracted, and unless you write the address down you might have to go through an extended search to find it again. Your browser—the software that lets you view all the Web pages—will also let you save the Web site's address. It's like bookmarking a page in the novel you're reading. Once you have it bookmarked, you can go back to it whenever you want, provided the address stays the same.

- Use your online service when it's not likely to be busy, that is, between the hours of 5 and 11 P.M.

- One of the more useful Web sites you might find is that of the *Wine Spectator*, which posts articles—covering the last five or six years—from the magazine. You can find it at http://www.winespectator.com. Robert M. Parker, Jr., also has a Web site, http://www.wineadvocate.com.

Good hunting!

State Alcohol Control Boards

The following is a list of state and territorial offices that administer and enforce laws regarding the manufacture, distribution, and dispensing of alcoholic beverages. It's a good idea to check the laws in your state before trying to buy wine by mail-order.

United States

Alabama

Alcoholic Beverage Control Board
2715 Gunter Park Drive West
Montgomery, AL 36109-1021
Fax: (334) 277-2150

Administrator Robert B. Leavell: (334) 271-3840

Alaska

Alcoholic Beverage Control Board
550 W. Seventh Ave., Suite 350
Anchorage, AK 99501-3510

Director Douglas B. Griffin: (907) 277-8638

Arizona

Liquor Licenses and Control Department
800 W. Washington St., Fifth Floor
Phoenix, AZ 85007
Phone: (602) 542-5141; fax: (602) 542-5707
E-mail: liqr@ll.state.az.us; Internet: http://www.azll.com

Director Howard G. Adams: (602) 542-9020

Arkansas

Alcoholic Beverage Control—Administration
Technology Center
100 Main, Suite 503
Little Rock, AR 72201
Fax: (501) 682-2221

Director Robert S. Moore, Jr.: (501) 682-1105

California

Alcoholic Beverage Control Department
3801 Rosin Court, Suite 150
Sacramento, CA 95834-1633
Phone: (916) 263-6900; fax: (916) 263-6912

Director Jay R. Stroh: (916) 263-6888

Colorado

Liquor Enforcement Division/Department of Revenue
1881 Pierce Drive, Room 108A
Lakewood, CO 80214
Phone: (303) 205-2300; fax: (303) 205-2341

Director David Reitz

Connecticut

Liquor Control Commission
165 Capitol Ave.
Hartford, CT 06106
Phone: (860) 566-4687

Chairperson Mark A. Shiffrin: (860) 566-4999

Delaware

Alcoholic Beverage Control Division
Carvel State Office Building
820 N. French St.
Wilmington, DE 19801
Fax: (302) 577-3204

Director Donald J. Bowman, Sr.: (302) 577-3200 ext. 16

Florida

Department of Business and Professional Regulation/
Alcoholic Beverages & Tobacco
1940 N. Monroe St.
Tallahassee, FL 32399-1020
Phone: (904) 488-3227; fax: (904)922-5175

Director Richard Boyd

Georgia

Department of Revenue/Alcohol & Tobacco Tax Unit
270 Washington St. SW
Atlanta, GA 30334

Director Chester Bryant

Hawaii

Department of Liquor Control
County of Hawaii
101 Aupuni Street, Room 230
Hilo, Hawaii 96766

Idaho

State Liquor Dispensary
7185 Bethel St.
P.O. Box 59
Boise, ID 83704

Superintendent Dyke Nally: (208) 327-7300

Alcoholic Beverage Control Division/
Department of Law Enforcement
P.O. Box 700
Meridian, ID 83680-0700
Phone: (208) 884-7003

Chief John Gould

Illinois

Liquor Control Commission
100 W. Randolph St., Suite 5-300,
Chicago, IL 60601
General information: (312) 814-2206;
fax: (312) 814-2241
TTY: (312) 814-1844; Internet: http://www.state.il.us/lcc

Chairperson Albert D. McCoy: (312) 814-3930
Commissioner Don W. Adams: (312) 814-3930

Indiana

Alcohol Beverage Commission
302 W. Washington St., Room E114
Indianapolis, IN 46204
General information: (317) 232-2430;
fax: (317) 233-6114

Chairperson John Hanley: (317) 232-2448

Iowa

Alcoholic Beverages Division
1918 SE Hulsizer
Ankeny, IA 50021
Phone: (515) 281-7407; fax: (515) 281-7385

Administrator Jack Nystrom: (515) 281-7407

Kansas

Department of Revenue/Alcoholic Beverage Control Division
4 Townsite Plaza, Room 210
200 SE Sixth St.
Topeka, KS 66603-3512
Phone: (913) 296-3946; fax: (913) 296-0922

Director Bernie Norwood

Kentucky

Alcoholic Beverage Control Department
1003 Twilight Trail
Suburban Park Building A2
Frankfort, KY 40601
Phone: (502) 564-4850; fax: (502) 564-1442

Commissioner Richard Johnstone: (502) 564-4850

Louisiana

Alcohol & Beverage Control
P.O. Box 201
Baton Rouge, LA 70806
Phone: (504) 925-4041; fax: (504) 925-3975

Commissioner Murphy Painter

Maine

Alcoholic Beverages and Lottery Operations Bureau
8 State House Station
Augusta, ME 04333-0008
General information: (207) 287-3721; fax: (207) 287-6769

Director Eben Marsh: (207) 287-3432

Maryland

Alcohol & Tobacco Tax Division
State Treasury Building, Room 310
Annapolis, MD 21401-3311
Phone: (410) 974-3311; fax: (410) 974-3201

Administrator Charles W. Ehart

Massachusetts

Alcoholic Beverages Control Commission
100 Cambridge St., Room 2204
Boston, MA 02202
Phone: (617) 727-3040; fax: (617) 727-1258

Chairperson Walter J. Sullivan: (617) 727-3040

Michigan

Liquor Control Commission
7150 Harris Drive
P.O. Box 30005
Lansing, MI 48909
General information: (517) 322-1345;
fax: (517) 322-5188

Chairperson Jacquelyn Stewart: (517) 322-1353

Minnesota

Department of Public Safety/Liquor Control Division
444 Cedar St., Suite 100L
St. Paul, MN 55101-2149
Phone: (612) 296-6212; fax: (612) 297-5259

Director Thomas Brownell

Mississippi

Alcoholic Beverage Control Bureau
P.O. Box 540
Madison, MS 39130-0540
General information: (601) 856-1301;
fax: (601) 856-1390

Director James Sullivan: (601) 856-1301

Missouri

Liquor Control Division/Department of Public Safety
P.O. Box 837
Jefferson City, MO 65102

Supervisor Hope Whitehead: (573) 751-2333

Montana

Revenue Department/Liquor Division
Sam W. Mitchell Building, Room 455
Helena, MT 59620
Fax: (406) 444-3696; TTY: (406) 444-2830

Licensing Bureau Chief Jeff Miller: (406) 444-2837

Nebraska

Liquor Control Commission
301 Centennial Mall South
P.O. Box 95046
Lincoln, NE 68509-5046
Phone: (603) 471-2571; fax: (402) 471-2814

Chairperson Jack Crowley: (603) 471-2571

Nevada

Nevada Department of Taxation–Liquor Division
Capitol Complex
1340 South Curry St.
Carson City, NV 89710
Phone: (702) 687-4820

New Hampshire

Liquor Commission
Storrs St.
P.O. Box 503
Concord, NH 03302-0503
Phone: (603) 271-3134; fax: (603) 271-1107

Chairperson John W. Byrne: (603) 271-3132

New Jersey

Department of Law & Public Safety/
Alcoholic Beverage Control Division
140 E. Front Street, CN087
Trenton, NJ 08625-0087
Phone: (609) 984-2830; fax: (609) 633-6078

Director John G. Holl

New Mexico

Department of Regulation & Licensing/
Alcohol & Gaming Division
P.O. Box 25101
Santa Fe, NM 87503
Phone: (505) 827-7003; fax: (505) 827-7168

Acting Director Robin Otten

New York

Alcoholic Beverage Control Division
State Liquor Authority
84 Holland Ave.
Albany, NY 12208
General information: (518) 474-3114;
fax: (518) 402-4015
TTY: (518) 474-9888

Chairperson Anthony J. Casale: (518) 474-4696

North Carolina

Alcoholic Beverage Control Commission
3322 Garner Road
Raleigh, NC 27610
Phone: (919) 779-0700; fax: (919) 662-1946

Chairperson George F. Bason: (919) 779-0700

North Dakota

Licensing Administration/
Office of the Attorney General
State Capitol, 17th Floor
600 East Boulevard Ave.
Bismarck, ND 58505
Phone: (701) 328-2210; fax: (701) 328-3535

Ohio

Department of Liquor Control
2323 W. Fifth Ave.
Columbus, OH 43266-0701
Phone: (614) 644-2472; fax: (614) 644-2480

Oklahoma

Alcoholic Beverage Control Board
4545 N. Lincoln Blvd., Suite 270
Oklahoma City, OK 73105
Phone: (405) 521-3484

Chairperson Robert V. Wilder: (405) 521-3494

Oregon

Liquor Control Commission
9079 SE McLoughlin Blvd.
Portland, OR 97222-7355
General information: (503) 872-5000;
fax: (503) 872-5266
TTY: (503) 872-5013

Administrator Pamela Erickson: (503) 872-5200

Pennsylvania

Liquor Control Board
Northwest Office Building
Harrisburg, PA 17124-0001
General information: (717) 783-7637;
fax: (717) 783-6614
TTY: (717) 772-3725

Chairperson John E. Jones III: (717) 787-5230

Rhode Island

Department of Business Regulation/Liquor Control
233 Richmond St.
Providence, RI 02903
Phone: (401) 277-2562

Acting Administrator Anthony Arrico

South Carolina

Department of Revenue & Taxation/
Division of Alcohol Beverage Control
301 Gervais Ave.
Columbia, SC 29201
Phone: (803) 734-0477

Supervisor Patricia L. Stites

South Dakota

Division of Special Taxes/Department of Revenue
Kneip Building, Third Floor
700 Governor Drive
Pierre, SD 57501
Phone: (605) 773-3311

Director James Fry

Tennessee

Alcoholic Beverage Commission
226 Capitol Blvd., Suite 300
Nashville, TN 37243-0755
Phone: (615) 741-1602; fax: (615) 741-0847

Chairperson James Exum: (615) 741-1602

Texas

Alcoholic Beverage Commission
P.O. Box 13127
Austin, TX 78711
General information: (512) 206-3333;
fax: (512) 206-3350
TTY: (512) 206-3270; E-mail: questions@tabc.state.tx.us

Administrator Doyne Bailey: (512) 206-3217

Utah

Alcoholic Beverage Control Department
1625 South 900 West
P.O. Box 30408
Salt Lake City, UT 84130-0408
Phone: (801) 977-6800; fax: (801) 977-6888
E-mail: kwynn@state.ut.us

Director Kenneth F. Wynn: (801) 977-6800

Vermont

Liquor Control Department
Green Mountain Drive, Drawer 20
Montpelier, VT 05620-4501
Phone: (802) 828-2345; fax: (802) 828-2803
E-mail: norrie@dlc.state.vt.us

Commissioner Norris Hoyt: (802) 828-2345

Virginia

Alcoholic Beverage Control Board
2901 Hermitage Road
P.O. Box 27491
Richmond VA 23261
Phone: (804) 213-4405; fax: (804) 213-4411

Chairperson: (804) 213-4402

Washington

Liquor Control Board
1025 E. Union Ave.
P.O. Box 43080
Olympia, WA 98504-3080
Phone: (360) 586-4826; fax: (360) 664-9689
TTY: (360) 586-4727

Chairperson Nathan S. Ford, Jr.: (360) 753-6268

West Virginia

Alcohol Control Administration
322 70th Street SE
Charleston, WV 25304-2900
Phone: (304) 558-2481; fax: (304) 558-0081

Commissioner Donald Stemple: (304) 558-2481

Wisconsin

Department of Revenue/Alcohol & Tobacco Enforcement
4610 University Ave.
P.O. Box 8905
Madison, WI 53708
Phone: (608) 266-3969; fax: (608) 266-6884

Chief Jim Jenkins

Wyoming

Department of Revenue
Herschler Building
122 W. 25th St.
Cheyenne, WY 82002
Phone: (307) 777-7961; fax: (307) 777-7722

Director Johnnie Burton

United States Territories

American Samoa

Alcoholic Beverage Control Board
Office of the Governor
Pago Pago, AS 96799
Fax: (684) 633-2269

Chairperson Logovii Magalei: (684) 633-4116

District of Columbia

Consumer & Regulatory Affairs/
Alcoholic Beverage Control Division
614 H St. NW, Room 807
Washington, DC 20001
Phone: (202) 727-7377

Program Manager Paul E. Waters

Guam

Department of Revenue & Taxation
BEQ 13-1-3 Mariner Ave.
Tiyan, GU 96916
Phone: (671) 475-1817; fax: (671) 472-2643

Director Joseph T. Duenas

Northern Mariana Islands

Commerce Department/Alcoholic Beverage Control Board
Caller Box 10007
Saipan, MP 96950
Phone: (670) 664-3058; fax: (670) 664-3067

Administrator Enrique A. Santos

Puerto Rico

Department of the Treasury/
Bureau of Alcoholic Beverage Taxes
P.O. Box 9024140
San Juan, PR 00902-4140
Phone: (787) 721-5245; fax: (787) 722-6749

Director Rafael Caraballo

Index

B

C

H

I

J

K

L

M

N

O

P

Q

R

S

T

U

V

W

Z